THE BEES OF THE INVISIBLE

THE BEES OF THE INVISIBLE

STAN DRAGLAND

ESSAYS IN CONTEMPORARY

ENGLISH CANADIAN

WRITING

COACH HOUSE PRESS

TORONTO

Copyright © Stan Dragland 1991

Published with the assistance of the Canada Council
and the Ontario Arts Council

Typeset and printed in Canada

Canadian Cataloguing in Publication Data

Dragland, Stan, 1942–
The bees of the invisible : essays in contemporary English Canadian writing

Includes bibliographical references.
ISBN 0-99810-400-X

1. Canadian literature (English) — 20th century — History and criticism.*
I. Title.

PS 8071.4.D73 1991   C810.9'0054   C91-094485-7
PR9189.6.D73 1991

For Marnie, Rachel, Simon and Toby

The Bees of the Invisible

PREFACE

"There are many kinds of both kinds"
bp Nichol

Why these writers?

Before I answer that, let me say who else would have been included, had there been time and space enough. Maybe this is the contents of Volume 2: Colleen Thibaudeau, Rudy Wiebe (especially *The Temptations of Big Bear*), Michael Ondaatje, Don McKay, Jay Macpherson, Wilfred Watson, Robert Kroetsch.

Add that list to the contents of the book in your hands, and the picture may still not be much clearer. That is because what draws these writers together is not their similarity but my having fallen in love with their work. The heart is a poor excluder, so I could make a much longer list. I name only those about whom I know I'll eventually have something to say.

A few of my extra-Canadian affections make brief appearances here—Borges, Dorn, Cage, Nabokov and others—but I'm most involved with Canadian literature. This gives me plenty of scope. After Michael Ondaatje's reading to launch *Secular Love*, Don McKay said to me that if a writer these days could choose any literary context in the world, he or she might well choose Canada. Don grew up in Cornwall, Ontario. As a youngster he may have felt something of the warm glow of Ralph Connor's Glengarry novels, but I have the impression that his awareness of Canadian writing at that time pretty much matched my own, gathered while growing up in various Alberta towns: almost nil. I do remember buying Hugh MacLennan's *The Watch That Ends The Night* off the drugstore rack in Oyen, Alberta, in 1959, lured by the blurb on the gold seal: "WINNER OF THE GOVERNOR GENERAL'S AWARD, THE CANADIAN COUNTERPART OF THE PULITZER PRIZE." It made a difference to me that MacLennan was Canadian, but only after I read those fabulous scenes of violence and flight set in northern Quebec. Now I look around at my contemporaries and see major writers. To have come from nothing to this in a matter of decades is a continuing source of wonder to me.

Not that there *was* nothing; it's just that nobody pointed me to what there was. Nobody pointed me anywhere. Perhaps that's why I grew up an indiscriminate reader, a print junkie. I know of a woman in Victoria who goes nowhere without the company of some words, keeps a supply of books in every room of the house and feels a little desolate walking from one room to another. Now *there's* a reader. I've never met her, but she and I are surely kindred spirits. Yes, Miss Hanson did read *Anne of Green Gables* to the Grade Six class I attended in Stettler, Alberta. I liked it much more than *Ben Hur,* which she also read aloud. I became for a time a mental citizen of Avonlea, Prince Edward Island, without caring if it was in Canada or not.

It's not to drop a name that I mention Don McKay. Critics of contemporary Canadian writing may well know their subjects personally. It's a large country, a small literary community; people naturally write about each other. The intertextualities so generated are labyrinthine. Constance Rooke plunges into this issue of personal contact in her book of essays, *Fear of the Open Heart,* and formulates a "theory of intimacy" (10) around it. Rooke is not just dropping names either, of course. Writing from her own heart, she is trying to deal with a fact of the contemporary Canadian literary scene (whether obstacle or opportunity) so obvious that few people acknowledge it, at least not in print. To me, knowing the writer is something to get around, but I'm not riding a high horse about this. After all, while Chris Dewdney lived in London I heard him read and talked with him many times and so was eased into his strange work. *That's* what I want to be intimate with, though: the work.

The Bees of the Invisible was assembled mostly from essays already written (all of these revised for the book), but there are some arguments connecting them. One is a running, glancing engagement with the modernist-postmodernist "dichotomy," which I prefer to stretch into a continuum. Postmodernism is a silly term to have found such purchase in literary studies. Sometimes it designates writing post-1945 (1970 for Canada), but I think it's more useful as a name for extensions of the experiments in discontinuous form and generally anti-linear technique that were carried on by modernists like Eliot, Pound, Joyce, Stein. For a couple of representative statements of postmodernist aesthetics, we might turn to John Hawkes and Charles Olson. Hawkes' often quoted assertion that he "began to write fiction on the assumption that the true enemies of the novel were plot, character, setting, and theme" (144), those comfortable staples of realism, is a rallying point for writers of postmodernist fiction. Olson's essay "Projective Verse," replacing "inherited line, stanza, over-all form" with "COMPOSITION BY FIELD" (16), with an open-form or process poetic, is one postmodernist answer to the "well-wrought" formalism of modernist poetry.

If this book were *about* postmodernism, it would hardly be adequate to begin with a couple of brief definitions. Since it's about the works of particular writers, not all of them postmodernist, and since at this point we need just a serviceable working definition, I don't scruple to simplify even further: if the work requires you to meet it half way and assemble it yourself, if it's self-consciously *in your face,* probably it's postmodernist.

But I have no special place in my heart for postmodernism, and I'm not interested in fashionable difficulty. Is Al Purdy postmodernist? Only in the crude and unreliable chronological sense (Gertrude Stein still looks avant-garde). *Reading* Purdy is easy, but describing how his poetry works, trying to engage the profundity in his simplicity, is not. I can't approach his poetry in the same way I approach the obviously difficult writing of Christopher Dewdney, but, writing on both of them, writing on anybody I take the trouble with, I'm like nobody so much as Alice in the Sheep's shop of *Through the Looking Glass.* "The shop seemed to be full of all manner of curious things—but the oddest part of it all was that, whenever she looked hard at any shelf, to make out exactly what it had on it, that particular shelf was always quite empty, though the others round it were crowded as full as they could hold" (178-179). What is on the "particular shelf" in all of the writers I look at in this book is a riddle. Each of them is as conscious as I am of reaching, with words, beyond where words will go.

I was moved, reading over the manuscript of *Bees,* to discover something I hadn't realized as I approached each writer separately: with what bravery they face and resist not only mortality but the darkness of contemporary times, including the possible demise of human life. Apparently what the wretched Consul says in Lowry's *Under the Volcano* is still true: "But it's amazing when you come to think of it how the human spirit seems to blossom in the shadow of the abattoir" (95)!

Works Cited

Carroll, Lewis. *Alice's Adventures in Wonderland and Through the Looking Glass.* Oxford: Oxford University Press, 1971.

Enck, John. "John Hawkes: an Interview." *Wisconsin Studies in Contemporary Literature* VI, 2 (Summer 1965), 141-155.

Lowry, Malcolm. *Under the Volcano.* Oxford: Jonathan Cape, 1947.

Olson, Charles. *Selected Writings.* Ed. with introduction by Robert Creely. New York: New Directions, 1951.

Rooke, Constance. *Fear of the Open Heart: Essays in Contemporary Canadian Literature.* Toronto: Coach House, 1989.

Acknowledgements

Most of the essays in this book are revised versions of essays that were published or will be published in magazines and books. I thank the editors for their hospitality.

A stripped version of "F.ing Through *Beautiful Losers*" will appear as Afterword to the new New Canadian Library *Beautiful Losers.* David Staines is the general editor of this series.

"James Reaney's 'Pulsating dance in and out of forms'" appeared in David Helwig's *The Human Elements.* Ottawa: Oberon, 1978.

"Reaney's Relevance" was an afterword written for *Approaches to the Work of James Reaney,* edited by myself for ECW Press (Toronto 1983), Jack David and Robert Lecker, editors and publishers.

"On Civil Elegies" appeared in Russell Brown, Donna Bennett and Karen Mulholland, eds. *Tasks of Passion: Dennis Lee at Mid-Career.* Toronto: Descant Editions, 1982.

A short version of "Al Purdy's Poetry," entitled "Al Purdy's Poetry: Seven Openings," was delivered at the Al Purdy Celebration, University of Toronto, 1987. The long version appeared in *Brick* 35, (Spring 1989), Linda Spalding and Michael Ondaatje, editors, and will be included in the proceedings of the Celebration, edited by Sam Solecki.

"Christopher Dewdney's Writing: Beyond Fear and Madness" was the "Afterword" to Dewdney's Selected Poems, *Predators of the Adoration: Poems 1972-1982* (McClelland and Stewart 1982), edited by Michael Ondaatje, Dennis Lee, Dewdney and myself. A slightly different version was published in *The Malahat Review* 66 (October 1983), Constance Rooke, editor.

"The Bees of the Invisible: George Bowering's *Kerrisdale Elegies* appeared in *Brick* 28 (Spring 1988).

The first section of "Creatures of Ecstacy" was a review written for *The Journal of Canadian Poetry*, David Staines, editor. It appeared in the first number (1986).

"Out of the Blank: *Ana Historic*" will appear in a festschrift for John P. Matthews, edited by Gillian Whitlock and Helen Tiffin.

&

I've been blessed by wonderfully tough and supportive readers over the years—Michael Ondaatje, Don McKay, Dennis Lee and, more recently, Marnie Parsons—but I really have to take not only all the blame but most of the credit for the contents of this book.

E.ING THROUGH *BEAUTIFUL LOSERS*

Not all readers in the free love sixties and early seventies could stand the kinky sex in *Beautiful Losers*, and I doubt that those few among the shocked who hung on long enough to realize what the sex was doing in the novel ("Hard cock alone leads to Thee") would have been reassured. Sex was not the only obstacle, when there was one. I remember people who should have known better feeding the rumour that *Beautiful Losers* had been a perfectly good straightforward novel until Cohen got on drugs and scrambled the damn thing. Not everyone was a convert, then, but *Beautiful Losers* was a holy book for many readers of the Age of Aquarius who simply inhaled it, as uncritically as those novel readers of Henry James's age who had the "comfortable, good-humoured feeling … that a novel is a novel, as a pudding is a pudding, and that our only business with it could be to swallow it" (165).

For me, at first, Cohen's novel didn't go down so easily. It was the first weird book I'd ever read. There wasn't much context for it in the Canada of 1966, not that I knew of anyway, nothing like the postmodernism of writers like Ondaatje and Bowering who owe something to *Beautiful Losers* and haven't forgotten that. Certainly no criticism like Linda Hutcheon's *The Canadian Postmodern*, which begins with *Beautiful Losers*. I made no connection between Cohen's experimentation and that of writers elsewhere. The most unusual other book I had read by then was *Ulysses*, and this was so literary as to feel familiar enough. Coming to *Beautiful Losers* cold (except for scarcely believable reports of Cohen's reading from it at The University of Alberta—"slof tlif, sounded the geysers of his semen as they hit the dashboard"—and Desmond Pacey's appearance there to declare it a masterpiece), it might have stumped me had I not been a more talented reader then than I am now. Then I read like an antelope grafted to a steamroller: I could leap the incomprehensible and flatten the complex. So I could jump from section to section, book to book, absorbed mainly by the chronological story of Catherine Tekakwitha. She was historical and thus "real." "This material has a power of its own, doesn't it" (212), says F. while he is finishing the story of Catherine (become a sort of collaborative hagiography) that his friend began. That's how *I* felt, and I still do. As Catherine is transformed into an Iroquois virgin, her uncle realizes that "Our heaven is dying" (94); the Christians are going to win. Catherine's achievement is a poignant anomaly in a religious tragedy which moved me.

But I wasn't paying much attention to wild cards: this material is actually joked through, annotated and infiltrated by anachronism, generally shunted around by narrators who have several additional matters on their minds. And the comprehensible seventeenth century plot begins inside a present-day fiction, the story of an unnamed narrator, a scholar, desperately courting the Indian Virgin with his words for solace from continuous grief, whose narrative is all over the place, as you might expect from a man whose "Brain Feels Like It Has Been Whipped" (58). "Cohen keeps about twelve incidents going at the same time," says Michael Ondaatje (*Leonard Cohen* 49), one of the reasons why Ondaatje's *Coming Through Slaughter* has haunted my recent reading of *Beautiful Losers*. In Buddy Bolden's music, "He would be describing something in 27 ways" (37).

The context of Canadian postmodernist fiction slowly grew up around *Beautiful Losers*, helping to make its discontinuities legible. But the first stage of critical response, when receptive, sifted and sorted through the novel under the influence of practical criticism, with its assumption of a text's underlying unity. Stephen Scobie's book on Cohen performs a sophisticated version of my leaping steamroller, offering a detailed chart of the novel, with everything joined to everything else, each motif pattern rendered about as significant as any other. Scobie wouldn't do that now. At least his (to use Rafael Barreto-Rivera's pun in *Nimrod's Tongue* 27) Derridative treatment of *Death of a Lady's Man* in *Signature Event Cantext* suggests that he too is not the reader he was.

My own first critical approach to *Beautiful Losers*, mercifully hidden in old lecture notes, was also bent to show how the novel made sense. For students, good inhalers short on analytic skills, this was maybe a service. But I see now how limiting it was. Especially I see how much my approach depended on a selective reading of the character of F. It was and is much easier for the reader to become a student of F.—to swallow his teachings as though his authority were not immediately limited by his fictionality—than it is for the reluctant disciple/narrator of Book I, suffering his bereavements and the apparent waste of his life. The reader, re-reading, may study at leisure the pronouncements of a guru reduced to the black of words on a white page.

The words are flesh to the narrator of Book One, "The History of them All," much of which is a howl not only of pain but of bewilderment because he was/is the reluctant disciple of a teacher whose classroom is hysteria (59) whose teachings are at once persuasive and incomprehensible. "Mindfucks," Dennis Lee calls them in *Savage Fields* (69). It's one thing to see as through a glass, darkly, and it's another to have to try to see as through a prism of funhouse mirrors, through F., best friend since orphanage days, charismatic charlatan. His rendition of the Platters' "The Great Pretender" is probably not merely a love lament. "Take one step to the side and it's all absurd" (37), the narrator realizes. What is it that tempts me (being, in my relationship to *Beautiful Losers*, something like this man to F.) not to take that side-step? F.'s "system," his outrageous salad of world myths and religions tossed with contemporary advertising, movies, porn, comics, cartoons, the Top Forty, you name it—all of it accepted as sacred material—is couched in such passionate rhetoric and poetry that it's almost possible to give in to it.

The fascination of F., this desire to believe what he says, is astonishing, provoked as it is by a novel so little bound by the conventions of realism. The stakes are high, of course. If F. were real and if he knew what he was talking about (forgetting for the moment the cracks in his consistency, forgetting that he's made of words), then everything in the modern world would make sense; the whole painful puzzle would be whole, as it once was, in "an eternal eye" (17), just as bracingly difficult of approach as ever. Any amount of suffering could be endured. Like the narrator of Borges' "The Library of Babel," crying the frustration of his search for so much as an inkling of meaning in his labyrinthine universe/library, many are lonely for the lack of such belief:

If honor and wisdom and happiness are not for me, let them be for others. Let heaven exist, though my place be in hell. Let me be outraged and annihilated, but for one instant, in one being, let Your enormous Library be justified" (*Labyrinths 57*).

Yes, F. is seductive; his system has its attractions. But not, I expect, when all things are considered, to the squeamish. A reader who listens to everything F. says, the depressive lapses in confidence as well as the manic persuasiveness, is going to draw away from him. A reader who ponders *all* the words, even the puzzling ones, in the system—the novel—that contains F., finds it quite like F.'s character at face value, inconsistent and undependable. Like looking at the northern lights when the spirits are particularly active: the whole design pulses to some configuring energy, but centre and all are constantly shifting. In fiction, isn't continual change more exhilarating to a reader (especially when s/he joins the process) than the centre holding (still)? If we stop expecting sense to be made in the old ways, it is. Form and chaos cohabit everywhere.

Reading all the words, trying to stay free. As a child I was the antelope, reading voraciously with a naive sort of rigour only the words that interested me. Never contemplating response in any making of my own, whether creative or critical. This much of that illusory freedom I wish to keep in these latter days: to honour theory in my writing only where it's wild, lifting hot off the critical occasions it collects and baptises reluctantly; theory in the bone. "Play with me, old friend" (159), F. says posthumously to his disciple. Join in, he means (to slide over the sexual connotation), go with it. Life is [*Beautiful Losers* is] a fabulous game with fluid rules and no possibility of winning.

But F. can't sustain his belief, if belief it is and not "a mood gone absolute" (Lee, *Civil Elegies* 55). Suffering and doubt is all the narrator of Book One possesses, so he thinks. He has no system, no theory. Sometimes he sees that F. suffers, but he doesn't seek an outlet from his own pain by reinterpreting F. in that light. To a reader standing somewhere between the two, a lot of what F. says comes to sound like bravado. "Oh,

F." asks the disciple of his master, "do you think I can learn to perceive the diamonds of good amongst all the shit?" "It is all diamond," F. replies, characteristically (9). Easy for *him* to say?

One way to read *Beautiful Losers* is as a journey—of the narrator, of Catherine, gathering other selves as they go—through the shit to the diamond. Another approach, unlinear, is suggested by the fact that the pain and the questions don't disappear, the shit doesn't go away. Neither is absent from the novel's ending(s), spoken by some survivor with a breaking heart. In Michael Ondaatje's rewriting of F., "The diamond had to love the earth it passed along the way, every speck and angle of the other's history, for the diamond had been earth too" (111).

Ꮪ

Not all sections of Book One advance the plot. Eight of them are tours de force with a rhetoric and a structure of their own, several others have large set-pieces embedded in them, and the text lurches or slides into a virtual anthology of briefer set pieces. There is, in general, such volatility of voice, such thoroughly polyphonic notation of the sounds of "the tinkly present" (75) that one might be reminded of the dolphin sonographs (depicting multiple simultaneous vocalization) in the epigraph to Ondaatje's *Slaughter* (6). Yes, but I was thinking of Cohen's bird: "Experts with tape recorders say that what we hear as a single bird note is really ten or twelve tones with which the animal weaves many various beautiful liquid harmonies" (117). Catbird, maybe: one of the avian parodists capable of alternating the dulcet with the dissonant.

Few sections of Book One are stylistically "pure," and few readers have made much of this pyrotechnique. Not surprisingly, Michael Ondaatje is an exception. He sees "the essential drama of the novel in the styles Cohen uses" (*Leonard Cohen* 47), and he reflects the critical consensus that the variety of Book One illustrates the narrator's failure to fit things together. It is true that his lonely limited first-person world must collapse before something familial and ecstatic may reassemble from the fragments (this is in F.'s syllabus) but we need also to consider the *behaviour* of this man's words. A character who can raise his normal colloquial style into elegant prose and also sink into gibberish or virtually speak in tongues is protean, and hardly the sad useless dead-end dummy he thinks he is. It doesn't even matter if his style has been "colonized" by the extravagant F., that much of his style and substance doesn't belong to him, to either of them. In this he is like people in general—derivative, "intertextual"—only more, and more obviously, so.

Book One's narrator is abulge with the babel of the world. He is too many for us. He spills over the edges of system. He enacts a freedom that is unfortunately no bloody good to him; hence the torment in so much of *what* he says. Like all the best clowns he is often hilarious with his breaking heart on his sleeve. To enjoy his Book Three performance of a "remote human possiblity" (101), a miracle, it helps to realize that the narrator of Book One *is* his style—as long as we're seeing him as a character in the conventional sense. In another perspective he is an ego too beautifully de-centered to be able to absorb and dissolve the traces of his culture that stream through him. They leave his style striated with their own signatures.

Book Two is "A Long Letter from F.," epistolary in form and pedagogical in intent. F. now exposes his aims and his method, sure that his pupil knows all that losing his mind can teach him. An irony retroactively spreads over Book One when F. reveals that he is only "the Moses of our little exodus. I would never cross" (178). "Go forth," F. says, "teach the world what I meant to be" (169). "I wanted to be a magician," he goes on, in a more generic metaphor, "That was my idea of glory. Here is a plea based on my whole experience: do not be a magician, be magic" (175). If the man with the system is merely the forerunner, we need to reconsider the value (without forgetting the pain) of the one who loses control.

Book Two is more continuous and stylistically less varied than Book One, though certainly not uniform. In his narrative of Catherine's last four years, F's style carries marks of his friend's style, with Jesuit originals and other source-styles layered in, but even in his letter proper he bursts into a poem, "God is Alive, Magic is Afoot," and inserts three quatrains of unattributed poetry (the same poem; different ones?) into the Argentine Hotel scene. And the novel's total anthology of styles is swollen by the catalogues, blurbs and samples of material generated by the pornography and sex aids industry that F. reads in the attempt to stimulate Edith to orgasm. Not even a recitation of the martyrdom of Brebeuf will work, however—and that extreme incongruity gives a clue why *Beautiful Losers* fails utterly as pornography: those not offended or simply aghast are more likely to be startled into laughter than aroused.

Between that epic sex scene and the sequel of Catherine's story two poems appear: a sonnet called "F.'s Invocation to History in the Old Style," and a quatrain entitled "F.'s Invocation to History in the Middle Style." The first could conceivably be read as a symbolic condensation of the whole novel, including Book Three ("I see an Orphan, lawless and serene, / standing in a corner of the sky" 200-201); the second is (very characteristic of F.) nonsense, "drug addict's argot" (201) compacted to meaninglessness and the joke extended by seven explanatory footnotes, with notes on the footnotes infiltrated by extensions of F.'s letter to his friend. F.'s photographic memory will have retained his friend's scholarly method as one more style to parody.

F. takes some pains with the remainder of Catherine's tale, which may seem inconsistent with advising his friend to "Read it with that part of your mind which you delegate to watching out for blackflies and mosquitoes" (200). Is he still giving with one hand and taking away with the other? Maybe not. He wants the mind's watchdogs drugged so there's no filter of the real. You see clearly only out of the corner of your eye. Anyway, the continuation of Catherine's tale is hardly that only. F.'s letter continues to flow through it, as F. explicitly draws the parallels between Edith's life and Catherine's. He almost imperceptibly shifts the setting to that of the final scene of the epilogue, as well. "We are now in the heart of the winter of 1680," says F., as he begins, "We are now in the heart of our pain. We are now in the heart of our evidence" (218).

Stan Dragland

Who is "we"? F. and Edith and her husband and probably you and me and the author,
the whole ensemble beginning to roll together towards the epilogue, as the "we are
now" motif survives the end of Catherine's story: "We are now in the heart of the
System Theatre. ...We are now in the heart of the last feature in the System Theatre"
(235,236). We are travelling forward to hook the events of the Epilogue to the end of
Book One, and back into F.'s memory of himself and his two friends watching a
movie, to the moment when his own attention is distracted to the projected ray itself.

In another refrain that links his letter and his narrative of Catherine, F. has been
showing his friend "how it happens." Some variation on this phrase occurs several
times. In fact the active presentness of both refrains chimes with the spirit of
beginnings invoked in Section 21, which is out in left field, having nothing to do with
Catherine:

Like a numbered immigrant in the harbor of North America, I hope to begin
again. I hope to begin my friendship again. I hope to begin my rise to President.
I hope to begin Mary again. I hope to begin my worship again to Thee who has
never refused my service, in whose flashing memory I have no past or future,
whose memory never froze into the coffin of history ... (228).

(I can't let this passage slip by without remarking slight turbulences in it: the myth of
America as promised land of equal opportunity is a banal Norman Rockwell vision
elsewhere in the novel; and who is "Thee?" The answer would seem obvious if the
flashing and the collapsing of time weren't so reminiscent of the transformed narrator
in the Epilogue.)

Just before the last scene in which F. is given up to the dogs he presents the question
he claims tormented him during the silvery hours he and his two friends spent at the
System Theatre (an appropriately named but nevertheless actual Montreal cinema):
"What will happen when the newsreel escapes into the Feature?"

The newsreel lies between the street and the Feature like Boulder Dam, vital
as a border in the Middle East—breach it (so I thought), and a miasmal mixture
will imperialize existence by means of its sole quality of total corrosion. So I
thought! The newsreel lies between the street and the Feature: like a tunnel on
the Sunday drive it ends quickly and in creepy darkness joins the rural
mountains to the slums. It took courage! I let the newsreel escape, I invited it
to walk right into plot, and they merged in awful originality, just as trees and
plastic synthesize new powerful landscapes in those districts of the highway
devoted to motels. Long live motels, the name, the motive, the success! Here
is my message, old lover of my heart. Here is what I saw: here is what I learned:
Sophia Loren Strips For A Flood Victim
THE FLOOD IS REAL AT LAST (237-238).

18

The Bees of the Invisible

This is the second epitome of F.'s system, "God is Alive" being the first. He seems to have forgotten having already summed everything up. It's good that F.'s old lover has been prepared to receive this new message (so might run a reader's first reaction), because it makes no sense to me. But the reader has also been learning, or should have been; we are reading F.'s letter over the shoulder of a man whose cluelessness (his own Book One contains a very high proportion of questions) is not foreign to us. Well *have* we been learning? Here is the relevant lesson: "To understand the truth in anything that is alien, first dispense with the indispensable in your own vision" (89). No sooner heard than accepted. On to Book Three.

Just kidding.

The newsreel is both a border and a tunnel, fencing out the Feature and also connecting with it, but underground, not obviously. My paraphrase turns simile into metaphor and conceals my guesswork. Nowadays the newsreel has been dignified with the name of documentary, a sort of buffer genre more or less halfway to fiction. When newsreel and Feature merge ... I'm blunting my mind trying to cypher this through and ending up in anticlimax every time. I guess you do have to be there. I feel on firmer ground saying that the text is using filmic analogies for what has been happening all through *Beautiful Losers,* a veritable Bible of miasmal mixture or generic instability. Just look at part of the exit from Book Two, which has escaped F.'s narrative control:

> (DOLLY IN TO CLOSE-UP OF THE RADIO ASSUMING THE FORM OF PRINT)
> —This is the radio speaking. Good evening. The radio easily interrupts this book to bring you a recorded historical news flash: TERRORIST LEADER AT LARGE.
> (CLOSE-UP OF RADIO EXHIBITING A MOTION PICTURE OF ITSELF)
> —This is the radio speaking. Eeeek! Tee hee! This is the ah ha ha, this is the hee hee, this is the radio speaking. Ha ha ha ha ha ha, oh ho ho ho, ha ha ha ha ha ha, it tickles, it tickles! (SOUND EFFECT; ECHO CHAMBER) This is the radio speaking. Drop your weapons! This is the Revenge of the Radio (240-41).

Typing out this passage (simpler to chuckle over than to analyse in terms of, say, the various genres playing in it) is a good reminder that *Beautiful Losers* never takes itself seriously, never plays the same game for long. Which is not to say that it should not be taken seriously. The novel is light-hearted as Eastern sages whose jokes may be doors to wisdom. The narrator of Book One would love to be able to "stand on some holy mountain of experience" and "sweetly nod [his] Chinese head over" the betrayals and outrages of his life (7). In the journey paradigm, he has achieved that stance as Book One winds down, but what I like best about the sentence-long section 51 is not the way it fits the journey-to-enlightenment pattern by detailing the narrator's empty-headed openness, his acceptances ("artificial limb accepted, Hong Kong sex auxiliaries accepted, money confessions accepted, wigs of celanese acetate accepted"); what

Stan Dragland

I really like is that somebody, whether author or narrator or both, cannot resist
inserting a brief satiric variation into this litany: "Zen Ph.D tolerated" (145). Thus the
hypnotised might signal the hypnotist that s/he has not completely relinquished
control. Thus the colonized might warn the imperialist of a stormy rule to come.

The style of Book Three, "Beautiful Losers, an Epilogue in the Third Person" is not
neutral. It borrows from both previous narrators, but is governed by neither of them.
So the narrative surface of most of Book Three is smooth and calm. F. and his friend
are and are not what they were. The borders between their identities have corroded
and they have merged. Edith had been revealed as a contemporary incarnation of Isis
in Book Two, and now she is and is not the woman in the fast car, naked below the
waist, who picks up the hitch-hiker who used to be her husband. The moccasins she
wears show that the identity of Catherine has been folded in. Understanding *how* the
newsreel walks "right into plot" may not be necessary; the corrosive results, in these
destabilized identities, are clear enough. Now the Feature is not going to stay put.

In downtown Montreal, next to the System Theatre at the Main Shooting and
Game Alley, the climax of the book plays to an audience of generic people drawn by
the sense that "Action was suddenly [not in the theatres but] in the streets" (256). They
are treated to an unusual experience as the composite old man begins to dissolve "from
the inside out" (259), and to reassemble himself,

And at that point where he was most absent, that's when the gasps started, because
the future streams through that point, going both ways. That is the beautiful
waist of the hourglass! That is the point of Clear Light! Let it change forever
what we do not know!" (258).

The finale of this virtuoso display is his reassembling of himself "into—into a movie
of Ray Charles."

Then he enlarged the screen, degree by degree, like a documentary on the Industry.
The moon occupied one lens of his sunglasses, and he laid out his piano keys
across a shelf of the sky, and he leaned over them as though they were truly the
row of giant fishes to feed a hungry multitude. A fleet of jet planes dragged his
voice over us who were holding hands.
—Just sit back and enjoy it, I guess.
—Thank God it's only a movie.
—Hey! cried a New Jew, laboring on the lever of the broken Strength Test.
Hey. Somebody's making it! (258-259).

Only a movie, eh? A movie must have got crossed with the northern lights. But there
would have been food lineups after that original miracle of loaves and fishes too, and
people urging others to "Eat up" and only much later wondering—then finally
realizing—Who was catering, and How. Linda Hutcheon complains that this

20

Montreal audience isn't taking the message (32), but I say give them time.

Meanwhile, this crowd of strangers, this melded cross-section of contemporary urbanites, is holding hands and enjoying themselves, and there is no missing the happy ending even if it *is* understated in contemporary slang. In *Savage Fields* Dennis Lee has no use for this ending, none for the whole Epilogue. In fact he feels the essential action of the book is over before the resumption of Catherine's story in Book Two. The rest is copout. But Lee's *Savage Fields* translates *Beautiful Losers* into terms that fit an argument: contemporary "world" and "earth" (roughly, technology and nature) are locked in vicious competition. The no-outlet argument itself is sobering in its plausibility, and there is much in *Beautiful Losers* that supports it, but the novel flies free of it, right to the end. I'm tempted to adapt (freely) the term polyphony (in "Polyphony: Enacting a Meditation," Lee's essay on poetics) to describe its flight: polyphony orchestrated as by the Queen of Hearts in Wonderland.

The happy ending is not the ending. Two brief unconnected passages remain, and they bounce out of the third person. One of them, "rented to the Jesuits" (259) puts a case for Catherine's canonization, and the other seems to me to wind back to the opening when everything was up in the air. The last sentence, as George Bowering points out in "A Great Northward Darkness: The Attack on History in Recent Canadian Fiction," is a couplet (7). It's also a very belated welcome to the reader, a welcome to melancholy and longing. It's an ending, calm but not restful, that wants to be played with. Or perhaps the whole novel needs to be played again with this ending in mind.

ↄჲ

The whole of *Beautiful Losers* seems to stream through certain set-piece passages composed of the contradictory stresses of existence that characters and readers alike must wrestle with. These passages are part of a self-reflexive inquiry into order and chaos in life and art. They interest a reader in something other than how the plot turns out. They magnetize a reader's attention with the prospect of meaning, even a "necklace of incomparable beauty and unmeaning" (18); with an offer of "the exercise of a kind of balance in the chaos of existence" (101); with "a dance of masks" in which "there was but one mask but one true face which was the same and which was a thing without a name which changed and changed into itself over and over" (140); with the lure of "the sound of the sounds [heard] together" (160).

The well-known passages so abbreviated, those wellsprings of aesthetic sense, supplement and connect with each other, and they might all be felt to meet in the statement of faith that F. calls "the sweet burden of my argument" (167). This is the poem, "God is alive. Magic is afoot," that has been wonderfully served in a musical setting by Buffy Sainte-Marie. Actually F.'s message involves a further leap, beyond faith in human creative capacity to the divine source of it all. But in this constellation of remarkable passages lies the meaning of *Beautiful Losers* for those who feel that the novel has something important to say, something the mind can hold and carry away. Both the narrator and F. (the latter in a weak moment), feel the pull of this sort of kernelized meaning. The appetite survives in the "part of [the narrator's] mind which buys solutions" (135), in the "American" part of F.'s mind that wants "to tie my life up with a visit" (45). Small wonder a reader should feel his/her desire for order exercised by this book.

The saint-artist's "exercise of a kind of balance in the chaos of existence," that visionary "necklace of incomparable beauty and unmeaning" and the rest—these are not images of easy harmony, or they wouldn't be as seductive as they are. But all the same they are reassuring figures which link or contain the members of chaos, lending them at least the illusion of coherence. If God is alive the whole shebang makes sense, because the lamented "transcendental signified" never really died. So it's plausible to read *Beautiful Losers* as a modernist novel with an underlying drive towards organic unity because the novel powerfully sponsors that sort of response. The "celestial manifestation" (75) of the "Epilogue" would then be the plot's fulfillment of the principle of harmony under whose influence one threads the parts of the novel as beads on a necklace. But if the novel were meant to inhere in those transcendent passages, I don't believe that, line by line, page by page, the experience of reading it would involve such continual readjustment and surprise and joyous evasion of a critic. *Beautiful Losers* will slake the thirst for meaning, for resolution, but only in a reader partially amnesiac.

A few passages that connect, however compelling, are not the book. Leonard Cohen has delegated no one to speak for him; neither do the collected voices of the novel add up to Writ. Sometimes the narrative mask all but dissolves to let us see through the words to the man who wrote them, as when a voice one almost seems to recognize cries,

O reader, do you know that a man is writing this? A man like you who longed for a hero's heart. In arctic isolation a man is writing this, a man who hates his memory and remembers everything, who was once as proud as you …" (108).

The suddenness of this, rather than any inconsistency with what else the volatile narrator has been saying, persuades me that the author is flirting with self-revelation (if such can be said of one who all but slides into the bones of Eliot's drowned sailor, Phlebas the Phoenician, "once handsome and tall as you") (85). It makes more poignant the appeal to a common experience of exile from bravery and purity of intention. A man like me, only too conscious of his limitations, made *Beautiful Losers* out of his longing. Writer and reader, narrators and characters—we're all in this wilderness together, and only the characters emerge.

Writer and reader are again together, abandoned, in the last passage of the novel, where the melancholy tone is heard again. Those reassuring passages with the family face are not the whole picture; F. speaks only for himself; there is no resting in, say, "God is alive. Magic is afoot;" meaning is not only fluid but collaborative, not only collaborative but reconstituted with each reading.

The desire for order is so palpable in the minds of both narrator/characters, those chips off the old block, that any conclusions they reach ought to be suspect. Their cries of metaphysical loneliness and prayers to silent gods ring through *Beautiful Losers*. Here is the narrator of Book One straining against mental and physical constipation to thread (or comma splice) some faulty logic into a charm against loneliness: "Please make me empty, if I'm empty then I can receive, if I can receive it means it comes from somewhere outside of me, if it comes from outside of me I'm not alone! I cannot bear this loneliness. Above all it is loneliness" (41). F.'s generalization of the theme appears in a prayer abruptly inserted into the letter to his friend:

> (O Father, Nameless and Free of Description, lead me from the Desert of the Possible ... Dear Father accept this confession: we did not train ourselves to Receive because we believed there wasn't Anything to Receive and we could not endure with this Belief) (190).

The joy of "God is alive. Magic is afoot" is not punctured but it pales beside the pain of a mind bereft of certainties in Book One, and it's undercut in Book Two when F. all but admits that spiritual loneliness scares human beings into affirmation. In the words of Don McKay, written in the margin of a draft of this essay, "the 'God is alive' passage is one spiritual posture among many, orally and aurally compelling but of no greater weight than the others in a democracy of spiritualities."

Beautiful Losers has a great deal to do with the response of artists like F. to the lonely wrack of contemporary life. The novel is largely about the principles and workings of the weird "system" that F. is using to mould out of the lumpen clay of his friends superbeings with perfect bodies and wide open minds. He wants things different, "any old different" (199), and not just for the hell of it. "What is most original in a man's nature," runs one of his aphorisms, "is often that which is most desperate. Thus new systems are forced on the world by men who simply cannot bear the pain of living with what is" (59). A poet's allegiance, the passage goes on, "is to the notion that he is not bound to the world as given, that he can escape the painful arrangement of things as they are" (59). F.'s examples are two "creators" not often associated: Hitler and Jesus.

Hitler? This might sound a little like John Cage saying that the music of Beethoven is every bit as acceptable to him as a cowbell, except that Cage is not putting the Holocaust into play, not introducing the "unspeakable" subject (Yanofsky 31). If you rethink music along with Cage, any noise is worth listening to, but is there a rethinking capable of erasing the difference between Jesus and Hitler? The plot shows that F. is not talking through his hat, at least. He and Edith would likely be as happy to go three in a tub with Jesus as with Hitler, though Jesus might not bring the soap. Hitler's soap is human soap; it's six million Jews. In what sort of system is this a comic turn? In the system called *Beautiful Losers*. F. is not laughing. His "lust for secular gray magic" (175) makes him covet that soap. He feeds on *any* power.

To write his letter, F. says, he has "had to stretch my mind back into areas bordered with barbed wire, from which I spent a lifetime removing myself" (164). He never suffered any scruples to interfere with the gratification of his lust for life, and the Argentinian hotel scene shows that he has erased the border between good and evil. Theoretically, He should be far from Jesuit territory, then, away from the Christian system with its tales of Hero and Adversary in settings of heaven and hell, but he isn't.

The Jesuits use ghastly paintings of hell (in the seventeenth-century narrative of Book One) to frighten the Indians out of their own less dualistic system into "a new kind of loneliness" (87), the death of their heaven. The novel makes this tragedy moving, as I've said, but it does not stay on the side of the losers. Renting the end of the book to the Jesuits is not the first sign that what they stand for, unfair players and winners though they are, may have its admirable side. The narrator of Book One includes in his paean of homage to the Jesuits ("because they saw miracles") a section it's easy to skip or forget, unless one comes to it thinking of F. and Hitler:

> Homage to the vaulted halls where we knelt face to face with the shit-enhaloed Accuser of the World. … Homage to those old torturers who did not doubt the souls of their victims, and, like the Indians, allowed the power of the Enemy to nourish the strength of the community (106).

Like F., though hardly in the same way, the Jesuits have congress with the devil. In a novel of collapsing identities it shouldn't be surprising that Hitler's exit leaves behind "the vague stink of [the Adversary's] sulphurous flatulence" (195). There is no passage celebrating the fact that the Devil is afoot, but the narrators of Books One and Two both fold into their thinking his energy of darkness.

If God is alive, is F. even on his side? In the orgy that climaxes with the Danish Vibrator, F.'s "Pygmalion tampering" (195) with Edith is revealed. "You've gone against God" (176), she says to him, placing him in the Archetypal Rebel camp, and that association is extended in a passage that darkly parodies his friend's vision of unity, early in the novel, created by the "needle" of his mind that when relaxed sews everything together: "everything which has existed and does exist, we are part of a necklace of incomparable beauty and unmeaning" (17-18).

This "comforting message, a beautiful knowledge of unity," has to be matched with the perspective of F.'s contrasting needle-work in Book Two. Then one understands why F. might consider it "some glimmering of a fake universal comprehension" (17). Maybe he hates to see a student backslide; maybe he's jealous. His ambition may be well-meaning but it's also, as overreaching always is, disastrous:

> Call me Dr. Frankenstein with a deadline. I seemed to wake up in the middle of a car accident, limbs strewn everywhere, detached voices screaming for comfort, severed fingers pointing homeward, all the debris withering like sliced cheese out of Cellophane—and all I had in the wrecked world was a needle and thread, so I got down on my knees, I pulled pieces out of the mess and I started

to stitch them together. I had an idea of what a man should look like, but it kept changing. I couldn't devote a lifetime to discovering the ideal physique. All I heard was pain, all I saw was mutilation. My needle going so madly, sometimes I found I'd run the thread right through my own flesh and I was joined to one of my own grotesque creations—I'd rip us apart—and then I heard my own voice howling with the others, and I knew that I was also truly part of the disaster. But I also realized that I was not the only one on my knees sewing frantically. There were others like me, making the same monstrous mistakes, driven by the same impure urgency, stitching themselves into the ruined heap, painfully extracting themselves (186-87).

Is he thinking of his failure when he shouts "connect nothing" in response to his friend's necklace vision of unity. "Place things side by side on your arborite table, if you must, but connect nothing!" (18). If F. were a contemporary writer/theorist like, say, Robert Kroetsch, he might shout "Metonymy, not metaphor!" You could see him touting the "postmodernist" fragmentary text over the "modernist" integral one, a stance more consistent with the message that borders between genres may be corroded than with the message that God is alive and the first term of meaning is still in place. But the point is that, given his confession, given his overreaching, who's going to put much faith in F. as a creator, as a saint? His system is a botch.

Or is it? Now we're only listening to the dark side. This reading has in fact risked abandoning balance in order to explore it. There comes a time to put aside the search for consistency in F.'s system and resolution in this novel, to put aside all that irritable reaching after fact and reason. "Shhh" is

the sound made around the index finger raised to the lips. Shhh, and the roofs are raised against the storm. Shhh, the forests are cleared so the wind will not rattle the trees. Shhh, the hydrogen rockets go off to silence dissent and variety (157).

Shhh, the trickster text will now behave itself. Resisting that step aside into irony doesn't necessarily mean deciding whose side F. is on. It means keeping the options open.

"We rejoiced to learn that mystery was our home" (164), F. recalls to his friend (and the pronoun welcomes the reader). Their home is this novel. With a true mystery there is nothing to do but play. Mystery is life in the best novels, those tests of the centre's cohesion, and play is the creative process at its most cooperative and least judgemental. Of course, by accommodating Hitler, Cohen becomes one of those heroes of the edge, in the words of Michael Ondaatje's "White Dwarfs," "who shave their moral so raw / they can tear themselves through the eye of a needle" (*Rat Jelly* 70). He pushes his system right up to the edge of the tolerable. He goes where I can follow him only in fiction, and even then not without a shudder.

Stan Dragland

What is it like to get near the Source, to move into "death," and return to tell about it? "I," in Ed Dorn's *Slinger*, sometime secretary to Parmenides, begins his account this way:

> First off,
> the lights go out on Thought
> and an increase in the thought of thought,
> plausibly flooded w/ darkness,
> in the shape of an ability
> to hear Evil praised ...
> (Book IIII)

Is it something akin to this detachment, this revision of priorities—radical as that of Lazarus, returned from the grave in Browning's "An Epistle of Karshish" and now indifferent to the deaths of children—that permits a reader to accept Hitler and his soap as integral to *Beautiful Losers*, as merely the most extreme of Cohen's many courageous outrages of convention and taste? Or is it slackness, failure of the imagination to grasp the enormity of Cohen's glibness about the Holocaust? The former, I think, after soul-searching, but my confidence on the subject is given to slippage.

℘

I find myself thinking how reluctant I have become to stand away and generalize about *Beautiful Losers*. But then I have always felt a perverse identification with an improbable character imagined by Jorge Luis Borges. Funes the Memorious suffered a knock on the head that left him with phenomenal capacities of perception and memory but with absolutely no generalizing capacity.

> With no effort, he had learned English, French, Portuguese and Latin. I suspect, however, that he was not very capable of thought. To think is to forget differences, generalize, make abstractions. In the teeming world of Funes, there were only details, almost immediate in their presence (*Labyrinths* 66).

In another sort of story, like *Middlemarch*, this is the mind of a human computer, the arid systematiser of the Key To All Mythologies. But Borges makes the mind and thus the world of Funes sensuously rich. Funes is totally attuned to the solid bloody landscape. It is almost as though when everything rearranged itself in his brain he found himself somehow again unfallen. I think it is true and maybe even valuable to say of *Beautiful Losers* that its life-blood is the love and pain that saturate it. If the final note of the novel were the only one that lasted, then pain would be uppermost, but I haven't been arguing the importance of that ending to assert its primacy or finality. The novel thwarts a teleological reading, after all.

I need the mind of Funes to detect how this novel means, as any novel means that teems enough to qualify as a world. From generalizing I lately feel the pull to plunge back in, especially into the riddling parts, like this bit of F.'s arousal script, with his commentary:

> "SEND ME ANOTHER Rupture-Easer so I will have one to change off with. It is enabling me to work top speed at the press machine 8 hrs a day," this I threw in for sadness, for melancholy soft flat groin pad which might lurk in Edith's memory swamp as soiled lever, as stretched switch to bumpy apo-theosis wet rocket come out of the fine print slum where the only trumpet solo is grandfather's stringy cough and underwear money problems (182).

This is writing of precision in the nonsense tradition of carnivalizing sense, very much alive in the work of contemporary inheritors like the so-called "language" writers. It isn't hard to contextualize these lines so, nor to connect words like "apotheosis" and "rocket" with the journey of the soul (in the "birchbark rocket") on which the narrator hopes he will be joining Catherine. But the mystery is local in passages like this. I know I could do something approximate, quite a lot actually, in the way of accounting for the madcap melancholy this one creates, but ultimately these crafted non sequiturs elude any zoo of language and I throw in the towel. I shut up, not in defeat but respect.

Works Cited

Barreto-Rivera, Rafael. *Nimrod's Tongue*. Toronto: Coach House Press, 1985.

Borges, Jorge Luis, *Labyrinths: Selected Stories and Other Writings*. New York: New Directions, 1964.

Bowering, George. "A Great Northern Darkness: The Attack on History in Recent Canadian Fiction." *Imaginary Hand: Essays*. Edmonton: NeWest, 1988.

Cage, John. *Silence*. Middletown, Conn.: Wesleyan University Press, 1939.

Cohen, Leonard. *Beautiful Losers*. Toronto: McClelland and Stewart, 1966.

Dorn, Edward. *Slinger*. Berkeley: Wingbow, 1968.

Eliot, T.S. *Collected Poems 1909-1935*. New York: Harcourt, Brace, 1936.

Griffin, Susan M. and William Veeder, eds. *The Art of Criticism: Henry James on the Theory and the Practice of Fiction*. Chicago and London: University of Chicago Press, 1986.

Hutcheon, Linda. *The Canadian Postmodern*. Toronto: Oxford, 1988.

Lee, Dennis. *Savage Fields: An Essay in Cosmology*. Toronto: Anansi, 1977.

—. "Polyphony: Enacting a Meditation." *Tasks of Passion: Dennis Lee at Mid-Career*. Toronto: Descant, 1982.

Ondaatje, Michael. *Leonard Cohen*. Toronto: McClelland and Stewart, 1970.

—. *Rat Jelly*. Toronto: Coach House, 1973.

—. *Coming Through Slaughter*. Toronto: Anansi, 1976.

Scobie, Steven. *Leonard Cohen*. Vancouver: Douglas & McIntyre, 1978.
—. *Signature Event Cantext*. Edmonton: NeWest, 1989.
Yanofsky, Joel. "Storytelling and the Holocaust." *Brick* 38 (Winter 1990), 30-38.

JAMES REANEY'S
'PULSATING DANCE IN AND OUT OF FORMS'

On 14 December 1975 the NDWT Company ended a national tour of James Reaney's *Donnelly Trilogy* with a marathon same-day performance of the three plays: *Sticks and Stones, Handcuffs* and *The St. Nicholas Hotel, William Donnelly, Prop.* The marathon, at Bathurst Street United Church in Toronto, climaxed over a decade of Reaney's research for and writing of the plays about the massacre of the Donnelly family by their neighbours in the Southwestern Ontario township of Biddulph. Posters invited the audience to share in "the agony of nine hours of theatre." Whatever the experience was for the actors it was anything but agony for me. It was one of the most enthralling experiences I've ever had in the theatre, and I wasn't alone in that opinion. I don't believe the importance of the event—if we see it as a crystallization of the whole tour and all that led up to it—has sunk in in this country. Only a small fraction of the potential audience can have seen the plays, and it's not a simple matter to produce a trilogy. When will those three plays next be performed together? Of course each play is self-contained and tells the whole Donnelly story from the perspective of a particular period of its unfolding. And the three plays are published. Books can't re-create the NDWT production, but the inclusion of production notes, photographs and a discontinuous essay composed of stage directions is a considerable help.

I was galvanized by the trilogy to read Reaney's work up to that masterpiece, seeing it all differently in the light of a dramatic and poetic technique that orchestrates an astonishingly rich flow of material. I wouldn't have been so surprised at the accomplishment had I been able to see productions of *Colours in the Dark* and *Listen to the Wind*, rather than reading them as texts, and had I been paying closer attention to the poetry and essays. But I needed a push to consider Reaney's whole prolific and various career to that point, and *The Donnellys* was it. Possibly the most astonishing thing about the trilogy is that, like Rudy Wiebe's *The Temptations of Big Bear*, it demonstrates that the heroic is still alive. Big Bear, James Donnelly Sr., Judith Donnelly and Will Donnelly are epic heroes, created out of a boldness that dares to be unironic in an age that is properly more than suspicious of heroes. There are such wonderful anomalies in Canadian literature which, as Robert Kroetsch hyperbolizes the matter, skipped the modernist period and arrived at postmodernism undaunted by monumental Canadian forebears (111-112). Neither *Big Bear* nor *The Donnellys* is formally archaic, of course. They're mixed-genre, multi-vocal, thoroughly dialogic works: postmodern enough.

When you stand within James Reaney's art as a whole, and concentrate not so much on the distinctive world that he creates or on his recurrent themes, but rather on the forms that contain it all and the techniques that make it work, you get a different impression from what most early Reaney criticism gives you. In a sense, form is *the* question with Reaney. Form has been evolving; the vision has remained pretty much constant and has been a staple of Reaney criticism. Reaney has always had something to say. He has been a vigorous proselytizer for the causes of regionalism, nationalism, romance as a viable form, the iconography of the imagination, a new theatre. His art has been successful very often in proportion to the submergence of the various "causes" within it, which is a way of saying that when Reaney is at his best it's the form that carries it off.

As a mythopoeic poet Reaney has gained an undeserved reputation for being more interested in art than in life. His less careful or less engaged readers have blamed his use of Northrop Frye's literary theory for what they feel is an over-systematization of experience, but the label of academic poet doesn't fit. There doesn't even seem to be a pigeonhole to put Reaney in. If you read him whole you find poems and plays that don't entirely work, occasionally because of an unresolved tension between "message" and the form it takes. But everywhere you find formal experiment, a true searching out of a strong centre that takes no account of what is fashionable, even though Reaney has always been abreast of what is current in literature and the other arts in and out of Canada. You have only to look at the formal distance between *A Suit of Nettles* and *The Donnellys* to realize that something revolutionary has happened to Reaney's art. If you look again you might see that at least in the Mome Fair eclogue of *A Suit of Nettles* there are formal experiments that feed into the later drama. Reaney's forms and techniques are always swapping around within his work. Even his essays, his little magazine *Alphabet*, his teaching at the University of Western Ontario—everything he does has a formal aspect that flows out of and back into his art as a whole. All of Reaney's preoccupations, formal and otherwise, seem to flow into *The Donnellys*, which is itself a world: everything is part of everything else.

Looking back through Reaney from the vantage point of the trilogy suggests some observations:

The connection with Frye can be overplayed. Reaney has been faithful to Frye's criticism, recognizing much that echoes and supports his own concerns, but he has been enough his own man to give Marshall McLuhan equal billing with Frye as a Canadian "thinker." Frye doesn't have much use for McLuhan, but Reaney does, and the connection with McLuhan has almost as much to say about the nature of Reaney's art as does the influence of Frye.

Reaney wants to do a great deal at once. Without sacrificing clarity, he challenges the reader or viewer with a three-ring circus in which many things happen at once. His art is cinematic in its range, flexibility and speed. He expects a lot of his audience (he wants us to complete his work for him), but there is nothing elitist about that work.

The evolution of Reaney's art has been metamorphic. His experiments with form have seldom been dead ends. One thing turns into another. Forms combine and recombine in different units. There is a flowing formal continuity.

Reaney aims at being comprehensive. He wants to reach us at all levels through all modes of representing reality. His centre is somewhere between myth and documentary.

Reaney's art is contemporary. His work as a whole makes an open form which is of our time, though it preserves much from times past and ultimately aims at getting clear of time.

ॐ

One of Reaney's recurring archetypal patterns structures *Colours in the Dark*. As he describes it in the author's note, the play has "the backbone of a person growing up, leaving home, going to big cities, getting rather mixed up and then not coming home again but making home and identity come to him wherever he is" (3). This is not original with Reaney. The story is the one Frye describes as the basis of all literature. But it's only part of what is going on in *Colours in the Dark*. The form is something else entirely: "The theatrical experience in front of you is designed to give you that mosaic-all-things-happening-at-once-galaxy-higgledy-piggledy feeling that rummaging through a playbox can give you" (3). There is much more McLuhan than Frye in this (McLuhan's image, along with Frye's, is projected on a screen above the action in the University College scene of the play). It sounds much like McLuhan's description of his technique, in *The Gutenberg Galaxy*, as a "mosaic or field approach" to "a mosaic of perpetually interacting forms that have undergone kaleidoscopic transformation—particularly in our time" (7).

McLuhan challenges his readers to make their own synthesis of the mosaic of materials he presents. Reaney is not so cool or detached as this, but you often see him using similar techniques of involving the reader. One of the forces behind Reaney's little magazine *Alphabet* was his interest in contemporary literary forms. He says in the editorial to *Alphabet* 1 that "the most exciting thing about this century is the number of poems that cannot be understood unless the reader quite reorganizes his way of looking at things, or 'rouses his faculties' as Blake would say" (3). Whatever else, *Alphabet* is an exercise in the use of the imagination, because the form it takes is a mosaic of myth and documentary out of which, as Margaret Atwood says in an article on the magazine, the reader is invited to make his or her own patterns. Six years after the last number of *Alphabet* appeared Reaney wrote that "perhaps it is changing into a theatre" ("A Letter From James Reaney" 10). That seems to have been the case.

Colours in the Dark and the Donnelly plays share the combination of mythic and documentary material, the juxtaposition of various forms, and the reader or viewer of the plays has again to "rouse his faculties" to assemble it all. The principle of involvement is explicit in Reaney's comment about the marionettes he made for *Apple*

Stan Dragland

Butter, one of his plays for children. They "are roughly made because I'm no Junior League seamstress, can't carve wood but also because I'm quite content with the resultant primitive effect which all the money in the world couldn't buy so far as forcing the reader to complete my work for me is concerned" ("A Letter" 3-4).

Alphabet may also have turned into the team-taught course in Canadian Literature and Culture that Reaney introduced at the University of Western Ontario. The structure of the course was certainly *Alphabet*-like. Students were obliged to make their own connections, not only between a mixture of Canadian "classics" and unorthodox, often non-fiction, offerings (art and life), but also between the styles and opinions of several lecturers as well as supplementary slides, films and records.

Every writer searches for the form that is what s/he has to say. There is little for Reaney in the form that Frye adopts (as distinct from the forms he discusses), the sequential and logically structured prose argument, however beautifully done. Frye's matter is there on the page. So it seems to me, at least comparing Frye to the gap-filled McLuhan, but Reaney feels it differently, referring in a review of Frye's *Fables of Identity* to

> a peculiar tension usually found in poetry rather than in critical prose. This tension, which one can continually feel in the progression of the sentences, results, I think, from the writer's never quite telling us all he means so that we are forced to think, tempted more than forced, and this makes for an agreeable kind of crackle and electricity" (77).

Ten years later, in *The St. Nicholas Hotel*, Reaney has the Protestant minister Dr. Maguire say of the Donnellys that "They were a very handsome, unusual family with a—as if there was something there they weren't telling you" (113). *They* certainly caused a crackle, not always agreeable. The unknown in their equation polarized their community: these loved them; those hated them. The fact that Reaney celebrates Frye and the Donnellys in almost the same terms would suggest the perversity of underestimating Frye's importance to Reaney, even if Richard Stingle's article, "'All the old levels': Reaney and Frye," hadn't been written. But even Stingle quotes Margaret Atwood saying, "I have long entertained a persistent vision of Frye reading through Reaney while muttering 'What have I wrought?' or 'This is not what I meant, at all' " (114). The *way* Reaney uses Frye is every bit as important as what he uses. To oversimplify the matter, we might say: Frye for content; McLuhan for technique, if McLuhan is allowed to stand for all that is exploratory, unfinished, darting in Reaney's work. In McLuhan and Reaney the page (or sometimes, in Reaney's case, the performance) is full of gaps that a reader or viewer has to leap. To put it another way, as Reaney describes John Hirsch's production of *Names and Nicknames* in the production notes for *Listen to the Wind*, "words, gestures, a few rhythm-band instruments create a world that turns Cinerama around and makes you the movie projector" (117).

The Bees of the Invisible

∾

In *Alphabet* 4 Reaney prints a concrete poem by the London artist Jack Chambers that he feels illustrates Charles Olson's idea of "composition by field" better than the poetry of the *Tish* group. In the accompanying review he shows himself to be no reader of Frank Davey's poetry, and a selective reader of "Projective Verse" as well, but his remarks on the relationship between poetry and contemporary reality are interesting nonetheless. The "images and meaning of the [Chambers] poem, as well as the mere surface format," he says,

> make up a beginningless, middleless and endless field of bubbling energy that reflects the current world picture. In short, if matter is a swarming cloud of electrons and landscape through air travel has become a continuous Jackson Pollock painting with no skyline and Mr. Glenn Gould says that the *Goldberg Variations* begin again as soon as they end, then poetry if it wants to express this reality has quite a job ahead of it ("C.P.R." 74).

This vision of contemporary life—a blur in which patterns are lost or blurred—sounds like the one McLuhan's techniques of probe and pattern-recognition were evolved to comprehend. One way to meet the present is to work in forms that have a speed and versatility of their own, but underlying whose complexity is a shape that may be felt and discovered. Reaney works with myth, insoluble but expansive, containing and redemptive. Myth is his answer to contemporary riddles of information overload and accelerating change. Long before he finds his own comprehensive form that "reflects the current world picture" I can see Reaney moving toward it.

I find the phrase "speeding it up" (275) in his pioneering article on the nineteenth-century Canadian poet Isabella Valancy Crawford. Reaney does for Crawford's poetry what she might have done for herself had she not lived in such cultural isolation. He puts her poems into his own mutascope and turns them fast enough that the underlying pattern, at least Reaney's version of her myth or vision, spins out of the dross that obscures it. Speeding it up means cutting down, simplifying, threshing, on a principle something like the one in the production notes for *Listen to the Wind,* where Reaney says "the simpler art is—the richer it is" (117).

In a similar way, when Reaney goes looking for the backbone of Canadian poetry in "The Canadian Poet's Predicament," he lists the passages out of two anthologies that hook him, and presents the list as an epitome of the whole. Later in the essay he refines even farther, choosing one line out of each of his quotations and making a composite Canadian poem, a grain of sand containing "the native tradition" (285). The date of this essay, 1957, makes Reaney the father of Canadian thematic criticism (see also "The Canadian Imagination," 1959) but he has probably escaped the blame because he's obviously more interested in encouraging others to play around with their own tradition than in establishing a definitive core of patterns. Also, he boils the

Stan Dragland

tradition down to the critical equivalent of haiku. Margaret Atwood, D.G. Jones, Gaile McGregor and the others made the "mistake" of elaborating in a thematic vacuum the poem that Canada writes. My point is that you can't turn Canadian poetry any faster than Reaney does, just as you can hardly do a quicker run-through of Canadian history or world philosophy than the Mome Fair eclogue of *A Suit of Nettles*. I admire the tour de force speed of Mome Fair without really getting caught up in it, but I feel something working in Mome Fair that Reaney takes quite some time to reach in his drama.

One reason the early drama doesn't work as well as the later is that it's too slow and deliberate, at least compared with what Reaney eventually comes to in his theatre. Too slow is one way of encapsulating some of the criticism of *The Killdeer, The Sun and the Moon, The Easter Egg,* and *Three Desks:* too much exposition, too linear and chronological a progression. Reaney himself has never given up on the early plays, though he has re-written some of them. He admits in "Ten Years at Play" that *Listen to the Wind* marks a change in his technique that splits his drama into two periods or styles, but he maintains that his audience only needed to give in to the "primitive" technique of the early plays to enjoy them. From the time of *Listen to the Wind* on, though, there is no question of needing to bring a certain openness to the plays; they demand it. Reaney makes it easier to "give in" because he makes it necessary.

Reaney says in "Ten Years at Play" that from the beginning of his career in drama he wanted to "tell as strong a story as I could devise, as richly as possible" (53). He seems to have discovered that richness requires speed, or "rapids," in the pun of his metaphor describing the later drama in "Ten Years at Play." He says that the early plays are "constructed like rivers in voyageur journals. You go smoothly along in an apparently realistic way, and then there is this big leap" (59) into the unusual. The later plays are "all rapids," which is to say that in them the richness Reaney aimed at has a formal dimension that incorporates swiftness and fluidity.

The Donnelly plays move at a terrific rate, as they must to make comprehensive sense and pattern of a complicated web of events spanning many years. Despite the speed, the plays never blur, and one interesting explanation is the "summary" or "epitome" scene which takes a whole play, or even the whole trilogy, and quickly passes it in review. Sometimes the elements of the summary are simultaneously verbal and visual, as at the opening of Act 3 of *Sticks and Stones:* "Behind [Jennie Donnelly's] narration the entire company mime groupings that go through the story backwards and forwards" (84). Or there is the wedding dance at the Donnelly School in Act 2 of *Handcuffs,* a "reprise that brings together the musical & dance themes of the whole trilogy" (238). Whether or not there is a direct and conscious line of influence, these condensing scenes seem to relate to the trilogy rather in the way Reaney's Crawford relates to Crawford unsifted, the way Reaney's Canadian "poem" relates to the whole tradition. Or the way the whole trilogy relates to the mass of its source material.

The summary scenes of *The Donnellys* are a kind of "shorthand," to adapt a word Reaney uses for the metaphorical technique he discovered while directing the first

34

production of the pivotal *Listen to the Wind*. The early plays sometimes left an audience feeling a bit manhandled by strange events unprepared for by the apparently realistic technique. *Listen to the Wind* introduced a radical solution to the problem of realism's resistance to carrying a poetic vision. It "broke with reality completely, used shorthand for everything, forced the audience to provide lighting and production and even ending ... " ("Ten Years" 60). The discovery of this shorthand was crucial to a workable combination of richness and speed. Shorthand means economy. It issues from a strong faith in the power of the audience's imagination to "complete" the metaphorical suggestions that Reaney's words and his actors' voices and bodies make. Reaney's basic verbal device has always been the metaphor but, as Wilfred Watson pointed out in a 1963 review of *The Killdeer and Other Plays*, "theatre form is *bilingual*—the language of the actor's voice is counterpointed against the language of his body. ... At present Mr. Reaney seems content to leave the second language of the theatre to his director" (65). It was a great advance to begin using the human body and various props metaphorically (mime, as in the Peking opera, is an influence), establishing his own conventions as he went along and inviting the audience to expand the images they suggest. Reaney sees one such visual metaphor, a wheel or carriage, as central to *Listen to the Wind*, and it recurs with increments and variations in *Donnelly*: "as the 'carriage' journeys with Maria to the station it should go on a journey that takes in part of the auditorium so that the boy running with the wheel 'enchants' itself into the onlookers' minds." The stage direction goes on to say of the wheel's artistic function that "in the original production this mime seemed to sum up the play. Devil Caresfoot limps over to the 'carriage' but once 'in' it he runs like a boy" (30). The wheel is a carriage. A row of chairs is a row of trees; a crossbuck, with sound effects, suggests a train. These are metaphors. The release from realism makes just about anything possible on the stage, an almost cinematic range, not to mention that it shrinks the budget considerably—so Stratford wouldn't be interested.

In *The Donnellys* we have a stagecoach duel, a horse race, trains, a threshing machine—all made with human bodies and capable of "dissolving" in a minute into something else—livestock or people. When the actors *are* props and scenery you gain a fluidity and flexibility that the static set and unwieldy scene change resist. On the stage you see what you see, unless you are asked to imagine it.

Reaney asks his actors to turn into things, and he multiplies their roles in another sort of economy move that also has psychological implications, two sorts of which are mentioned in separate stage directions to *Colours in the Dark*. The first explains the business of multiple characterization in this way: "The whole play is going to be like this—six actors playing many different roles—suggesting how we are many more people than just ourselves. Our ancestors are we, our descendants are us, and so on like a sea" (10). There are two sorts of visual symbol in the play which embody this formulation, two family tree pyramids (or, on the page, concrete poems); one supports a child, the child supports the other, suggesting in turn the sustenance and the burden of containing other people and earlier times.

The second direction suggests that multiple characterization is a symbolic way of handling psychological complexity, the individual as a nexus of many lives. The growing boy in *Colours in the Dark* discovers "how many colours and selves he broke up into ... finding out how both hostile and loving the most normal figures in one's life could be" (59). If the continual shifting of identities in *Colours* is not confusing (and it isn't except to those who don't recognize that the convention is symbolic), it's partly because one comes to feel the containment of all the symbolic personages inside the head of the boy whose story is the backbone of the play, and also because the splits are not random. They happen in permutations of an archetypal pattern that Reaney tells us in "An Evening with Babble and Doodle" is behind *Night Blooming Cereus*, "Carl Jung's division of the human soul into four parts represented by an old woman, an old man, a young man and a young girl" (39).

In *The Donnellys* a few actors still play many characters, but the Jungian scheme is not so much in evidence because the emphasis of the story is more historically particular, and because there are in a sense two complex protagonists, a family and a community. In fact more than one community: Ontario and Canada as well as Biddulph. But still, however fast moving and inclusive the technique, it never blurs because these communities tend toward polarization: Grits and Tories, Orangemen and Catholics, friends and enemies. And the neutrals, Donnellys and others, always hemmed in between the antagonistic factions. The "design images" of the trilogy help to reinforce the recurrent sense of conflicting oppositions, so that if the name and particular identity of a minor character slides by at first reading, or after one performance, there is little confusion about the total picture of people in opposition to one another.

❧

A natural corollary of "speeding it up" and "shorthand" is the combination of forms and, perhaps as an outgrowth of that, ultimately a metamorphic technique. If the current world picture is an "endless field of bubbling energy"—this sounds like what television *might* be—it makes sense that contemporary forms are going to be flowing and energetic too. When I look at Reaney's work as a whole I'm always conscious of what he calls in his introduction to *Masks of Childhood* (and repeats in his essay "Long Poems" 118), "an organism, a pulsating dance in and out of forms" (viii). In Reaney's art, forms are tried on that only a liberated imagination would think to use in literary ways (Robert Kroetsch makes a ledger and a seed catalogue into two long poems), forms mate with other forms, individual poems combine and recombine in different ways. This means that despite Germaine Warkentin's admirable anthologizing work, *One-Man Masque* and *Colours in the Dark* are still the best Reaney anthologies (joined now by *Performance Poems*) because the poems in them take the sort of place they have in Reaney's work as a whole—as parts of a large, mixed-genre, active design.

From his collaboration with John Beckwith on the chamber opera *Night Blooming Cereus* Reaney dates his birth as a "craftsman with words" (40). It may be that he learned something else from working with Beckwith. His early attempts at the libretto, he tells us in "An Evening with Babble and Doodle," were too complicated to be set to music; the words made too many claims for themselves. It sounds as if the boundary between poetry and music was too firmly fixed. "Since the librettist is supposed to write something which the music completes and extends," Reaney writes, "the lines have to be cleaned and scraped until there is nothing to stop the music flowing around them" (40). Then a marriage of forms is possible. A librettist is something slightly different from a poet, at least a poet of "involved, complex intellectual lyrics" (41); the latter must become a builder of "verbal structures, each one of whose sounds has been weighed and patterned" (40). There is a sacrifice of the isolating ego that makes it possible to combine your words with something else—or your person. The actors in Reaney's "workshop" drama discovered what it means to contribute to something larger than self. They were asked to leave off being people to turn into a stagecoach or one of a herd of pigs, cows, horses—in order to metamorphose into something else, as Reaney did writing *Night Blooming Cereus* (the poet became the librettist), as distinct forms tend to break down with Reaney in order to combine with others.

It's interesting to see what happens when music merges with poetry in "Letter Eight" of *Twelve Letters to a Small Town*. Music was important to Reaney before he met Beckwith, of course. He cites lessons in counterpoint (as well as the example of film and the three-ring circus) as instruction in multi-level composing. Music lessons gave him the idea for the two-part invention of "Letter Eight," which uses words as notes: left and right hands separately first, then together to play a year in town. Here's part of "Spring":

> Bud bud budling
> Bud bud budling   The spring winds up the town
> Bud bud budling
> Bud bud budling
> Buddy blossoms   The spring winds up the town
> Blossom buddies
> Budding blossoms (23)

This is fascinating on the page, but it isn't only a page poem. It wants to lift off the page into the ear, as so much of Reaney does, and maybe it does so more readily than the text of *Night Blooming Cereus* because it makes, or suggests, its own music. Of course one way to listen to *Night Blooming Cereus*, as Reaney puts it in "Babble and Doodle," is as "a pattern of sounds, some of them repeated many times, an arranged stream of babble … " (41).

Patterns of sounds are what you get from time to time in *Geography Match*, *Names and Nicknames*, *Colours in the Dark* and *The Donnellys*, which sometimes break into word lists, catalogues, chanted magically in the sound poetry "borderblur" between

Stan Dragland

words and music. In fact, by the time of *Donnelly* there is not only chanted words and phrases—sounds made with the voice—but sound effects made with sticks, stones, fiddles, a train whistle, a record-player needle—pre- or un-verbal sounds. Chants, assorted mimetic and mysterious sounds, and the music of songs and dances (see Gerald Parker's essay on Reaney's "sonic environment") combine to make the soundtrack weave of *Donnelly* a score that would be fascinating to hear on its own. I expect it would be intelligible, though more partial than the music for *Night Blooming Cereus* or the recent opera *Serinette*. Perhaps another recent collaboration with Beckwith, *Crazy to Kill*, would be more illustrative, with music made by

Piano
Percussion (one player): washboard, cabaza, wood block, sleighbells, two cowbells (high, low), suspended cymbal, Chinese opera gong, medium tam-tam, three drums (high, medium, low), marimba, vibraphone, chain/metal bucket.
Sound Tape (iii)

In *Gyroscope* there are further experiments with sound. Henry, alone of the characters, speaks in "a repertoire of subverbal hummings, authentic sounding burbles, blurred monotones and unfamiliar phonemes" (ii), and the poetry contest climax is inspired by the "spinning circle of sounds" ("Introduction") generated by sound poetry performances of The Four Horsemen.

Reaney adds his own musical counterpoint to the poems he was asked to read on tape for the Canadian Poets series issued by the Ontario Institute for Studies in Education. Reaney's tape opens with his piano rendition of the hymn "Beulahland," which he then calls the first poem he ever heard. He hasn't been singing, so he almost seems to be calling the tune a poem. The point is a small one, but it does notice a certain creative absence of discrimination as regards the boundary between forms.

Reaney was fiddling with the form of the poetry reading for OISE. He had done so earlier when he was asked to read some poems to "raise the curtain" (41) for the hour-long *Night Blooming Cereus*. Reaney gave the audience more than its money's worth by producing a hybrid form that combines elements of poetry reading (or anthology), drama and masque. *One-Man Masque*, which Reaney now sees as the first of his "performance poems," is a poetry reading, but the reading has the shape the poems are given by their arrangement in sequence, and the poems are "orchestrated" by Reaney's prose bridges, "a series of comic and macabre monologues to be performed in between the poems" (42) that come alive and stand on their own, unlike the connectives in Tom Wayman's *Money and Rain*, another book that borrows formally from the reading. Then Reaney uses the stage, or the space around the "reader" that sags during the usual reading, and fills it with visual symbols or mileposts along the two roads or journeys in life and death the poems make. Later, with more experience and some help, Reaney will liberate his static props to join that "pulsating dance."

The performance of the masque by Reaney himself erased the lines often drawn between writer, performer, director and producer; dramatist doubled as properties manager when Reaney created his own marionettes for *Apple Butter*. Without formal training, but with an avid amateur's devotion, Reaney has become a wonderful draughtsman and water colourist. A work in progress is the animation of a series of water colours, one of which appeared on the cover of the Reaney issue of *Essays in Canadian Writing*. Anywhere you look in his life you see these burgeoning transformations. *Performance Poems* comes with suggestions, in the "Author's Preface, A Letter to the Reader & the Performer," for joining the flow: "[The Poems] can be read silently, they can be read aloud, they can be scored for many voices along with all sorts of illustration and commentary from mime, dance, musique concrète, manipulation of props and body movement. ... Not all of the poems are finished," he goes on, "but challenge you to expand their patterns into larger works with your own local reference."

Performance Poems ("poems and prose-poems [grouped] into a calendar" 7), *One-Man Masque*, "Letter Eight" of *Twelve Letters* and to some extent the OISE tape—these are not standard forms. They make something new in the space between the forms they combine. Two or more forms are turning into something else. There is a guessing game called "Chinese Pictures" in the first version of *The Killdeer* that suggests how Reaney transposes forms, really to create a sort of metaphor identifying form with form. The game, played by Harry and Rebecca, is a riddle whose clues involve imagining the answer in different modes. "If it were / A flower what kind of flower would it be?" (47). Change it into something else. Play a poem on the piano. Elevate stage directions into an orchestral role, as in *Night Blooming Cereus*. Expand epigraph into anthology, like the goose alphabet that opens *A Suit of Nettles*. Make a metaphor without words, and not only on the stage. Here's a visual metaphor, one of Reaney's own drawings, which illustrates "The Bicycle" in *Twelve Letters:*

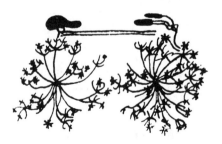

Reaney's art may be connected to a thematic stable faith in the source and ultimate unity of archetypes, but the form it takes is protean. That's one reason why it's so hard to get hold of it—his elusiveness is sometimes taken for a lack of centre—and why it's difficult to catch the essential Reaney in anthologies.

Stan Dragland

છ

If Reaney as a whole is metamorphic, *Donnelly* is quintessence of Reaney, an amazing amalgam of forms. It's so fluid in its shift in and out of forms (and within them) that you can hardly pin down its primary debt to any mainstream of drama. Film techniques, including silent film or slapstick , offer important points of comparison. The cinema's "cast of thousands" is approximated in the technique of multiple characterization, and the shorthand with props makes almost the same range of imagery available on stage that real life offers the cinema, except that the film-maker needs no help from the audience in creating his image; the art is less involving. The "dissolve" or "melt" from one scene or character into another has a great deal to do with the pace and fluidity of the trilogy. In fact there is enough of a cinematic nature in *The Donnellys* (the long shot, the closeup, the split screen) to make that worth an article in itself. But the novel is present too in the shape of various first-person retrospective narrators. *The St. Nicholas Hotel* is contained within the framework of Will Donnelly's account of the Donnelly story to Rev. Donaldson, and other narrators speak from time to time in this and the other plays. The address is sometimes directly to the audience within the plays. Then there are poems, not to be too sharply distinguished from the "poetry" of the whole, as the prose of speech is heightened, with accompanying changes of rhythm. There are songs—like the ballad "John Barleycorn" of *Sticks and Stones,* which contains the whole story and is used both entire, before the play begins, and piecemeal as one sort of recurrent motif which underlines the action at various stages. There are dances, not simply for entertainment or variety, though they provide that. The dances arise out of the community of Biddulph, as one of the chief sources of amusement in nineteenth-century Canada, and their shapes—parallel lines or a circle—are also the forms of antagonistic opposites or unified oneness that are poles of possible relationship to the Donnellys between which the members of the community swing until what we have left is a perversion of the circle of plenitude—a dark circle of the joined shadows of all Biddulph engulfing the Donnellys. There is puppet theatre, mime theatre, detective fiction, the classical chorus, the trial scene (actually originating in the documentary record that Reaney exhaustively researched). Dramatic use is made of almost the whole Roman Catholic liturgy, which is one of the main backbones of the trilogy. We are never very far away from a mass or some other ritual of the Catholic faith, even when the Donnellys are forced to become their own priests, their family an outcast congregation.

The formal variety, the borrowing from likely and unlikely sources and models, makes a new form in which the most diverse elements are whirling around a story-core. Perhaps one may nowadays safely look at this variety as something Northrop Frye accounts for in *The Anatomy of Criticism,* since it has been getting clearer all the time, and more people are recognizing, that Reaney isn't tied to Frye's apron-strings. But I'll approach the idea in terms of something Reaney says about Jay Macpherson's

40

The Bees of the Invisible

The Boatman. He admires her ability to transpose (something, as we've seen, he likes to do himself) a theme from one key or mode to another. One way to put it, in Frye's terms, is that Macpherson turns her book through the modes of tragedy, irony, comedy, romance. *The Boatman* would read like a mechanical versification of *The Anatomy of Criticism* (some readers think it does) if the poems in it hadn't sung themselves into being, section by section, out of the common chaos. Anyway, the modal completeness is partly behind Reaney's enthusiasm for the structural coherence of *The Boatman*:

> Not only is this poet able to arrive at a skill with a very important symbol;
> she also knows how to deal with a great variety of topics in a carefully modulated
> variety of ways. The variety of methods or ways or tones is so cleverly arranged
> that by the time the reader has finished the volume he has boxed the compass
> of the reality which poetry imitates (24-25).

Reaney gets this sort of modal inclusiveness too, not in a long poem constructed of orchestrated lyrics, not by occupying each mythos sequentially, but in a whirling, churning encyclopaedia of effects. All the modes of representing reality make their appearance in *Donnelly.* Irony thrives in such characters as the implacable *Sticks and Stones* antagonist James Carroll, impenetrable by love, as chilling a villain as Iago though not so motiveless in his obsession with bringing the Donellys down. Irony grows throughout the trilogy in proportion to the power of such men, as the gap widens between the complex truth of rights and wrongs in Biddulph and the blindered single vision of the vigilantes. We watch the vicious myth of The Black Donnellys created before us, as a combination of racial, personal, religious and political pressures first infects and then destroys the capacity of normally fair-minded people to exercise powers of ordinary eyesight and common sense.

Parallel and opposite to the Satanic mindset of irony and the hell it spreads is romance, the vision of freedom, harmony, community, imagination and love that Donnellys and others were seeking in the new world, fleeing the covert factional hatreds of Ireland. Throughout the trilogy Mrs. Donnelly embodies this ideal with such gentle strength that she terrifies the bully James Carroll and increases his determination to get at her and her family secretly. Her power has its seat in the soul, and the souls of the righteous are under divine protection, so her soul is invulnerable. The Donnellys may be murdered and their killers go unpunished by law, but the romance vision isn't touched.

The trilogy has the classic tragic trajectory, the inevitable decline into the dark world of disintegration and death. It ends (such is its cyclical construction, and that of each play within it) again and again with variations of the massacre. And yet a comic resolution is implicit from the very beginning in the fact that it's, after all, the Donnellys who return to tell most of their story retrospectively. And where they return from may be seen in the words of Bridget Donnelly as she describes her end, yearning out an upstairs window of the invaded Donnelly house:

> When I got upstairs I went to the window and knelt by it hoping to see a star if the one cloud that covered the whole sky now would lift. I knew they would come to get me and they did. They dragged me down the stairs. The star came closer as they beat me with the flail that unhusks your soul. At last I could see the star close by; it was my aunt and uncle's burning house in Ontario where— and in that star James and Judith and Tom and Bridget Donnelly may be seen walking as in a fiery furnace calmly and happily forever. Free at last (266).

In this gentle heartrending speech by the innocent victim—February 1880 was a terrible time for a niece to visit the Donnellys—all the modes are active. The power of good (romance) to defeat evil (irony) is concentrated; listening to Bridget, it takes an effort to recall the brutality of what is actually happening. And these tragic murders are a victory, a comic ending. "Lo," says Nebuchadnezzar, "I see four men loose, walking in the midst of the fire, and they have no hurt; and the form of the fourth is like the Son of God" (Daniel 3:25). The Donnellys are kin to Shadrach, Meshach and Abednego. Epic, according to Frye, is the genre that contains all the modes, all the other genres. Epic is what Germaine Warkentin calls *The Donnellys* in her introduction to the new edition of *A Suit of Nettles*. At the same time, what Manina Jones says of *Sticks and Stones* is true of the whole trilogy: "the play qualifies as the kind of multi-styled, heterovoiced, stylistically disjunctive writing Bakhtin attributes to the 'novelized genres,' which operate in opposition to an 'epic' version of the past, closed off from change, and impossible to revise" (16-17).

Reaney uses a range of fictional techniques from poetic to realistic to box the compass of reality. He has always been known for his use of "strong" archetypal patterns, not so much for rooting those patterns in everyday reality, as he does in *The Donnellys*. Actually his grip on the so-called "real" has always been stronger than has much been appreciated. For eleven years *Alphabet* placed documentary side by side with myth, as in various ways do the "Seventh Letter" ("Prose for the Past") of *Twelve Letters to a Small Town, Colours in the Dark* and an article, extending the work on media of H.A. Innis and Marshall McLuhan, called "Myths in Some Nineteenth-Century Ontario Newspapers." Of course these newspapers often disguise myth as fact. The connection, the interpenetration, is what Reaney finds fascinating.

The Donnellys is full of documentary material that doesn't call attention to itself, being subject to the demands of the flow of the plays just like everything else. We keep hearing an authentic voice of the past, often a down-to-earth emotionless voice that impassively punctuates a story full of passion. George Stub calmly and smugly recites the statement of expenses for building a gallows while Mrs. Donnelly urgently hikes to Goderich with the petition she hopes will save her husband from it. During the fight in which Donnelly kills Patrick Farl an "inquest voice" breaks in with a description of the murder weapon, a "certain common handspike the value of one penny" (49). The irrelevance of the spike's value underlines the sort of mentality that undervalued the Donnellys, the "on the ground quality which materializes everything," as Reaney puts it in a stage direction, "while with the Donnellys there is just the opposite feeling" (38). Detail after detail like this, whirled out of the flow of the plays, strikes home by being both sharp and specific. Gradually we have built up a detailed picture of what it was like to live in nineteenth-century Biddulph. The people, too, down to the minor characters, are sharply realized, and often through their language, which is one of the most amazing things about *The Donnellys*. The tricks of Irish-Canadian speech are caught and contrasted with more "poetic" English in one direction, and burlesque stage Irish in the other. The handling of densely layered varieties of speech is remarkably sure, seeing that the trilogy marks the first time Reaney used dialogue to compose an authentic history-based complete world. It isn't necessary to "give in" to the world of the Donnellys; it's all there in front of you, the local detail fleshing the archetypes.

It's one thing to identify the forms contributing to *The Donnellys* and to suggest some of the ways in which the trilogy is comprehensive, and it's another to get the feel of the trilogy as it bends old forms to new uses. The triumph in *The Donnellys* of Reaney's metamorphic slide from metaphor to metaphor, whether visual or verbal, his "pulsating dance in and out of forms," is that it sharply registers the edges of things (scenes, characters, images) before moving on, merging them with or dissolving them into something else. If one were looking for the spirit of this technique elsewhere in Reaney, one might find it in the poem called "Near Tobermory, Ontario" which describes the landscape in terms of a favourite organizational scheme, the four elements. Fire in this poem is light, not only the cardinal element, but the principle of the coexistence of all:

> But light, you're quite another thing.
> Indeterminate,
> You hold them all yet let them slip
> Into themselves again
> (*Poems* 190).

There is also a horse (Boehme) on the philosophical merry-go-round of Mome Fair in *A Suit of Nettles* that sounds as if it bears the spirit of the trilogy's technique.

> ... what a pretty snow white horse tattooed with stars, mountains meadows real sheep moving on them it seems & fiery comets & ships in a harbour & little horses dancing in a barnyard. This horse's eyes—oh the angelic wonder of its gold red mane. Every once in a while this horse's colour completely changes.

People shy away then I can tell you! Storms break out in the tattooed skies and a fiery fire burns in the eyes. However it bubbles over—a light comes into his eyes and the world changes back again (43).

I would have said that the Heraclitean horse, whose "whole form keeps flowy-changing," is also illustrative, but in Reaney you *can* "sit in the same saddle twice," because a principle of recurrence controls the flow.

If *The Anatomy of Criticism* contributes something to the form of *The Donnellys*, so does the galaxy or mosaic technique of Marshall McLuhan, but McLuhan as he might be interpreted by the film animation of Norman McLaren. McLaren painted his visual accompaniment to the Quebec folk lullaby, "La Poulette Grise," directly on blank exposed film, so eliminating the frame. I saw it first as a member of Reaney's Canadian Literature and Culture teaching team.

One reason why *The Donnellys* seems to me to concentrate all of Reaney formally is that he appears to have brought to the story all that he feels about life and literature, everything he had learned about writing, and sunk those things into the play, so that one not only feels less of Frye here than elsewhere but, for all the intricacy of the mechanism, less of Reaney too. I think that is because the form does so much.

Almost everywhere in Reaney we find, sometimes quite schematically, the conflict between the antipoetic materialists and the "identifiers," the unthinking advocates of progress versus the believers in subtler laws of existence, educators of the soul as opposed to educators for practical life. These conflicts, or variations on the one conflict, are present in *The Donnellys*. They help to define the Donnellys not only as individualists but as people who buck the common assumptions of their time and place. The conflict is central, but set in such a wealth of flowing event and detail that it doesn't obtrude, as it does for example in the post-Donnelly *Baldoon*, a delightful play which nevertheless reverts to mere lobbying for the value of love and the imagination.

The Donnellys is an extremely complicated machine whose working parts are open to view. There is the feeling Jay Macpherson got from *Listen to the Wind* of "creation before one's eyes" (viii), perhaps even stronger in the trilogy because the dramatic metaphor ("how do we make this play" within the play?) is assumed. There is nothing hidden by a backstage. The actors sit on the stage and move into their parts when required. Or they make sound effects using everyday objects that are also visible. All this contributes to the audience's co-creation of the trilogy and is worth a great many Reaney exhortations to go out and make our own plays, rouse our slumbering imaginations.

The Donnelly trilogy is an anti-environment, in McLuhan's phrase, the form of which is familiar to us, whether we recognize it or not, from our experience of speeded up, bewildering modern life. But the metamorphic form is shaped to the expression of permanent values and has a shape (one of those values) that may be discovered, that controls its constituent parts centripetally, while the fragments of contemporary existence seem centreless, centrifugal. But a better way to account for the form of the trilogy is to say that it is *of* the Donnellys. It has their wit, their verve, their openness, their humour; it has their wings, their refusal to kneel. Even the simultaneity of the story seems to be of the Donnellys. The murder happens in *Sticks and Stones* and happens again and again one way or another throughout the trilogy, and there are other ways of dislocating and contracting time that only the Donnellys, of all the protagonists, seem connected to. For one thing the ghost selves of the Donnellys know all the story, having "passed into source" ("The Ghost," *Poems* 122). But sometimes we see them even in the "present" of the play living fleetingly in the future, as when Mrs. Donnelly predicts that she will come once more to Father Connolly's church after she had decided, in this life, never to enter it again, or when she dimly senses the presence of her "deep down dead leaf self" (81) in Act 2 of *Sticks and Stones*. The trilogy has the largeness of spirit, extending even to breaking the barriers of time, of the Donnellys themselves. Which is to say that you may tell almost all there is to tell about *The Donnellys* by talking about form. That isn't inevitably true of other individual Reaney works, but it seems true of Reaney read whole as, to adapt some words of Irving Layton, his forms "swap, bandy, swerve" in an overall shape that is free.

Works Cited

Jones, Manina. " 'The collage in motion': Staging the Document in Reaney's *Sticks and Stones.*" *Canadian Drama* 16.1 (1990), 1-22.

McLuhan, Marshall. *The Gutenberg Galaxy.* Toronto: University of Toronto Press 1962.

Parker, Gerald D. "The Key word ... is 'listen': James Reaney's 'Sonic Environment.' " *Mosaic* XIV, 4 (Fall 1981), 1-14.

Reaney, James. *A Suit of Nettles.* Toronto: Macmillan, 1958.

—. "The Canadian Poet's Predicament." *University of Toronto Quarterly* XXVI, 3 (April 1957), 284-295.

—. Isabella Valancy Crawford. Robert L. McDougall, ed. *Our Living Tradition.* Second and Third Series. Toronto: University of Toronto Press, 1959.

—. "The Canadian Imagination." *Poetry* (Chicago) 94,3 (June 1959), 186-189.

—. "The Third Eye: Jay Macpherson's *The Boatman.*" *Canadian Literature* 3 (Winter 1960), 23-34.

—. "An Evening With Babble and Doodle: Presentations of Poetry." *Canadian Literature* 12 (Spring 1962), 37-43.

—. "C.P.R. (Canadian Poetry Railroad)." *Alphabet* 4 (June 1962), 71-74.

—. *Twelve Letters to a Small Town.* Toronto: Ryerson, 1962.

—. *The Killdeer and Other Plays.* Toronto: Macmillan, 1962.

—. "Frye's Magnet." *Tamarack Review* 33 (Autumn 1964), 72-78.

—. "Ten Years at Play." George Woodcock, ed. *The Sixties: Canadian Writers and Writing of the Decade.* Vancouver: University of British Columbia Press, 1969.

—. *Colours in the Dark.* Vancouver: Talonbooks, 1969.

—. *Listen to the Wind.* Vancouver: Talonbooks, 1972.

—. *Masks of Childhood.* Toronto: New Press, 1972.

—. *Poems.* Ed. and introd. Germaine Warkentin, Toronto: New Press, 1972.

—. *Apple Butter and Other Plays for Children.* Vancouver: Talonbooks, 1973.

—. "A Letter From James Reaney." *Black Moss* Series 2, No. 1 (Spring 1976), 2-10.

—. *Gyroscope.* Toronto: Playwright's Canada, 1980.

—. *The Donnellys.* Victoria/Toronto: Press Porcepic, 1983.

—. "The Long Poem." Frank Davey and Ann Munton, eds. "The Proceedings of the Long-liners Conference on the Canadian Long Poem." *Open Letter* Sixth Series, 2-3 (Summer-Fall 1985), 115-119.

—. and John Beckwith. *Crazy to Kill: A Detective Opera.* Guelph: Guelph Spring Festival, 1989.

—. *Performance Poems.* Goderich, Ontario: Moonstone, 1990.

Watson, Wilfred. An Indigenous World. "Rev. of *The Killdeer & Other Plays.*" *Canadian Literature* 15 (Winter 1963), 64-66.

REANEY'S RELEVANCE

My favourite words in the "Long-liners Conference Issue" of *Open Letter*, the proceedings of a conference I didn't attend, are some that James Reaney spoke in the discussion following the panel of which his paper was a part:

> The way I read Derrida is quite different. What Derrida is doing is he wants a reaction. He doesn't want you to agree with him, surely. No one could agree with that! [Laughter.] It's intended to arouse the old, whatever it is—the old Martin Luther, or something, or Ezekiel, or Isaiah, or those Old Testament prophet kinds of thing. Sure the role is absolutely all illusion. Nothing means anything; it's just a fog. But, by God, *I'm* not a fog. I see a living chariot with four wheels on it all covered with eyes! How about that? [Laughter.] (123)

"[Laughter]" is sprinkled through the transcripts of discussions following each panel. One-liners at the Long-liners. The conference participants seem to have enjoyed themselves. But what sort of laughter was greeting these pronouncements of Reaney? Supportive? Patronizing? Because his paper, "Long Poems," was still citing the old theory hero, Northrop Frye: "There has to be, if I read my recent Frye aright (and I'm particularly indebted to *Modern Century*), something outside of ourselves that inspires and orders" (118). No wonder he reads the new theory hero as rhetorical provocateur. "Something outside of ourselves" ("I feel that we're going to have to revive God" 118) is the transcendental signified or origin or presence that Derrida denies metaphysics. It's the Word made flesh. It's logocentrism, humanism; it's the old order.

It's not the rejection of Derrida that delights me when Reaney suddenly, improbably at an academic conference, enters the prophet's role he had written many years ago in Part VI of "A Message to Winnipeg" (*Poems* 137-139). It's the style, the energy, the *conviction* in the words. One way or another, Reaney has been grabbing me for over twenty years. The poem that stood out for me when I first read *Poetry of Mid-Century* was the May Eclogue of *A Suit of Nettles*. For almost twenty years Reaney and I have been colleagues at The University of Western Ontario.

Not that we've always been close, over the years. We've often enough been annoyed with each other. His work has sometimes annoyed me. I had mixed feelings about

Wacousta, Traps, Baldoon. I wasn't taken with the chapbook *Imprecations: The Art of Swearing,* despite these wonderful lines from the first page:

My own father never swore except—'the dirty beggar!'
Never *bugger. Beggar*—as damn becomes darn, and God
Is always Golly where the bright angel feet
Of Elwy Yost have trod,
But my stepfather was quite another story:
'Great Judas Iscariot—that fart in a windstorm!
Get off my toes, you bloody cocksucker!'—to a horse.
'Son of a sea-cook' was his mildest imprecation.
On a daily basis *shit-ass* and *piss-willie*
Were levelled at neighbours, relatives, those
Who deserved this, those who did not (NP).

At certain irritated moments I've almost taken seriously Louis Dudek's charge of "strange infantilism" (20) in the poetry, or W.J. Keith's of "technical uncertainty at all stages of Reaney's poetic career" (32). Mostly, though, I feel that what occasionally bothers me in the work, what we used to call unevenness in the days of pontificating, is original, individual Reaney. His work is not smooth and it's anything but bland. Sometimes it's intentionally unfinished. He often takes the supreme risk, among adults, of sounding like a child. He risks preaching. Yet he has a spiny commitment to the creative imagination that reminds me of some words of John Cage in "Composition as Process;" perversely, because the two are on opposite sides of the art/ chaos divide: "IF THERE WERE A PART OF LIFE DARK ENOUGH TO KEEP OUT OF IT A LIGHT FROM ART, I WOULD WANT TO BE IN THAT DARKNESS, FUMBLING AROUND IF NECESSARY, BUT ALIVE." (46). Alive: passionate, unpredictable. I won't recite everything I like about what Reaney does. If all that, and all the rest, were merely preparation or context for *The Donnellys,* it would be valuable for that reason alone, though unfair to some wonderful work written since: *Gyroscope, The Boy Actors* (yet unpublished), the opera *Serinette,* with music by Harry Somers.

Being alive: being open. That ideal of postmodernist poetics often seems not to extend to the possibility that humanism, modernism, may have something to say to us still. Literary modernism and postmodernism disentangle with great difficulty, in fact, even when we stop trying to divide them chronologically—absurd, I suppose, given that both words originate in chronology—and speak instead in terms of opposing approaches to genre, form, technique. Of course isms never speak themselves. We construct isms by connecting examples. If it untidies postmodernism— whose instabilities of form, genre, and technique in general are based on convictions that the word, the self, the *world* are nowhere near as solid and unitary as we once thought—to insist that Reaney is part of it, at least in terms of form, that's tough. It's true that I've sometimes felt patronized by Reaney's didacticism and winced at unlikely lines, but I've also, in my heart and belly and mind, been deeply moved by his words. When that happens, the categories dissolve. They return, the critical terminology flows back (and welcome enough) to settle over the texts in discussions like this one, but grounded in deeply sustaining silence.

Contemporary theories of randomness, indeterminacy, deferral of meaning, and the poetics of writing that expresses or in some way responds to such contingencies, are no longer news. Kurt Vonnegut's popular and accessible anti-novel *Breakfast of Champions* plays with the proposition that chaos is reality and God is a writer fighting depression. Unsettling ideas and unsettled technique are not just the private concerns of far-out artists and intellectuals. And it's valuable to discover an anti-form that helps you to stand outside and question inclusive (totalizing, we now say) theoretical systems like Northrop Frye's, those coherencies that are also the basis of Reaney's art. It's valuable to feel the hazards of the crude naming language permits, illusions of identification, control, ownership. "[L]anguage of course is a kind of lullaby," says Charles Simic (25). That's certainly not how Reaney sees it, though. To him the alphabet (words, poetry) is a reveille. To me, both stances feel true and problematical, and I believe they should stay that way. Reaney's model of the gyroscope, over-neatly self-correcting though it is, suggests how a mind might be divided on such matters and still remain sane:

> Yes, the gyroscopic idea applies to souls as well as voice boxes. It does so in the following ways: if you keep spinning, that is, moving from where and what you are now to the opposite of that and then immediately to the opposite of that, then you have power, flexibility, love, energy, community—in short BALANCE —even in our absurd world where the real horizon is often obscured (*Gyroscope* "Introduction").

I find BALANCE elusive. My mind wobbles, though it does gyroscopically embrace the poetry (and so entertains, as foundationally valid, the world view) of writers who'd squirm to find themselves in the same category. George Bowering and Jay Macpherson, for example: an unlikely couple? Reaney is often enough admitted, as by Bowering, to have escaped Northrop Frye's orbit, but Macpherson seldom is. I find her two long poems, *The Boatman* and *Welcoming Disaster*, at once satisfying and daunting. Running *The Anatomy of Criticism* through them would only be a beginning. I'm also a lover of Bowering's *Kerrisdale Elegies*, and have made a critical start on that poem. To me, obviously, the result of interrogating established forms and systems is not necessarily rejection of the writing they nourish. Working systems are as grains of sand on the literary beach. Some of the ones you can't sign your name to may still clarify the world and your place in it. They can still delight.

"Something in him so loves the world," says Leonard Cohen of his saint/artist, "that he gives himself to the laws of gravity and chance. Far from flying with the angels, he traces with the fidelity of a seismograph needle the state of the solid bloody

Stan Dragland

landscape. His house is dangerous and finite, but he is at home in the world" (96). Giving himself/herself, categories suspended, to the itch of what is. Listening hard to "the tinkly present" (*Beautiful Losers* 12) in irritation or delight or puzzlement. Certainly, but why not choose, reading Reaney, to fly with the angels as well? Meaning what? Reaney says that "an angel [in Jay Macpherson's *The Boatman*] is anything ... at ... its most expanded" ("The Third Eye" 24), a poetic interpretation of anagogic being. In Jay Macpherson's complementary version, "Beings capable of ... transformations—emblematic of 'the power to see the universe as the content of the poet's mind'—in Reaney's work are sometimes called 'Angels'" ("Educated Doodle" 81).

Anagogy reaches the status of commonplace in Reaney criticism in articles by Terry Griggs, Colin Browne, Jay Macpherson, and Richard Stingle published in *Approaches to the Work of James Reaney*. Anagogy, once the mystical level of the four levels of interpretation in Medieval criticism, becomes to Canada's mythopoeic poets the imaginative plenitude achieved in absorption of the outer world by the human mind. The world out there is worded, named; things so identified merge one with another in metaphor, the basic combinative trope of a myth of absorption, the myth that renders everything, according to Reaney, as the Indians see it. To them, he says, "the outer world means very little; it is the inner world of dreams and visions that is all" ("An ABC" 2). Or the Inuit: "Not me in the world, but the world in me" ("A Letter" 4). "More than anyone else," Germaine Warkentin says, "Reaney has recognized the profound moral and social centre of Frye's theory. ... Frye's vision ... is of a universe made completely intelligible. It is one which we can live in contentedly because we have possessed it with our minds and it can never henceforth be lost to us" (*Poems* XII).

The imagination can draw "the world below" into what Frye and Reaney call the verbal universe, or literary tradition, to mimic a coherent whole as seen "in God's eye" or dreamed by a sleeping giant. Culture is "The study of words," says Professor Dale in *The Dismissal*, refuting Professor McQuaild, of Political Science, to whom "culture is the study of things" (19). *Alphabet* was dedicated to the proposition that mankind answers "the terrors of the inner and outer world with a symbolic fruit and an iconic seabeast" (I, 14), answers, that is, with names—the forbidden fruit, for example, or leviathan—with metaphors, symbols, which grow into myth, the structures of the imagination that serve relationship or family and defy discontinuity, chaos.

Reaney makes an interesting analogy in the Editorial to *Alphabet* 2 for the way his magazine's juxtaposition of myth and documentary, words and things, was meant to work:

> ... take the face cards out of a card deck; then put a circular piece of cardboard near them. Curves and circles appear even in the Queen of Diamonds and the Knave of Spades. But place a triangular shape close by and the eye picks up corners and angularities even in the Queen of Clubs. What every issue of *Alphabet* involves, then, is the placing of a definite geometric shape near some

50

face cards. Just as playing about with cubes and spheres can teach an artist and a critic a better sense of composition, *Alphabet's* procedure can have the same result with iconography and symbolism (2).

Each issue of *Alphabet* revolved around a myth or archetype intended to suggest a shape or pattern or common backbone to its contents (fiction, essays, poetry, reviews, music, visuals—quite varied, really, so that editorial control never usurped the reader's creative role). This is in the spirit of Frye's *Anatomy of Criticism*, with its encyclopaedic design; the ultimate collection of edifying shapes, as far as Reaney is concerned.

The *Anatomy*, like *Fables of Identity*, he says in a review of the latter, offers "a number of very powerful designs—theorem-image might be a name for them. Once you expose yourself to these designs or images you may soon find that anything you read arranges itself around them as—iron filings around a magnet" (73). Life or the present is opaque unless clarified by the organizing powers of art, especially when boosted by the magnet of theory. A complex little riddle/concrete poem/advertisement Reaney composed for *Alphabet* says it tightly:

LIFE IS BMQIBCFU
ART IS ALPHABET

BMQIBCFU looks at first like a typographical scramble, a metaphor for chaos—life makes no sense; art does—until you notice (reading from A to B, L to M, and so on) that it's actually ALPHABET in code. The message is that art reads life; with this key life is much more intelligible than at first it seemed, and the implication is that it always *was* so, except to uneducated eyes.

It's sometimes felt that Reaney spends all his time with the angels: opting out of life as it is, explicitly structuring his works with archetypes, and creating a closed, artificial world that never really touches the one we live in. The same is often thought of Frye's system. I can understand how the backs of some writers go up, hearing this talk of absorption, control, subordination of chaos to order, nature to man. In distilled form, it's repugnant to me too. I'm suspicious of control. At times my desire is exactly that of Daphne Marlatt's character Ana Richards: to be "simply eyes" (97). But one test of the theory is the work it sponsors. *The Donnellys* helps me to relax, if guardedly, to Frye's theory and Reaney's extensions of it, and to endorse the caring social vision that they share. The trilogy proved that Reaney can recreate the texture of an actual world down to its subtlest low mimetic nuances.

It shows that Reaney's words and things need not circulate in separate vortices. The words of the trilogy are charged with respect for things, and chaos has a powerful voice in characters like Tom Cassleigh and Jim Carroll. *The Donnellys* is partly the fruit of Reaney's long fascination (notwithstanding his claims that the inner world is the real one) with the shape of things as they are that he calls "documentary." Life is shown to school art in an important passage in *14 Barrels from Sea to Sea*. At the Winnipeg

Stan Dragland

stop of the national tour, Reaney met two families whose ancestors had come from Biddulph, Donnelly country:

> Only a fellow researcher could understand the excitement I felt at meeting these people; previously they had been just a scrap of paper in the Chancery Court files under B for *Blackwell vs Brown*; now in Row S of the Salle Pauline Boutal the verbal universe dissolves into human figures and faces telling me things that enable me to go back into the patterns I am weaving in the world of words and adjust here, shade more here (42).

The sampler of Reaney might come away with the impression that he has no use for Cohen's "solid bloody landscape," but a more thorough reader knows that his writing bears out the claim, in "An ABC to Ontario Literature and Culture," that "precise knowledge shows love and breeds the same quality" (2). This is not to deny that sometimes, as Margaret Atwood observed of the *Poems* (157), the archetype and the actuality do not dissolve in one another, but are simply associated without much release of energy. The strain apparent at such moments is presumably what made Frank Davey, almost twenty years ago, argue that Reaney is one of those who imposes pattern on life rather than discovering it there, one of a "school of poets" "who have retreated from the reality of themselves and their country into an emasculated international world of myth and archetype" (64). Robin Blaser endorses Davey's anti-humanistic stance in his introduction to George Bowering's *Particular Accidents: Selected Poems*, where he persuasively defends Bowering from coherence-seeking misreaders in terms that implicitly reject work like Reaney's:

> The unwitting demand is that Bowering give us a unity—this is the word for a nostalgia or sentiment of form in so many writers and readers—which in his work is not lacking, but is relentlessly questioned ... 'It is important not to be deceived,' Geoffrey Hartman writes, 'by the sophisticated vagueness of such terms as *unity, maturity, coherence*, which enter criticism at this point. They are code words shored against the ruins. They express a highly neo-classical and acculturated attitude; a quiet nostalgia for the ordered life; and a secret recoil from aggressive ideologies, substitute religions and dogmatic concepts of order.' The nostalgia and sentiment of form are no answer to the conditions in which we live (11-12).

Bowering's poetry does answer, Blaser thinks, with its "restlessness of meaning," with its form that is "alive and difficult of access because it is not before or after the fact of writing, but within it. That is to say, the movement of life into language—a marvel that begins childishly where we all begin—is not formulaic or expected. It is perhaps a surprise" (10).

Since *The Red Heart*, Reaney has been writing the story that turns up as something

52

of a formula in everything he writes—heroes of the imagination vs. "the anti-anagogy gang" (*Alphabet* 1, 4); his writing is not restless of meaning in Blaser's sense. But Reaney is formally eclectic and protean, and his more recent plays have embodied his myth in techniques that have to be called restless. He keeps surprising writers as different from him as bp Nichol. Nichol's reading of Reaney, in fact, his defence in an open letter to Frank Davey, makes the man sound postmodernist plain and simple.

> Reaney's concern is also with language with the materials of language   you can see the jump in consciousness in difference between 12 LETTERS TO A SMALL TOWN & EMBLEMS   in 12 the drawings illustrate the text   in EMBLEMS the text & the emblem are inseparable   the materials of the poem are no longer external   it *is* the object it describes   no more duality   here reaney comes close to writing writing   he has finally done in his poetry what he has done in his plays which is to say he has made them self sufficient   they exist as real objects in the real world (5)

Nichol, naturally reading Reaney in the light of his own concerns with language and form, recognizes another experimenter. His Reaney is not invented, though the drive to explicitness in meaning is being filtered out. Perhaps that drive is an occupational hazard of Reaney's solid stance on faith in the power of words to proceed to anagogy, in the permanence of the verbal universe with its resources for interpreting life. Or perhaps the hazard for Reaney's art issues from self-consciousness about what he's doing and the impulse to let the reader in on that. Behind this, in turn, has always been his desire to improve his country and the world. "I wonder," he asks in *14 Barrels From Sea to Sea*, "if there's some sort of special firewater you could feed people in this country just to get a more loving feeling started?" (139). Whatever the cause, Reaney sometimes spells out for his reader or viewer things that the resources of his art are perfectly adequate to embody. I don't believe he is naive about this. I think he accepts the risk of assuming a didactic stance and sometimes even pulls it off. But not always.

ço

When Reaney wrote, in "The Canadian Poet's Predicament" (1957), that "no one seems to be able to tell you ... whether you should be self-conscious or unconscious about the craft of poetry ..." (111), he was already coming down on the self-conscious side. He has been reflecting on his own art ever since, in essays that can't be touched as Reaney criticism. In fact his essays, editorials for *Alphabet* and the series of occasional theatrical newsletters called *Halloween*, the journal-based *14 Barrels*—these are extensions of his art. Polemicizing may sometimes impair the effectiveness of his plays, but it flowers in these pieces. The *Halloween* essays are wonderful to read, because Reaney is one of the best prose stylists in the country, and because he is passionately persuasive on behalf of his theatre and the cultural contexts it focuses. But I sometimes turn from one of these essays to certain of the plays and wonder what happened to such excellent theory.

To the reader who hears Reaney preaching in certain plays, it seems ironic to hear him talk so convincingly, in his first newsletter, about how the reading of Frye encourages the wrapping of meaning in concrete formal envelopes:

> ... as Frye points out in his latest book, *The Critical Path*, all "isms" come out or go back into myths, or STORIES, so why not present the concrete version of your favourite "ism" rather than try to jam existentialism or Maoism or naturalism down your audience's throats the way ministers used to dose us with Calvinism. Maybe if we get used to seeing our society as being based on a story, we'll wake up and realize that we can get a better story ... ("A letter from James Reaney" 4).

The occasion for these remarks is reflection on the nature and origin of *The Donnellys*, "A story, a story that matters very, very much," in which something that happened in nineteenth-century Biddulph, and happens still (a dark power, a rat growing larger and larger by feeding on the lives of imaginative individualists) is very movingly counterpointed by the "better story" of what could and should have been, its theme the "world of power and love" that, in *The St. Nicholas Hotel*, "might have been [Maggie's] forever" (114). That better story runs through Reaney's work and takes some lovely shapes, but is no more palatable than existentialism and the rest when the audience feels forced to swallow *it*. This is what happens in *Traps* and, to a lesser extent, in *Baldoon*.

Traps, "a mime play," was not wordless, though there was a higher proportion than usual of Reaney's trademark mime. The vision of the rat in this very dark play is literally embodied in a race of rats bred by mind-control experiments of behavioural psychologists in a fictional North American university. In the production I saw, the "concrete" mime made it so clear what was going on that young children had no trouble understanding it. Still, the anti-rat lesson was spelled out in the harangue of a South American woman whose husband fell victim to the mind-controllers. She was so clearly the author's voice that, sadly, it was difficult to sympathise with her.

Founded on a tradition sometimes known as "the Baldoon mysteries," *Baldoon* has to do with a ghost or demon that tormented a house occupied by a family near Wallaceburg, Ontario, and with Dr. Troyer, the witch-finder. The play begins with the mystery of the haunting; from then on much of the action involves Dr. Troyer's exorcising activities, his probing for the source of the problem. The responsible party, McTavish, has to be turned inside out before he can see the selfishness which made him commit wrongs that laid him open to supernatural harrassment. By the end of the play everything is clear and resolved, and the Baldoon mysteries have evaporated as surely as they would have under a materialist treatment. That is so even though the explanation replaces the mystery with another mystery—the shamanistic powers of Dr. Troyer and his access to the world above. To put it baldly, one might say that Reaney doesn't explore the Baldoon mysteries so much as smother them under the formula of his own myth of good triumphing over evil, the same one that is charged with real and lasting tension in other plays.

To put it baldly is to put it too harshly. It's possible to complain about overall heaviness of touch in *Baldoon* and still like the way both McTavish and Dr. Troyer are lovingly and particularly rendered, especially in their speech. But in the two plays I've singled out, the author seizes the gentle reader or viewer too firmly by the elbow. He is very much the guide, very clearly spelling out the lessons, in his children's plays and novels too.

A much more interesting manifestation of the helping hand in the adult plays and libretti is the stage directions in the published texts. They are so helpful, even with interpretation, that critics of the drama are almost as likely to quote them as they are the text proper. Of course a Reaney play, so rich in performance, is inevitably thinner on the page. The stage directions help with filling in something of what's missing; they become part of the text, and in fact their augmented use is typical of Reaney's activation of genres not usually recognized as genres. One of Reaney's signatures is a directness of approach which is appealing rather than irritating, then, when the context naturalizes it.

Statements, quite overt messages, sometimes appear in *The Donnellys*, for instance, where to my ears they usually sound right. There's an example in Act III of *Handcuffs*, when the metaphor of the title is spoken by the ghosts of Mr. and Mrs. Donnelly to a "soft tough" representing the simplistic but powerful Black Donnelly myth that the whole trilogy refutes. The 1970s youth has made the mistake of drunkenly standing on the Donnelly grave on the anniversary of their murder and inviting them to rise up. They do, handcuffing him, and reacting with indignation to his appeal to be set free:

BOTH:
UNDO THE HANDCUFFS, Indeed! First unlock the handcuffs in your mind that make you see us as

MR. DONNELLY:
that fierce harridan

MRS. DONNELLY:
that old barnburner!

BOTH:
We weren't that/this! (254)

Why does the explicit message work here and elsewhere in *The Donnellys*, while in certain other plays messages are almost patronizing? For one thing, the moment in Act III of *Handcuffs* is not the only one in the trilogy when the "curtain ... between life and death" (132) has wavered, allowing the Donnellys to act as audience in plays within the play about them. They are permitted their opinion of the nasty myth they have become. For another thing, this is not the only time Reaney metafictionally punctures the illusion that the Donnelly story is merely an entertainment, a fiction performed by actors for an uninvolved audience. Further, addresses of characters to the audience are whirled out of a three-ring circus of multiple techniques (narration, mime, song, dance) all layered into the standard stratagems of the drama. The trilogy sparkles from technique to technique so quickly and persuasively and clearly, in "a pulsating dance in and out of forms" (*Masks of Childhood* viii), that the direct approach is folded into the variety, and seems not only permissible, but extremely effective.

There is some difference of opinion among Reaney's critics as to which of his works succeed best, and, when there is dissatisfaction, about what sorts of artistic problem have not been satisfactorily solved. His son, James Stewart Reaney, finds *Listen to the Wind* Reaney's greatest play, feeling that the trilogy whitewashes the historical Donnellys. This seems to me as naive an argument (in a very useful book) as W.J. Keith's that *A Suit of Nettles* is not fair to F.R. Leavis. Fair satire is a contradiction in terms; historically accurate art is another, given that even straight history is a construction and a version of the whole. My own biggest problem is with Reaney's didacticism. But this I see in a field of passionate commitment, grounded in concern for the cultural past and future of this country, to education.

∽

I fell into the Reaney vortex between 1970 and 1972 as a member of the large teaching team assigned to a new course, called Canadian Literature and Culture, that he had designed. I found him a wonder during that time, a fabulous teacher who gave his imagination free rein. His language was almost totally free of critical jargon; he was learned without any parade of learning. The "Fryekit" (70), to adapt Jay Macpherson's neologism, may have been at the core of much of what he said, but there was little sense of his leaning on it. If it helped him to structure his eclectic originality, it never seemed burdensome to me as system, and really his pedagogical technique came much closer to the McLuhan "probe," the brief unpondered flash into a subject, than to the systematics of Frye. I've heard him say he sold his soul to Northrop Frye, but only a free man given to hyperbole would say such a thing in public.

Reaney is always teaching, not only in the classroom but in his essays, his poetry, his dramatic workshopping, his plays. Education is one of his most important themes. His poems and plays are full of teachers, good and bad. The good ones are usually some variation on Old Strictus, the traditional education goose in *A Suit of Nettles*, while the ones Reaney mistrusts are often utilitarians with very little method to speak of, if they aren't actively "anti-anagogy." Reaney espouses with and in his own work the traditional values of discipline and standardization in education, and his aim is to reach, child and adult, as wide a student body as possible across the country.

The purpose may well be incompatible with the creation of works in which form and meaning are, as Blaser puts it, "difficult of access." Indeed, it's an apparent contradiction between the accessible and the arcane, the simple and the profound, that troubles Louis Dudek in an article on Reaney called "A Problem of Meaning." Dudek takes an elitist line in trying to account for some of the poetry he finds embarrassing, and in explaining why he thinks Reaney, addressing himself to a general Canadian audience, is up against it: " ... I would say that faced with an audience of mindless biddies and croquet intellect, such as we may have in Canada in the outlands, the poet has taken drastic means to simplify" (21-22). Punch-pulling ("I would say," "may have," "in the outlands") aside, Dudek's article combines the reasonable assumption that an artist's first obligation is to him or herself with the snobbish opinion that Reaney compromises to reach people not worth the trouble. Perhaps there *is* a compromise, when content overrides form, but I doubt that simplification is the root of it.

An answer to Dudek might divide into two complex parts:

a) "The simpler art is—the richer it is" ("Production Notes," *Listen to the Wind* 117). Reaney is expecting the educated members of his audience to relate to his "complexity in simplicity" (Noonan, "Foreword," *The Donnellys* 8), rather than levelling his art to reach the simple-minded. It's a fact that simple art need not be impoverished, that "STORY" may embody complicated "isms," which is why romance, whether in folk-tale or sophisticated versions, can still be so satisfying, and why it's no criticism of Reaney to say that his work is based on romance. But Reaney's *Listen to the Wind* statement should be read along with this one in the editorial to *Alphabet* 1: "The most exciting thing about this century is the number of poems that cannot be understood unless the reader quite reorganizes his way of looking at things or 'rouses his faculties' as Blake would say." The richness of *Finnegans Wake* and Dylan Thomas's 'Altarwise by owl-light' sonnet sequence, the exciting examples offered, is not owing to simplicity, so is Reaney being contradictory? Not if we sort out the relationship of simplicity and complexity in his own work.

Reaney would probably say that *Finnegans Wake* is simple once you see that it's built on an old story of The Sleeping Giant. That's his way of containing the book in a nutshell—hardly all there is to say about *Finnegans Wake*, but then you don't contain most Reaney volumes in a grain of subject either. In one sense it's easy to handle *Colours in the Dark* by calling it an archetypal growing-up story, but what about the techniques of multiple characterization, of mime, even the use of properties?

> When *Colours in the Dark* was done professionally, one of my friends was babbling on to the prop-design lady, "Reaney's stuff is so simple," and she said "Simple! Do you realize there are 120 props in this show and I've had to make eighty of them," including a Luna moth (McKay 143).

Reaney's later plays are highly complex, multi-levelled compositions, the elements of which in themselves, the words, the sound and visual effects, the basic patterns, are often simple enough. Watching *The Donnellys* painlessly rouses the faculties to appreciate very complex art, because the simple and the complex in the trilogy are one. *Gyroscope*, by contrast, is dramatically straightforward, a simple, delightful comedy, quite unlike the galaxy-in-motion of *The Donnellys*. Like *The Boy Actors*, it seeks a truce in the battle of the sexes by exploring androgyny, an uncommon male stance even in the days of feminist revolution. Very accessible, this play, but the text also sustains Richard Stingle's extremely complex analysis, "'all the old levels': Reaney and Frye."

b) The "democratic impulse" (22) Dudek speaks of is certainly strong in Reaney, whose political sympathies are socialist. He has made every effort to create an audience for his work as well as a context for it in other art and thought that he endorses and discusses. Rather than staying with private artistic concerns, and perhaps producing what is accessible only to the few (a penalty paid by many postmodernists), he has gone public. The "theory" of aggressive approach to the audience is there in the "Invocation to the Muse of Satire" that begins *A Suit of Nettles*:

> Beat them about the ears and the four senses
> Until, like criminals lashed in famine time,
> They bring forth something ...
> (xxi).

You can hear it also in something Reaney says in "An Evening with Babble and Doodle" about his own performance of "One-Man Masque": "I particularly enjoyed directly attacking an audience with my poetry ... " (43). It's not just that he wants to get at them. "I shall never forget the thrill of having a reaction of 400 people at a time to my spoken voice," he says of that performance almost thirty years later, in the "Author's Preface" to *Performance Poems*, "almost as many as had bought my first volume of poems" (3). That thrill has nothing to do with being the centre of attention. The wheels must have begun to turn in Reaney's mind when he realized how many people he could reach at once, and how directly. Did I say that Reaney "improbably" assumed the role of prophet at the Long-liners Conference? That used to be part of the poet's public function, an obligation that Reaney still accepts. It involves rising to milder occasions than the imminent destruction of Babylon and Nineveh (Winnipeg). In the organized miscellany of *Performance Poems* he introduces two "private public poems" this way:

> Here are two public poems performed only once at friends' funerals and never to be performed again, but I print them to show you what public duties a poet should be able to perform when asked, as we have been, to write epitaphs, elegies, epithalamia, christening songs, etc. Why should this be surprising? Get rid of the old romantic cliché of the poet being interested only in expressing his or her self.

The Bees of the Invisible

For these important gateways to other states—life, union, death, coming of age, betrothal, society needs words arranged as well as they can be (84).

Listening to bill bissett read his earthquake poem at the Forest City Gallery the day after the earthquake hit London on January 30, 1986, I remember feeling a complex pang—of pleasure that the poet had not been completely replaced by the newspaper; of regret that still, as far as the general public is concerned,

> he who unrolled our culture from his scroll—
> the prince's quote, the rostrum-rounding roar—
> who under one name made articulate
> heaven, and under another the seven-circled air,
> is, if he is at all, a number, an x,
> a Mr. Smith in a hotel register,—
> incognito, lost, lacunal.
>
> (A.M. Klein, "Portrait of the Poet as Landscape" 50)

I want everybody to hear bill bissett. I want everybody exposed to Reaney. There's nothing quaint about this poet, with his bag of occasional poems, writing as though post-Victorian poets hadn't, often intentionally, parted company with a wide audience.

The drama is a much more public forum than poetry (even performance poems) and fiction, especially when the plays are workshopped, as Reaney's are, by the author himself. See *14 Barrels* for details of his operations to plant "root ideas that uncurl in a community" (*Apple Butter* "Preface"). There is no writer more selflessly ambitious than Reaney. He has worked so hard to naturalize the play of the imagination, to rouse the artist in all those he meets, that his efforts in this line must be called heroic. No wonder the compulsion to cajole and, failing that, to sting his fellow Canadians into bringing forth something occasionally reaches overkill in his art. It must be frustrating to see your contemporaries as lost princes, knowing you have news that could bring them home. What news? What curriculum, that is to say? The question might be answered in many ways, but drawing a line between two complementary poems, "The Ghost" and "July" in *A Suit of Nettles* (about the lost and the found, respectively), might serve.

"The Ghost" concerns a confrontation between everything (anagogy) and ignorance (doltishness) in the persons of ghost and farmboy. The ghost speaks at the beginning of the second stanza:

> The awkward doltish low I.Q. farmboy shambles down the steps,
> The empty pitcher in his hand:
> I am!
> Ha ha! And his hair stands straight up like brambles.

Everything—Egyptian hieroglyphs and crystallography,
Diary of shadows,
Vast God and the interiors of tree trunks, snowflakes
All spin like a fiery corkscrew into his psychology.

For I know everything now having passed into source,
Even
Through me he knows himself—a kidnapped prince.
It is too much for him—he falls down—hoarse
As they shriek and lift him up—I am not
                    (*Collected Poems* 122).

The ghost has presumably been reduced to playing such macabre practical jokes because his "knowledge has been chopped from [his] ... power." The dolt whose intellectual circuits the ghost overloads is a kind of opposite. His body works, but his head is as empty as the pitcher he carries. What is the princedom he has lost? His tradition, his culture, the words and the forms that carry it—just what suddenly fills the airy space in his skull, and what is restored by Polly to another lost prince, Kenneth, in *The Easter Egg*.

I doubt that the graduates of Old Strictus's school would be so vulnerable to a sudden perverse infusion of everything. For the price of intensive educational discipline they receive the power to identify themselves out of such perplexing situations. "When I was a gosling," Valancy tells Anser, a "progressive educationist" who teaches "the young gosling what he likes" (*Nettles* 31), Old Strictus

taught us to know the most wonderful list of things. You could play games with it; whenever you were bored or miserable what he taught you was like a marvellous deck of cards in your head that you could shuffle through and turn over into various combinations with endless delight. At the end of the year we each made ourselves little huts of burdock leaves, lay down on our backs with large stones on our bellies and recited the whole thing over to ourselves forwards and backwards. Some of the poorer students were in those huts till November but even those to whom it was an agony, when they at length did know that they knew all that a young goose was supposed to know, the moment when they rolled the stone away and climbed out of their burdock hut—it was a joyous moment as if they had been reborn into another world (30-31).

Here is a goose version of traditional university education, modelled on the old University of Toronto honours system. "My goodness, how useless so far as the actual living of life is concerned" (31), is Anser's scornful comment on the "list" that Valancy recites for him, not believing that education of the inner self gives the power to transform the outer world, not understanding that "if we get used to seeing our society as being based on a story, we'll wake up and realize we can get a better story ... " ("A Letter from James Reaney" 4).

Reaney usually doesn't address the sceptics in his audience as dolts or mindless biddies (though he comes close once, addressing a Blakean "idiot questioner" poorly disguised as his other self in an imaginary dialogue that structures one of the *Halloween* essays, "Topless Nightmares"); he wants to persuade them to join him in the city of words he so much believes in. He welcomed David McFadden to the cause, responding to a Hamilton production of *The Collected World of David McFadden* that he saw during the national tour of *The Donnellys*:

> That McFadden is becoming interested in the City of Words as well as the City of Hamilton means that we may finally be able to see that latter place, part of whose identity problem is that it can so easily sink into the unverbal, American megalopolis stretching up from New York State (*14 Barrels* 162).

This is a backhanded compliment, of course. David McFadden had written several books full of words by that time, "becoming" an important writer on his own terms (*The Poet's Progress* was published in 1977, same year as *14 Barrels*), unconcerned with Reaney's agenda.

Reaney's own identity-making projects start with the ground under his feet, and move from there through the national and beyond. He's interested in identity at all levels, but doesn't "believe you can really be world, or unprovincial or whatever until you've sunk your claws into a locally coloured tree trunk and scratched your way through to universality" (*14 Barrels* 162). In "Reaney's Region," George Bowering points out how old and settled Souwesto seems, compared to British Columbia, and Robert Kroetsch and Rudy Wiebe have said much the same about the prairies, but like those Western writers Reaney nevertheless sees himself starting from scratch—naming his country, often for the first time, naming and helping to "cross reference" it (*Alphabet* 4, 3).

Reaney's naming efforts have their firmest base in his own region, but there is a surprising amount of coverage of the whole country, in what might be called the *a mari usque a mare* structure. A journey across the country is the geographical backbone of *14 Barrels from Sea to Sea*, of the Maclean's article "James Reaney's Canada," and of the centennial year children's play *Geography Match*. It also figures in *Ignoramus* and in the Canadian history and geography sideshow of Mome Fair in *A Suit of Nettles*. From sea to sea is a difficult literary pattern to keep from becoming as artificial as the nation, geographically speaking, itself. That's no argument against trying; in fact hosts of people, from composers of popular songs to the CBC's Cross-Country Checkup to Terry Fox, *keep* trying, as if obeying a sense that Canada was not created once and for all in 1867. Obviously in his cross-Canada works, at any rate, less directly in others, Reaney is a teacher of citizenship in Canada as well as in the country of words. He wants Canada to mean not abstractly, but as a poem means. Like Frye, writing in the Preface to *The Bush Garden* (vi), Reaney doesn't confuse unity with uniformity. He would endorse what Frye says about "liberal or 'open' mythology" in *The Modern Century:*

> I call it a structure, but it is often so fluid that the solid metaphor of structure hardly applies to it at all. Each man has his own version of it, conditioned by what he knows best, and in fact he will probably adopt several differing versions in the course of his life. Myths are seldom if ever actual hypotheses that can be verified or refuted; that is not their function: they are co-ordinating or integrating ideas (115).

"Any national identity, any identity," Reaney says, "is a web of adjusting visions" ("A Letter from James Reaney" 7).

☙

The myth of coherence may be a deconstructionist's amusement, but in Reaney and even in Frye it doesn't always cater to those who like their systems not only simple, but static and rigid. Reaney may not always play quite as good a game as he talks, failing to trust his audience enough, but a fair-minded listener familiar with most of what he has done will be able to pass between his work and that of his postmodernist contemporaries (those "goddamn postmodernists" Audrey Thomas calls them somewhere; maybe that's where Reaney learned to use 'postmodernist!' as an imprecation), with a healthy feeling of dislocation—also noting points of deep agreement. George Bowering extends his hospitality to Reaney's writing across quite a gulf in his essay "Reaney's Region," without observing that he and Reaney agree on abandoning the lyrical ego as a source for poetry, and also on what Reaney calls, in the "Author's Note" to *Colours in the Dark*, the importance of "play" in an "Age of Dread" (iv). Bowering is "interested in some kind of [postmodernist] reconstruction beyond despair" (109), a literary dead end, he says, unless you absurdly write against the grain. The identity of contemporary literature is a "web of adjusting visions" too.

There's too much agreement on the meaning and the centrality of postmodernism when writers like Reaney are left out. Too much agreement that humanism is a dead horse. I do have qualms about speaking as though I think Reaney should be "in." The poems and plays of Wilfred Watson (I risk insulting a small group of devoted readers) are the undiscovered south sea isle of Canadian literature. You hesitate to mention this for fear the tourists in the lit. crit. industry will flock there. Perhaps, with his three Governor General's Awards, his Chalmers Award, Reaney has already had his share of attention, his phase of centrality. But some of his readers, like myself, still feel that his work is bigger than its blemishes, that he's a major writer now.

Afterthoughts
Earlier this year I had softened on *Imprecations*, having re-read it and responded more positively to a colloquialism I'd first felt as looseness. Today (Friday, November 9, 1990)

62

The Bees of the Invisible

I heard the poem read, or rather performed, by James Reaney and his wife Colleen Thibaudeau. Why hadn't it come home to me that the poem alternates two voices, one cursing up a satiric storm and the other quietly lamenting the split of the speaker's parents? The poem's energy finally reached me today. Sitting in University College Room 84, suffering from a bad cold, I still felt mentally and physically lifted by Reaney's poems, by Colleen Thibaudeau's poems, by their collaborations, by their indelible personalities. Poetry is good for you.

∽

Finally having read *Traps* in manuscript, as distinct from seeing it performed, I still find it the least satisfying of any Reaney text. But I have misgivings about my criteria for saying so. Concluding that his most overtly political text is his least satisfactory text has lately tended to rebound in some uncomfortable reflections on my own comfortable Canadian freedom to pursue purely aesthetic questions. Here is the germ of *Traps*, in *14 Barrels From Sea to Sea*:

> At St. Joseph's High School, we did an improvisation about rats in an experiment; one of the tragic stories heard on tour was of a man who had for years experimented in sensory deprivation, no doubt doing some of the things the actors and the students thought of acting out in the rat-mazes; when he learned that the CIA was using his published papers to train torturers in Uruguay, he jumped into the river (82).

Might not the oppressed people of Uruguay, Colombia, Chile, El Salvador, if we could imagine them reading Reaney, find *Traps* the *most* satisfying of his works?

Traps is a direct attack on abuses of academic freedom—publishing not to extend and share knowledge but merely to gain status and power and to hell with concern about social applications. Ironically, the play was first performed at The University of Western Ontario where tenure now shelters Phillipe Rushton (as it shelters me). Rushton's theories of racial differentiation are supported by white supremacist groups. They are psychologically damaging to the black people who consistently appear in the least desirable categories (smallest brain, for example, greatest sexual activity) generated by his statistics. He shows no signs of conscience, social or otherwise.

I haven't changed my mind about *Traps*. It's no *One Hundred Years of Solitude*, after all. I value it for addressing a need which it might serve better, but which most Canadians simply ignore.

Works Cited

Atwood, Margaret. "Reaney Collected." *Canadian Literature*

Blaser, Robin. "Introduction." George Bowering, *Particular Accidents: Selected Poems*. Vancouver: Talonbooks, 1980.

Bowering, George. "Sheila Watson, Trickster." *The Mask in Place: Essays on Fiction in North America*. Winnipeg: Turnstone, 1982.

—. "Reaney's Region." *Approaches to the Work of James Reaney.* Ed. Stan Dragland. Toronto: ECW, 1983.

Cohen, Leonard. *Beautiful Losers.* Toronto: McClelland and Stewart, 1966.

Davey, Frank. "Reflections While Reading Canadian." *Open Letter* Second Series No. 5 (Fall 1972), 62-65.

—. and Ann Munton. *The Proceedings of the Long-liners Conference on the Canadian Long Poem. Open Letter* Sixth Series, Nos. 2-3 (Summer-Fall 1985).

Dudek, Louis. "A Problem of Meaning." *Canadian Literature* 59 (Winter 1972), 16-29.

Frye, Northrop. *The Modern Century.* Toronto: Oxford, 1967.

—. *The Bush Garden: Essays on the Canadian Imagination.* Toronto: Anansi, 1971.

Keith, W.J. "James Reaney, 'Scrutumnus' and the Critics: An Individual Response." *Canadian Poetry* 6 (Spring/Summer 1980), 25-34.

Klein, A.M. *The Rocking Chair and Other Poems.* Toronto: Ryerson, 1948.

Macpherson, Jay. "Educated Doodle: Some Notes on One-Man Masque." *Approaches to the Work of James Reaney.* Toronto: ECW, 1983.

Marlatt, Daphne. *Ana Historic.* Toronto: Coach House, 1988.

McKay, Jean. "Interview with James Reaney." *Approaches to the Work of James Reaney.* Toronto: ECW, 1983.

Nichol, bp. "Letter re James Reaney." *Open Letter* Second Series No. 6 (Fall 1973), 5-7.

Reaney, James. "The Canadian Poet's Predicament." *University of Toronto Quarterly* XXVI, 3 (April 1957), 284-295.

—. *A Suit of Nettles.* Toronto: Macmillan, 1958.

—. "Editorial." *Alphabet* 1 (1960), 3-4.

—. "The Third Eye: Jay Macpherson's *The Boatman.*" *Canadian Literature* 3 (Winter 1960), 23-34.

—. "An Evening With Babble and Doodle." *Canadian Literature* 12 (Spring 1962) 43.

—. "Frye's Magnet." *Tamarack Review* 33 (Autumn 1964), 72-78.

—. *Colours in the Dark.* Vancouver: Talonbooks/Macmillan, 1969.

—. *Poems.* Ed. and Introd. Germaine Warkentin. Toronto: new press, 1972.

—. *Listen to the Wind.* Vancouver: Talonbooks, 1972.

—. and C.H. Gervais. *Baldoon.* Erin, Ontario: The Porcupine's Quill, 1976.

—. "A Letter From James Reaney." *Black Moss* Series 2, 1 (Spring 1976), 2-10.

—. "Topless Nightmares, being a dialogue with himself by James Reaney." *Halloween.* London, Ontario: James Reaney, 1976.

—. "An ABC to Ontario Literature and Culture." *Black Moss* Series 2, 3 (Spring 1977), 2-6.

—. *14 Barrels From Sea to Sea.* Erin, Ontario: Press Porcepic, 1978.

—. *The Dismissal: or Twisted Beards & Tangled Whiskers.* Erin, Ontario: Press Porcepic, 1978.

—. *The Donnellys.* With scholarly apparatus by James Noonan. Victoria/Toronto: Press Porcepic, 1983.

—. *Gyroscope.* Toronto: Playwrights Canada, 1980.

—. *Imprecations: the Art of Swearing.* Windsor: Black Moss, 1984.

—. "The Long Poem." Frank Davey and Ann Munton, eds. "The Proceedings of the Long-liners Conference on the Canadian Long Poem." *Open Letter* Sixth Series, 2-3 (Summer-Fall 1985), 115-119.

—. *Performance Poems.* Goderich, Ontario: Moonstone, 1990.

Reaney, James Stewart. *James Reaney.* Toronto: Gage, 1977.

Simic, Charles. *Return to a Place Lit by a Glass of Milk.* New York: George Braziller, 1974.

ON *CIVIL ELEGIES*

Commitment

He has discovered, feature by feature, the thing we knew beforehand
but which we cannot believe until its particulars are made real in
words ... ("Running and Dwelling" 14).

Margaret Atwood's map of the Canadian imagination in *Survival,* as she realizes, is
drawn on a very large scale. When she says that Dennis Lee's *Civil Elegies* is about
"cultural castration" (244), she is being as accurate as she can be about the poem as
it fits her swift thematic overview. Of course if we read her book, its technique, as a
part of the map she is making, then her bleak view of the total poem of Canada is
contradicted by the lively style in which it's presented. Lingering on *Civil Elegies,* I find
that nothing *it* does—not the structural armature of nine elegiac meditations on the
problematics of living authentically in Canada, nor the mosaic sectioning of each
elegy, nor the movement of the language—is divisible from what it says. Making a
detailed map of *Civil Elegies* shows something that Atwood understands full well,
though she kept her knowledge on hold to write *Survival:* the poem means all along
its body, not simply in what may be abstracted of theme. Having survived the
paraphrase, in Frank Davey's term, having entered the post-thematic stage of
Canadian criticism, presumably we all know this now—though handling technique
becomes no easier when the way is cleared for it. No wonder some critics leap from
theme right to theory.

For all its basic accessibility, indispensable in a public poem, *Civil Elegies* is tough,
meaning both that it's a strong poem and a tricky one to meet squarely. To put it baldly,
for a start, the poem shows what we always knew but cannot be told enough: to be
alive in Canada in this century is to be lodged in paradox; we have nothing to stand
on, but must—and can—stand there. Reading *Civil Elegies* whole, it turns out to be
unnecessary to shield the scrotum with the hand that is not holding the book.

If what I say about *Civil Elegies* is to come from within the poem, I must mediate
what Lee probes with his nerve-ends as well as with his mind. There is nothing
dilletantish about his preoccupation either with concrete things or difficult concepts.
The poem's urgency rises from the whole being of the man who wrote it, and that

urgency is passed to the reader in poetry, not in the "high abstraction" that Lee is also very much drawn to. So I will stay close to the poem itself, without ignoring certain contexts of direct relevance, like Saint-Denys-Garneau's *Journal* and the thought of George Grant and Saraha touched on by the two epigraphs. *Civil Elegies* works extremely well as a poem, and offers plenty of scope for one who wishes to concentrate on the performance, particularly if he reaches out to Lee's other writings for help.

So the poem is the thing. But even if the poem didn't resemble much of Lee's other work in having an autobiographical dimension, it would still be important to say that *Civil Elegies, pro patria*, stands for no abstract commitment to Canada. The man who wrote it has made a difference to this country. The poem has partly to do with a divided individual, Lee, "spinning off many selves to attend each / lethal yen as it passed me" (52); the poem is the more moving in light of the fact that Lee *attended*, he took care, he acted. He followed his conscience along a difficult route—very tough for a writer—out of the University of Toronto into Rochdale College and Anansi, always trying to think and feel his way out of cramping or sold-out structures, even to the apparent impasse of *Savage Fields*. Much of this is public knowledge. Since *Tasks of Passion: Dennis Lee at Mid-Career*, Lee's editorial shaping of texts by some of the country's best writers is also known, but there have been no published testimonials from the scads of lesser-known and downright deservedly obscure writers that Lee has generously pushed to be the best they could. What went on between Lee and Harold Ladoo, documented to a degree by Lee himself in his elegy for a friend, produced in Ladoo's novels two peaks of an editorial iceberg. By no means all of the manuscripts Lee laboured over saw publication, and many of those that did appeared elsewhere than with Anansi. Lee was singled out for his literary influence in an uncovering of the hidden power-structure of Toronto that was published a few years ago in one of the weekend supplements to newspapers across the country. He might have been embarrassed by the revelation, knowing himself to be one of a network of literary workers; otherwise, it will have left him as cold as he says in "Cadence, Country Silence" he is left by the "chance to be a *poet*" (36)—with the reputation, not necessarily with the goods. This is no power-broker, but a man whose life has been lived in the service of the "deep tough caring" he says in "The Death of Harold Ladoo" he shared with many others during the Anansi years.

Lee might appreciate the paradox that, while he often mentions the muddle he lives in, the tracks he has been leaving are very clear to read. They read like a poem. That is not the whole truth about the man, whose modest perspective on himself, however limited, must be allowed to be a part of the picture, as even Dr. Johnson periodically fell into fits of depression in which he reproached himself for laziness among other signs that his life was falling apart. But if Lee's life is not worth dying (in the words of "Civil Elegy 2") then I hold out little hope for the rest of us.

Stan Dragland

Civil Elegies 1968 and 1972

[P]oet writes artificial early work, some of it being a log-jammed attempt to write in a cadence he has heard in Hölderlin and elsewhere; unexpectedly, he finds it possible to write in a rather stilted version of that cadence, and does a book-length poem (published as *Civil Elegies*); throughout this period, he is reading George Grant in dribs and snatches; for no reason he can see, he stops being able to write; after four years, again for no apparent reason, he starts writing in cadence again and revises the long poem ("Cadence, Country, Silence" 49).

To stay close to his sense of the warts-and-all of life, Lee always resists patterning anything so as to squeeze out the "anomalies" the pattern would ignore. Thus he warns us in "Cadence, Country, Silence" that he sees no "ten-year coherence of purpose" in the period he summarizes: "What I have most often felt as a writer is a sense of beleaguered drifting" (48).

Still taking the outsider's view, though, I should say before passing to a comparison of the two versions of *Civil Elegies* that while the free sonnets of *Kingdom of Absence* are not very successful as poetry, they make interesting reading in the light of what Lee has written since. As the title implies, the void that is so important in *Civil Elegies* and after is already being explored as the ground of being. The sense of neither-here-nor-thereness of the later poem has already appeared, even in Lee's self criticism that he is "hung between styles" (29). Besides other thematic constants, some of Lee's characteristic diction outlives the book too: sacrament, void, botched, lethal, *tremendum,* manic, kazoo, caring, cessation, measure, carnal—even the alligator shows up. There some tricks of phrase ("my flint-eyed, you inconsolable") that Lee is still using as late as "The Death of Harold Ladoo." But the Lee cadence is not fully occupied until *Civil Elegies* II, and *Civil Elegies* I marks a transition towards that accomplishment.

In *Civil Elegies* I the mind is very much in play, but it is not being jacked off, as might be said to the the case in *Kingdom of Absence.* In fact it's said by Lee in the "hung between styles" poem. Perhaps it's the civil audience he is now addressing that permits him to speak in a way much less cramped in style and form—though the sonnets seldom rhyme and though they move through various unconventional combinations of fourteen lines. Whatever the reason, Lee is freer in *Civil Elegies* I. The lines which invoke shared Canadian experience have greater amplitude and flexibility. Although it needed revising, the poem is already recognizably the poem it ended up being, which means that there is a lot of marvellous writing in it.

Between *Civil Elegies* I and II a great many changes of word, phrase, sentence and line-break were made. Material was omitted, notably twenty-eight lines from the final elegy about Sir John A. MacDonald's struggles and successes. (Lee may have felt that some of this had been anticipated by E.J. Pratt's "Towards the Last Spike.") A lot of material was added, whole elegies (2 and 4) for instance. Most altered are Elegies 2 (now 3) and 7 (now 9). In the second version the positions of Elegies 4 and 5 are reversed. There are changes enough that someone might attempt a detailed comparison of the two versions, perhaps as part of a study of the evolution of the poem. Between 1968 and 1972 (to leave aside the matter of worksheets), for example, "Elegy 5" appears in a form not quite final in Al Purdy's *The New Romans*, as "The Children in Nathan Phillips Square."

Besides the improvements in the actual writing, which I will glance at shortly, the main effect of the revisions is to clarify the movement of the poem as a whole. The reader is more easily drawn through the revised sequence, which had been somewhat jerky because truncated. The added elegies contribute to the structure, and also expand the perspective on void. The "Master and Lord" elegy (2) is particularly important because it grounds the concept of void in personal experience of the disappearance of God. The thorough overhaul of the final elegy means that the reader is left both with a more affirmative, more concretely realized experience of where Lee has arrived, and with a more tentative feeling about the function of void in the exploration. I think this latter result more thoroughly and clearly holds to the logic of certainty in uncertainty that was implicit in *Civil Elegies* I. So a welcome loss is this rather prosaic spelling out and deflation of the mystery of void,

> redemptive in that the movement of spirit by which we
> face unwilling into darkness, letting it
> break over us, permitting it to
> utterly unmake us—that movement
> brings us through a purgation of unmeaning to
> a source within ourselves, though not
> accessible to will and wordlessly it speaks oneself ... (NP).

Lee had a clear sense of what he had accomplished with stylistic revisions when he wrote David Helwig (who preferred *Civil Elegies* I), in an exchange about the two versions that became a review for *Quarry*:

> There are a lot of places where I defused the language slightly, dewhorled the syntax, etc. The reasons I did it were not for polish; it was because the earlier version sounded spurious to me in places. I thought the sense of anguish and everything-bursting-through-at-one was in places laboured, worked at, formularized. What replaced it was more limpid, usually because that is apparently how that part of myself senses these things now (it wasn't at all a matter of striving for that effect, just trying to make what sounded for real) (70).

Even without the help of *Civil Elegies* II, a reader with an ear will notice a startling variation in the quality of writing and the consistency of cadence in *Civil Elegies* I. Dewhorling certainly helped such passages as this:

Stan Dragland

> Many were born in Canada, and died
> of course but died truncated, stunted, not yet
> naturalized in their birthright dimension,
> native members of a human body of kind.

The jargon of the third line is not the work of a poet sure of his voice. Four years later Lee recasts the passage, adding a clarifying phrase and a paradox to the first line and condensing the last line while he's at it:

> Many were born in Canada, and living unlived lives they died
> of course but died truncated, stunted, never at
> home in native space and not yet
> citizens of a human body of kind (33).

The same unpuzzling effort fixes a sentence in the initial "Elegy 2," so that "we may not / malinger among the upward evident blisses" becomes "we cannot / malinger among the bygone acts of grace." These examples may stand for the sorts of local improvement Lee made by way of clearing away what remained of the *Kingdom of Absence* logjam. He does other things, of course, such as eliminating from the final elegy a reference to *Kingdom of Absence* containing a rather embarassing homespun reflection on the unreachable void: "How many toes does it have? Does it eat corn flakes?" (Asking "what would a god be *like?*" in "The Gods," Lee virtually recycles the earlier lines, now successfully: "would he shop at Dominion / Would he know about *DNA* molecules? and keep little haloes / stars for when they behaved? / ... It is not from simple derision / that the imagination snickers") (29). The odd quite interesting passage is sacrificed for the sake of polyphonic consistency, like a sudden lyricism following immediately on those marvellous ironic lines about "the first / spontaneous mutual retreat in the history of warfare./ Canadians in flight."

> And all their avatars, Jenny
> sang we clapped. Bird sang, Time sings we clap. Life sings and
> Lullaby my country now and all.

The dramatic shift in tone here, both barrels fired almost at once, seems to me like different strengths in conflict. The second version of *Civil Elegies* is slyer. Lee has found out how to sustain the notes he hits, and how to modulate between them. The cadence is hardly monotonous now, but it's orchestrated.

A few lines in "The Death of Harold Ladoo" help to pinpoint another innovation of the second *Civil Elegies*:

> People, people I speak from
>   private space but all these

70

The Bees of the Invisible

civil words keep coming and they
muddle me (*The Gods* 56).

In *Civil Elegies* II, it's the private, inward voice (short sentences, plain words) that very quietly enters at the opening and close of The "Master and Lord" elegy (2), and it can then be heard meditating on renunciation in the other new elegy, the fourth. In fact, the four sections of this elegy first alternate and then, in the last two, weave the public and private voices together. This is a step towards polyphony as Lee will later theorize and practice it. The public voice still predominates in *Civil Elegies* II, but it has been joined by the private voice that will predominate in the later "Harold Ladoo," the two long poems being complementary in stance and voice.

There are notes appended to *Civil Elegies* II, to explain some local allusions to readers outside Ontario and Canada. These are expanded in *Élégies civiles* by Marc Lebel, Lee's Quebec editor and translator, who also makes the interesting point that *Civil Elegies and Other Poems* is a "long poème en vingt-cinq parties" (7). (It's true that a structural connection between the two major divisions of the volume is created by the dedications, *Illisque pro annis uxore* for "Coming Back," and *Pro patria*—supplanting the earlier dedication to George Grant and Dave Godfrey—for "Civil Elegies." And the lyrics of "Coming Back" cover much of the territory of the elegies from more personal angles.) But the most important addition outside the poem proper is the epigraph from Saraha, also known as Saroja-vajira.

According to Robert Bringhurst, this epigraph "consists of two conflated sentences from the *Dohakosha* of Saraha, a Buddhist text written in one of the ninth-century Prakit vernaculars of eastern India" (73). Possibly Lee met Saraha in the Penguin *Buddhist Scriptures*, in a translation (by D. Snellgrove) borrowed from *Buddhist Texts Through the Ages*, both anthologies edited by Edward Conze. The whole poem is not presented in *Buddhist Scriptures*, but the two stanzas that Lee conflates (improving the poetry) are:

75 Do not cling to the notion of voidness,
   But consider all things alike.
   Indeed even the husk of a sesame-seed
   Causes pain like that of an arrow (*Buddhist Texts* 234).

90 I used to recite (the textbook which begins with the words),
   "Let there be success."
   But I drank the elixir and forgot it.
   There is but one word that I know now,
   And of that, my friend, I know not the name (236).

It's possible that the epigraph from Saraha brings with it more than the specific words. Robert Bringhurst says that

71

the verses collected under [Saraha's] name speak eloquently of the central thesis of the Mahayana: that *śunyata*, meaning voidness, emptiness, the unreality of the real—*and* meaning the wisdom of knowing that what is is empty—is inseparable from *karuna*, meaning compassion, the deep love of what is, standing open to the pain and glory of the living world. These two together, *śunyata* and *karuna*, say the Mahayana masters, are the principles of *bodhicitta*, the enlightened mind (74).

Whether it derives from Saraha or from Rilke, the enlightenment *Civil Elegies* earns does involve a difficult clasping together of meaning and unmeaning. It's less conjectural to say that the words of Saraha help soften the harshness of Grant's remark about being "cut off" from citizenship, "one of the highest forms of life" (77), while it adds an oriental perspective to those (from Athens and Jerusalem) Grant brings to bear on the bankruptcy of the dominant Western puritan-backed liberal cosmology. Perhaps more importantly, the addition of Saraha's mysticism helps Lee to catch more of the essence and the structure of his poem between the two epigraphs.

Civil Elegies begins with Lee's version of being cut off, but it moves back into the possibility of citizenship. The Saraha passage does not explicitly signal that movement, except perhaps in tone, but it foreshadows the end of the poem in the rejection of void which is explored in recoil from civil and metaphysical emptiness. Saraha's last two lines also sound like a version of "negative capability," which is the state of mind in which *Civil Elegies* ends—reasonably contented, but not resolved. What has been achieved by that point is a difficult clarity, still complex enough as it now stands forth, as free from obfuscation as Lee can make it: "Je prends un certain recul face aux choses; je vois qu'elles cohabitent, quelles ont entre elles des harmonies et des dissonances. Voila le quotidien" (110).

An *I* in Nathan Phillips Square

> This undercutting of a past he would have liked to make exemplary is a characteristic moment in Grant's thought, and it reveals the central strength and contradiction of his work. He withdraws from the contemporary world, and judges it with passionate lucidity, by standing on a 'fixed point' which he then reveals to be no longer there ("Cadence, Country, Silence" 43).

Two sorts of centre draw in to themselves and focus the heterogeneous matter of *Civil Elegies*. One is the speaker of the poem, a persona whom I will call "Dennis Lee," though I know he speaks in a voice quite different from that of Dennis Lee in his essays, or his letters, or over the phone. The other centre is the setting, Nathan Phillips Square, with the ordinary activities that go on there. In the square are Viljo Revell's City Hall architecture and Henry Moore's sculpted Archer, and within these Lee unsettlingly locates opposite impulses (say World and Earth, to borrow terms from

The Bees of the Invisible

Savage Fields). The square, then, along with the *I* whose mind ranges a long way out from Toronto, east and west and north and south, as well as backwards and forwards in time, becomes a container as well as a core for the whole poem. It's "hard to stay at the centre when you're losing it one more time" (46), Lee says about the Canadian will to fail, but, as we'll see, what he's explicitly saying and what he's doing very often contradict or qualify each other, so it's clear that technique as well as thought is something he shares with George Grant. Nathan Phillips Square, for example, is so vividly, if cumulatively, realized, in a poem that usually seems to be talking about loss and unreality, that it becomes permanently fixed in a reader's mind, and in consequence turns out to be very hard to lose. Of course, neither the Square and its contents nor the man who speaks from this "place of meeting" (33) is static. Both sorts of centre change in the dynamism of the poem, because of the need to register how comforting and treacherous both the mundane and momentous in life may be.

The Square is a public place in which Lee sits or stands, apparently always at noon, a temporary refugee from the work force, from the jobs which he so often links with kids and home, endangered decencies in the poem. As a middle-class presence, he is concerned with finding out how to maintain the simplest continuities of ordinary life, but at the same time he also explores regions miles from that ordinariness—with an intensity not normally attributed to the average citizen. Thus a tension is established: this *I* is an ordinary citizen and also a person apart who articulates what the average person cannot, one who undertakes the probing and naming of the disease ("fear of life, the mark of Canada" 54) that is generally submerged in our unexamined lives.

The Square is frequented not only by kids racing about, lunchers, and idlers, but also by a swarm of "furies" (33), uprooted ancestors who haunt the place, loading the weight of responsibility upon the man who sees them. These ghosts will not be laid until their descendants find a way through their fear of life to occupy the land in more than body. Meanwhile

> the dead persist in
> buildings, by-laws, porticos—the city I live in
> is clogged with their presence; they
> dawdle about in our lives and form a destiny, still
> incomplete, still dead weight, still
> demanding whether Canada will be (34).

For a people in desperate need to get moving into authentic lives, these spectres contribute to the inertia of daily "miscellaneous clobber" (53) of "friends and lacerations" (50)—a devastating play on "friends and relations"—suffering and failing in their relationships, and of the vortex of American empire sucking us south: "every year attaches itself behind and we have more to drag" (51).

But the Square's ordinariness, with its continuity and serenity, relieves the weight of responsibility at times. Sometimes Lee is caught up in its "placid continuance" (39), its "blessed humdrum" (46). In spring (1), summer (3 and 5) and fall (9) much occasional feeling of well-being is provided by the noon-time sun which warms everything. The dailiest sources of satisfaction may turn sour, however, and so does the peaceful, sunlit Square in the 5th Elegy. This passage lulls the reader into expecting a more comforting analogy than s/he gets:

> In Germany, the civic square in many little towns is
> hallowed for people. Laid out just so, with
> flowers and fountains and during the war you could come and
> relax for an hour, catch a parade or just
> get away from the interminable racket of trains, clattering through the
> outskirts with their lousy expendable cargo.
> Little cafes often, fronting the square. Beer and a chance to relax.
> And except for the children it's peaceful here
> too, under the sun's warm sedation (47).

The irony of "lousy expendable cargo" is not so pronounced (one hardly notices having slipped into a Nazi mind) as to undercut totally the portrait of German civic squares: they *are* attractive; perhaps they need not have been avoided ("Does the sun in summer pour its light into the square / for us to ignore?" 48), even by a people who were being undermined by atrocities done in their name. Indeed, the seventh line of the passage seems almost to let us off the hook, by acting with the fifth to sandwich the "lousy expendable cargo" between two thoughts about the pleasantness of civic squares. Two lines later, however, the poem bites again, in "sun's sedation": the innocent sun, like the placid square, can drug the conscience. And Lee shows us we had no cause for complacency here, either, because Canada's "clean hands" were making napalm to fry Vietnamese. If that era of American imperialism has now passed, the relevance of *Civil Elegies* has not, and will not as long as the U.S. extends its single-minded power all over the world (unless—but how?—we disentangle our affairs from theirs). "Sun's sedation" therefore recalls the ambiguity of the 1st Elegy in which the square "takes us in" (33)—gathering and fooling both—and looks ahead to the word "copout" (57) in the 9th Elegy.

Less ambiguous than the sunny square which is both enjoyed and resisted are Revell's towers, though the Archer undermines what they represent. These City Hall towers are "luminous" (54) and beautiful. With the humdrum of the square, they provide relief: this "spare vertical glory of right proportions" (52) has a calming effect, creating a respite from desolation. The towers are a

> sign, that not
> one countryman has learned, that
> men and women live that

they may make that
life worth dying (36).

"Revell's sign" is thus an achievement that reproaches the general rule of botched city architecture, maps jammed "with asphalt panaceas" (35), "banks of dreary high-rise" (55), which urban men make out of the domination of number and the profit motive. Like Moriyama's Metropolitan Toronto Library or Cardinal's Museum of Civilization in Hull, it says that people meet more wholly in beautiful surroundings, that mere functionality does nothing to feed the spirit. Which must be fed.

Revell's towers, the urban at its best, are associated with the human spirit making models for life as it might be lived harmoniously. Moore's Archer does something else. Revell the Finn and Moore the Englishman together express one of the major contradictions of Canada. Moore's Archer matches those Apollonian towers with its own chthonic reminder of the untouched nature whose power the pioneers felt and which can still be felt not very far north in any part of the country. The Archer

Was shaped by earlier space and it ripples with
wrenched stress, the bronze is flexed by
blind aeonic throes
that bred and met in slow enormous impact,
and they are still at large for the force in the bronze churns
through it, and lunges beyond and also The Archer declares
that space is primal, raw, beyond control and drives toward a
living stillness, its own (39).

The energy of the verbs helps to create an impression opposite to the serenity in square and towers. It's a feat of concentration to locate in downtown Toronto, in the Archer, the primal wilderness of Canada, the Shield that Lee links with the urban setting to express his sense of Canada, the barbaric land that broke so many settlers: "despotic land, inhuman yet / our *own*" (40)—ours, and yet completely independent of us. Like Pratt's Laurentian dragon in *Towards the Last Spike*, and his more ominous "paleolithic iceberg" in "The Titanic," the Archer occupies a space "which violates our lives, and reminds us, and has no mercy upon us" (41). The presence of the Archer is so powerfully established, in the third elegy, with its primitive refutation of the beautiful or botched civilization that formed our settlements, towns, and cities, that it declares to the gut how complicated a matter it is to claim this country as a whole. So Lee brings into his urban poem a northern reality which generates all those works like Atwood's "Progressive Insanities of a Pioneer" or Birney's "Bushed" that express the vulnerability of civilized men confronting nature alone.

Technological man, given to conquest of the alien, can triumph in such confrontations; *Civil Elegies* acknowledges what is more fully mapped out in Grant's *Tech-*

Stan Dragland

nology and Empire and in Lee's own *Savage Fields*. It takes time to create even an uneasy bond with "brute surroundings" (40) *made* of time, and it can be done only by accepting what we can of the land's own terms—but time is not one of our luxuries. Not only is the country "pelting very fast downhill" (49) in a decline that makes Lee think of Rome, but the resources torn from the north race "toward us on asphalt across the Shield" to be "shipped and / divvied abroad ..." (40). The country is being sold out from under us in so many ways that the determination to claim it is undercut before it is even seized. And something *can* be claimed from the wilderness. Lee ranges out from his centre in the square to show us how Tom Thomson did it.

Thomson claimed the north before it claimed him, drowned him, by becoming "part of the bush" and making art of it. He showed that wilderness could be captured by respect, just as Revell showed that urban architecture could transcend its function. In the Third Elegy the unity of Thomson's art with its subject, the landscape, is expressed in the image of a painting of sunrise. This image is powerful because the continuous sentence which contains it makes nothing of a great leap from wilderness canoeing into art:

> Often when night
> came down in a subtle rush and the scorched scrub still
> ached for miles from the fires he paddled direct through
> the palpable dark, hearing only the push and
> drip of the blade for hours and then very suddenly the radiance of the
> renewed land broke over his canvas (41).

The word "renewed" is significant—beyond the redemption of the land from darkness by light—because such acts as Thomson's merging with the bush and making art of that are the sort that claim the land for us, and therefore for the truncated ancestors who failed to claim it. No such act, however, roots us once and for all. "We cannot / malinger among the bygone acts of grace" (41). *Civil Elegies* is therefore an act of sustaining and extending what Thomson and others did, making the art that grows out of one's personal search a basis to claim his country.

If the main axis of this poem which centres on Nathan Phillips Square extends north to the wilderness and south to the U.S., Lee also makes a gesture west in the 1st Elegy ("the prairies, the foothills" 35). He later reaches east into Quebec by introducing the figure of Saint-Denys-Garneau, moving "across / two decades and two nations" (54) into another of the defining tensions of Canadian life. Characteristically, Lee both recognizes the cultural integrity of Quebec and claims Garneau (and implicitly Quebec) for Canada by calling him "*our* one patrician maker" (53, emphasis added).

A great deal of Canada is present in Nathan Phillips Square, then, and in the *I* who meditates from that centre, even though the further east and west Lee moves from home ground, as one might expect, the thinner the country appears. Garneau can

76

hardly bring with him the whole texture of Quebec because he spent much of his life weaning himself from that. Still, if not exactly writing *a mari usque ad mare,* Lee is claiming a large chunk of the country (taking it by giving to it), partly by reaffirming the local and regional basis of Canadian identity. This reaffirmation is consistent with his lament in the 6th Elegy over "the continental drift to barbarian / normalcy" (49), because the assertion of a presence alternative to that of the U.S. in North America, "a presence which is not sold out utterly to the modern" (34) would mean very little if it were uniform from coast to coast. Part of our dilemma thus is that while we could much more easily resist the downhill continental slide if we were anchored in a unified front of native normalcy, resistance to homogenizing is much of the alternative we, like other "post-colonial" countries, have to offer.

Void

For always standing within us
A man not to be beaten down
Erect within us, turning his back
                    to where our looks are turned
Erect in his bones, eyes fixed on the void
In a fearful dogged facing and defiance.
                    (Saint-Denys-Garneau)

All the details of the poem—the cumulative portrait of Nathan Phillips Square; the particularized portraits of, or scenes involving, "exemplars" like Thomson, Garneau, Chartier, MacKenzie and even Paul Martin; the shifting orientation of the speaker within the dramatic moments that focus his experience (those moments that appear in the 1st, 3rd, 5th and 8th Elegies, usually announced by the word "once")—are there to celebrate the integrity of specific things and people. But the mass of detail also grounds the generalizations about Canada and its problems, and helps to ground the most mysterious aspect of the poem, the encounter with void (absence, emptiness, silence, non-being) which makes a continuous thread through the poem. Void is difficult to catch partly because it is as unapproachable a ground of being, or measure of existence, as God, for whose absent governance void supplies to Lee a kind of alternative. But void is also elusive because, like so much else, it is protean within the poem. "We do not encounter Void," Lee says in "Cadence, Country, Silence," "we encounter this void and that" (52). Void takes on various identities in *Civil Elegies* as Lee makes it as palpable as possible.

Void is least ambiguous when it is identified with the evil done in the name of empire; it is both attractive and dangerous in its pervasive form as the context of being. In approaching it, Lee approaches the edge of the abyss, pushed by the complex of negatives embodied in Canada. Before he turns back, he follows Garneau a good distance into his void with the hope of sacrificing attachment to things that they might live more fully in their own being. When he subsequently turns back to this world, it's not that he has escaped the inescapable void, but that he has managed to reorient himself to life and the emptiness that surrounds it all by finding a difficult but possible way to live in the world as a Canadian. He has availed himself of the "lore of emptiness" (53) to honour void, and has returned from his "lonely inward procession" (53) with the promise to himself that he will "honour each one of my country's failures of nerve and its sellouts" (55). Thus he reaffirms a truth about identity that everyone has to learn for himself, the one expressed by James Reaney in *Colours in the Dark*: "things you've lost are inside things you don't like" (83). Lee doesn't renounce void as the dominant pull on him until the 8th Elegy, which is thus the turning point of the poem. The 9th Elegy is the dénouement and the consolation of a traditional elegy.

There is no better source than "Cadence, Country, Silence" for a gloss on what void means to Lee (unless it is the end of the first section of the elegy for Harold Ladoo, where Lee movingly clarifies what it means to die by reckoning up the wonder of "all that / sweet cross-hatched bitter noble aching sold-out / thrash of life" (51). In the essay Lee reflects on an epiphany which simultaneously undercuts life and gives it value:

> There is a moment in which I experience other people, or things, or situations, as standing forth with a clarity and a preciousness which makes me want to cry and to celebrate physically at the same time. I imagine many people have felt it.
>
> It is the moment in which something becomes overwhelmingly real in two lights at once. An old man or woman whose will to live and whose mortality reach one at the same instant. A child who is coursed through with the lovely energies of its body, and yet who is totally fragile before the coming decades of its life. A social movement charged at the same time with passion for decent lives and with the pettiness, ego-tripping and lack of stamina that will debase it. A table, at once a well-worn companion and a disregarded adjunct.
>
> Each stands forth as what it is most fully, and most preciously, because the emptiness in which it rests declares itself so overpoweringly. We realize that this thing or person, this phrase, this event, *need not be*. And at that moment, as if for the first time, it reveals its vivacious being as though it had just begun to be for the first time (51).

If it were possible to crawl into the empty surround of being, freeing other people, things, situations, to burn more brightly and continuously as themselves, that would be one way to clear "a space" (35) in which everything presently cut off might take root again. Everything, that is, but the martyr to void who made it possible. Lee comes to realize that what the space is cleared *of,* by pushing towards void, is oneself. He does manage a qualified clearing by the end of *Civil Elegies,* but he turns away from the "barren route" (53) to void for a less narrow one that permits simultaneous being and letting be.

Although the word "void" does not appear in *Civil Elegies* until the 3rd Elegy, the 1st and 2nd Elegies lament emptiness left by the loss of civil and divine presence—the latter lost, and the former never completely found. Void gets its most complete treatment only retrospectively, in the 9th Elegy after the escape from its domination. By then it has been defined and re-defined in the context of each particular elegy, so that it's seen to lurk everywhere. After the ironies about a Canada that scarcely exists (in the 1st Elegy) and the plaintive lament of the disappearance of a "Master and Lord" who supplied a measure to all things (in the 2nd Elegy), the conclusion of the 3rd Elegy begins an active exploration of void:

> We have spent the bankroll; here, in this place,
> it is time to honour the void (42).

These lines announce a determination to deal with void rather than passively being dealt with by it, and the 4th Elegy begins to explore one of two possible sources of action. Perhaps void is "our vocation," perhaps there are regenerative possibilities in it:

> Dwelling among the
> bruised and infinitely binding world
> are we not meant to
> relinquish it all, to begin at last
> the one abundant psalm of letting be (43)?

This is a question, not a statement of certainty. But what might happen if we took up this possible vocation, as people once undertook to serve God? (The association is made not only in the image of "vocation," but in "psalm"—and later in "beatitude" [56] as well.) Perhaps we might be acting on the spirit of reverence for everything that aches through the passage I quoted earlier from "Cadence, Country, Silence":

free to cherish the world which has been stripped away by stages, and with no
reason the things are renewed: the people, Toronto, the elms
still greening in their blighted silhouettes—some dead some
burgeoning but none our property, and now they
move at last in the clearness of open space, within the
emptiness they move very cleanly in the vehement enjoyment of their bodies (44).

The model of detachment is Saint-Denys-Garneau, "master of emptiness" (45). We get a fuller and more critical view of his example in the 8th Elegy, but for now it seems plausible to follow him into the ground of every thing, "oblivion" (45).

Even while he is expressing his attraction to Garneau's way, Lee never suggests that it would be easy to let go one's purchase on life. And he doesn't ignore the complication that might well render a successful quest for void useless. How should Canadians

> clutch and fumble after beatitude, crouching for
> years till emptiness renews an elm-tree,
> and meanwhile the country is gone (44-45)?

What good is a "psalm of letting be" (43) sung with the head in the sand? Thus the 4th Elegy invites a regenerative void and then undercuts it with an evil—empire (explicitly called void in the last section of the 6th Elegy)—after Canadian complicity in the Vietnam war has been starkly established: "And this is void, to participate in an / abomination larger than yourself. It is to fashion / other men's napalm and know it … " (48). Here is a void that must be actively resisted, even if in another aspect it's a spiritual discipline. The void of empire must be confronted, if there is to be any basis for resolve to fight it.

These two movements—toward regenerative void and away from void as abomination—come together in the 9th Elegy, still contradicting each other but held together in uneasy tension:

> To rail and flail at a dying civilization,
> to rage in imperial space, condemning
> soviet bombers, american bombers—to go on saying
> no to history is good.
> And yet a man does well to leave that game behind, and go and find
> some saner version of integrity,
> although he will not reach it where he longs to, in the
> vacant spaces of his mind—they are so
> occupied. Better however to try (56).

The poem doesn't let go, even as it reaches its most affirmative stage. Activist raging is good, though one rages to improve what is doomed; it's good to look inward for what is impossible to find.

While in the 2nd Elegy the familiar and reverent address is to the "Master and Lord" of an obsolete order, like Rilke's to the angels, still the allure of that order is made palpable at the same time as attachment to it is rejected as crippling nostalgia. Might a new order rest on void? Meeting the emptiness, Lee says to the absent "Master and Lord,"

> is a homecoming, as men once knew
> their lives took place in you (38).

The unreachable absolutes, God and void, are parallel if opposed. If the void is to serve the same function as God, it must be without the comfort of anthropomorphism, without a personification like "Master and Lord." And it does not take centuries to come to mistrust the reliability of void as home. "What if the void that compels us is only / a mood gone absolute" (55), Lee asks in the 9th Elegy, where again we meet the analogy between God and void. There neither is denied a continuing influence; instead both are naturalized. Rather than inhabiting "the realm above our head" God "must grow up on earth" (56) and at the same time the void must "re-instill itself in the texture of our being here" (57). Given quite natural human thirst for absolute measure, it's not very reassuring to conclude that what can be discerned of this is diffused throughout existence and recognized only fitfully. But the poem sets out to win what reassurance it can without glossing over the obstacles in its way; one would not expect the weight Lee has been carrying suddenly and finally to fall away, like the burden from Christian's back in *Pilgrim's Progress* or the albatross from the Ancient Mariner's neck. Nevertheless the mood of the 9th Elegy is celebratory. Taking his "right to be from nothingness," but "no longer held by its negative presence," Lee has found that the clearing away of illusions still leaves him access to "many things in the world / including Canada" (55).

Since at one point in the 8th Elegy Lee says "I will not speak of where I have not been" (53), which would seem to include void, one important thing remains to be said about that. Not much is made of the fact that Lee appears to enter void, perhaps so that his public poem does not get usurped by his private Dark Night of the Soul (St. John of the Cross is here called the "patron of void" 53), but 9th Elegy mentions that "when the void became void I did / let go," "derelict for months" (55). This reference to an emotional nadir, paradoxically the point of release that makes him finally "easy," is I think the experience dramatized in the 3rd Elegy in a scene that adds to our understanding of what the Archer represents. Lee normally comes to the square to be soothed by placid continuance, calmed by the beauty of the towers.

> But once at noon I felt my body's pulse contract and
> balk in the space of the square, it puckered and jammed till nothing
> worked, and casting back and forth
> the only resonance that held was in the Archer (39).

Lee describes a few lines later how one may easily stray into void in the "brute surroundings" of the hinterland, where "men who had worked their farms for a lifetime / could snap in a month from simple cessation of will" (40), but void may also yawn its abyss in the city as well. Fortunately the Archer, shaped by primal space quite other than man, saves Lee from being bushed in Nathan Phillips Square:

> Great bronze simplicity, that muscled form
> was adequate in the aimless expanse—it held, and tense and

waiting to the south I stood until the
clangour in my forearms found its outlet.
And when it came I knew that stark heraldic form is not
great art, for it is real, great art is less than its necessity.
But it held, when the monumental space of the square
went slack, it moved in sterner space (39).

This is a thorny passage. What is "stark heraldic form" that it could be more real than "great art?" Is it that great art, art period, draws away from the chaos (void) that never ceases to be a fact of existence, making a human order profoundly satisfying *because* it distances the chaos? The Archer seems not to have been created by Henry Moore, but by the earth itself, like the Laurentian Shield; it has therefore somehow directly tapped energies almost always outside man's jurisdiction. Lee has mentioned this force elsewhere, in a generalization which should be helpful here.

Canadian literature has long included an experience which the theologians call *mysterium tremendum*—the encounter with holy otherness, most commonly approached here through encounter with the land—to which an appropriate response is awe and terror. It is a very different thing from alienation ("Rejoinder" 33).

This is not the place to pursue the possibilities Lee opens up for a reinterpretation of the "threat" of the wilderness, the "stark terror" evoked by the land in Canadian poetry according to Northrop Frye, so I will just mention what good sense his comments make of a line which catches all that has seemed problematical about nature in Duncan Campbell Scott's "At Gull Lake, August 1810": "After the beauty of terror the beauty of peace." Surely this is the double hook of *mysterium tremendum*. Glorious and dangerous, the Archer is of it. So it holds, and Lee holds on to it when everything else goes slack, a mysterious artifact of void.

Cadence

Je vois ces emmêlements et ces noeuds du champ de l'existence dans notre continuum, et les rejoindre et les définir nécessitent que mes vers décalquent clairement et simplement ces remous, ces tourbillons et cette nodosité. Les vers et les mots servent à cela, et dans le cas où cela viole la syntaxe normale, pour moi, c'est que la syntaxe dite normale n'est pas à la hauteur de la trame de l'existence. Je ne vois aucune raison de démembrer et de sectionner l'être des choses pour le subjuguer à la syntaxe. Je ne cherche pas non plus à hacher et à démembrer la langue par pur fantaisie, mais pour la façonner jusqu'à ce qu'elle soit apte à exprimer ce que les choses sont. Si cela signifie que j'aurai parfois l'air excentrique dans ma langue et ma syntaxe, je suis bien prêt à cela (110-111).

So Lee writes in the afterword to *Élégies civiles* called "Lee, poète du processus," in which he talks about the challenge of recording a reality "très nébuleux et multiple" (110). Much of that reality as caught in *Civil Elegies* should be apparent by now. But the "eccentricities" of its style demand a share of the attention for two reasons. For one thing, the style may well seem uneconomical and perhaps unnecessarily strained if it isn't made clear how flexibly and purposefully it is manipulated. More importantly, all that I have said about the themes and structure of the poem also takes place in the style.

The term cadence means differently in different contexts, literary and musical. Analysts of prose style use the term to designate the fall to rest of the end of a sentence. Lee perhaps starts from a more general definition than that. In the glossary of the *Anthology of Verse* that he edited with Roberta Charlesworth, at least, cadence is defined as an aspect of rhythm, "the product of three elements: the natural grouping of words, the length and syntax of the sentence unit, and the speed of the line" (506). For my purposes cadence is the local and cumulative patterning of units of sound and sense that make up what we usually think of as "voice." I need a practical working definition so as to avoid a scorching by the immensity the word names for Lee. In "Cadence, Country, Silence" he says that he is trying to heed in his poetry a cadence which has a source independent of him but which he recognizes in "Hölderlin and Pindar. As in Henry Moore, The Brandenburg Concertos, Charlie Parker, John Coltrane, early Van Morrison" (35). What sort of rhythm links these diverse artists? The answer is in "Polyphony: Enacting a Meditation," an essay in poetics so tight that it resists quotation. But its cumulative, inconclusive definition of cadence is hinted at in this: "To be tuned by cadence is to vibrate with the calamitous resonance of being. And that is what is mimed in the polyphonic voice of meditation" (98). My own essay doesn't presume to handle cadence on this scale; the best I can hope for is to obey it in my own limited, local way.

A poet of process is not a poet of content (if there is really any such thing), even if his product is as full of ideas as *Civil Elegies*. When we catch the eddies and undercurrents in its flow from line to line, we engage the poem on the level at which it most engaged Lee while he was writing. The language at work in the poem is one of the ways in which Lee roots the experience his poem presents. That style is an animal—a fox—instantly responsive, in its moves, to any situation, always *engaged*, totally at one with its environment.

Lee writes free verse, so he can be abrupt or hesitant (as in the 2nd Elegy) with short lines and frequent punctuation, but the characteristic line is a long one which creates a flow of thought and feeling, spilling across the page in an all-at-onceness defying conventions of grammar and syntax. Commas might conventionally separate clauses and phrases (though an ambiguity is sometimes created when one of those expected commas is missing) but a comma might also join complete sentences. Or punctuation might disappear entirely, as it does to create the tight-lipped jamming of "yank and gook and hogtown" (48) in the 5th Elegy. So punctuation has more to do with pacing than with syntax.

The conjunction "and" is omnipresent, often appearing at the beginning of new sentences. The frequent use of conjunction is one of the techniques that some might find annoying, though its function seems to arise out of Lee's vision of life as a continuum of contradictions. In a normal sentence "and" links; it gives elements equal value because it does not make one a modifier of another. So when Lee makes a verbal chain with "ands" he implicitly asserts a relationship between often quite different grammatical units and their contents, while at the same time recognizing their integrity. He never bashes a sentence completely beyond recognition, though, so a reader can hear the normal punctuation shadowing what appears on the page. Two systems working at once keep a reader loose. Lee's syntax is not an inherited closed system; it responds to the nature of what it carries, no more a fixed measure than God is a fixed definer of identity or anchor of conscience.

Lee is inclined to work in lengthy, elastic, portmanteau units that, while they may begin with a capital and end with a full stop, contain a range of syntactical relationships in between. The internal structure of some of these units is tightened by the repetition of a word or phrase that moves, like the backward curl of a wave, in a direction contrary to that of the main thrust of a passage, enacting the internal tensions and contradictions that Lee wants to embody whole. For example, the phrase "our own" is repeated three times with different emphasis in a passage about the land (in the 3rd Elegy, 40), which mainly shows how the land is *not* our own. How can it be ours when it is our "adversary" and when it is "occupied" by empire, and when we have never fully claimed it? Well, it both is and is not, and that will always remain the case, even though the 9th Elegy clarifies the terms by which fuller possession may be taken.

Similarly the word "goodbye" crops up twelve times in the passage in the 4th Elegy about the prospect of acting on the assumption that void is regenerative, and everything should therefore be let go. Yet each of these "goodbyes" is contradicted by the gathering field of images they punctuate, images that firmly fix the tenacity of the flawed and precious things that are ostensibly being abandoned, so that the simultaneous effect is of letting go *and* holding on.

> If only
> here and now were not fastened so
> deep in the flesh and goodbye, but how should a man
> alive and tied to the wreckage that surrounds him,
> the poisoned air goodbye, goodbye the lakes,
> the earth and precious habitat of species,
> goodbye the grainy sense of place, worn down in
> words and local ways of peoples, goodbye the children returning
> as strangers to their roots and generations,

and cities dying of concrete, city goodbye my city of passionate bickering
neighborhoods the corner stores
all ghosts among the high-rise, like bewildered nations after their
surrender as their boundaries
diminish to formalities on maps goodbye, so many
lives gone down the drain in the service of empire,
bombing its demon opponents though they bleed like men, goodbye
and not that all things die but that they die meanly, and
goodbye the lull of the sun in the square, goodbye and
goodbye the magisterial life of the mind, in the domination of number every
excellent workaday thing all spirited
men and women ceaselessly jammed at their breaking
points goodbye who have such little time on earth and constantly fastened
how should a man stop caring (43)?

The "goodbyes" supply the glue of this passage as it meanders designedly through much of the matter of the poem on its way back to where it began, in "fastened," finally completing the framing question which has been suspended for nineteen lines. The "goodbyes" are so variously placed in this shapely unit, sometimes with the sense of verbs, that they create surprise as well as continuity (which is true of the line-breaks as well). Because leave is being taken not only of people but of the air, the city, the country, empire and so on, another sort of link is made between highly diverse things—the care for them all felt by the man who addresses them.

If the passage from the 4th Elegy is full of tender feeling, a very different effect of repetition occurs in the second section of the 5th Elegy, where Lee is again maintaining two contrary things at once. Good men, honourable men, necessary men, who by proxy fry "the skin of kids with burning jelly" (43), are criminals. One sentence will exemplify the basic—and repeated—structure: "Even though he loves children he is a criminal" (47). The passage is an accusation that begins in short-sentence bursts, then quickens and swells in an outraged rush, "he is a criminal" hammering through it, before drawing back into shorter lines and irony about "a nation's failure of nerve":

> And the consenting citizens of a minor and docile colony
> are cogs in a useful tool, though in no way
> necessary and scarcely
> criminal at all and their leaders are
> honorable men, as for example Paul Martin (47).

Lee fingers a decent man; he is perfectly serious about the bind that good men may find themselves in: service of an abomination dirties the hands. The end of the section reinforces the irony that began it, an irony rather slow to break and more devastating for that: "In a bad time, people, from an outpost of empire I speak" (47). There may be visions of exiled Chinese poets raised by this; one may even think of poor Ovid sending elegy-letters to Rome from his place of exile on the Black Sea, but the irony here is that this outpost of empire is our home, a supposedly independent nation.

Such examples demonstrate the necessity of watching what the language of *Civil Elegies* does, because it gives muscle to what is being said. A beginning is all that can be made here, because the richness of the poem defeats the attempt, in a foray no longer than this one, to catch more.

Home

> It is not much to ask. A place, a making,
> two towers, a teeming, a genesis, a city.
> ("Elegy 1")

It's ironic that so much has to be gone through to gain even the chance to begin accomplishing the very little asked for in *Civil Elegies*. Never underestimating the barriers that block the way to true independence, Lee deliberately sets his sights low. He begins a passage of the 1st Elegy quite clogged with punctuation—commas, semi-colons, periods and dashes—by saying "In the city I long for, green trees still / asphyxiate" (35), and goes on to describe his yearned-for city exactly as it is now—the breeding ground of emptiness—before introducing what would make all the difference: "but in the city I long for men complete / their origins":

> they clear a space in which
> the full desires of those that begot them, great animating desires
> that shrank and grew hectic as the land pre-empted their lives
> might still take root, which eddy now and
> drift in the square, being neither alive nor dead (35).

"Not much to ask." So how much closer is Lee to getting what he wants, after agonizing his way through all the problems to the 9th Elegy? Given that what he longs for cannot be made by one man, or a few men, he is light years away from achieving his minimal desire. And yet there has been a kind of enharmonic change in his position, because he has found his own shaky ground to stand firmly on, with the will to reenter his home and greet the very coffee mugs of it as though for the first time. This is good news for those miserable, gawking, ancestral spectres of the 1st Elegy, because now in taking up his own civil life, Lee takes on theirs and becomes pioneer and explorer:

> And I must learn to live it all again, depart again—
> the storm-wracked crossing, the nervous descent, the barren wintry land,
> and clearing a life in the place where I belong...

[find] a place among the ones who live
on earth somehow, sustained in fits and starts
by the deep ache and presence and sometimes the joy of what is (57).

So the poem ends in the exhilaration of a new beginning, "in the early years of a better civilization" (56), and in the sort of prayer that would never pass the lips of those who believe that the way to take care of the devastation and alienation caused by technology, "progress," is to lay on more technology. But it is the sort of prayer that would be understood by the swindled Indians of this country, because they had this kind of reverence for earth before its spoilage had begun:

> Earth, you nearest, allow me.
> Green of the earth and civil grey:
> within men, without me and moment by
> moment allow me for to
> be here is enough and earth you
> strangest, you nearest, be home (57).

Homage

A serious criticism of [*Lament for a Nation*] has been that to write in terms of inevitability (call it if you will fate) is to encourage the flaccid will which excuses the sin of despair in the name of necessity. By writing of the defeat of Canadian nationalism, one encourages in a small way the fulfillment of the prophecy (George Grant xi).

Of course Grant also writes that "When a man truly despairs, he does not write; he commits suicide" (3). But if Grant is to be reproached by readers of little heart who miss both his rhetoric and his passion, so is Al Purdy, writing in the introduction to his anti-American anthology *The New Romans* (iv) that it's too late to stop the sell-out of Canada. This is the same Purdy whom Lee salutes as the most Canadian of poets, a man who gets bored with all the clamour about Canadian identity because he knows what it is instinctively. *Civil Elegies* must hit many Canadian readers hardest as it first hit me—with rubbing of the nose into the "colonial mentality" first diagnosed years ago by E.K. Brown in *On Canadian Poetry*. Unwitting acceptance of a colonial reality contributes to the notorious Canadian diffidence, the feeling of second-rateness Lee exaggerates into a need to fail. A nation of colonial (Brown) victims (Atwood) cowed by an Old Testament God (Jones) or by nature into garrisons (Frye): some self-image we've had. When Wilfrid Laurier predicted that the twentieth century would belong to Canada he must have been counting on Christ's assurance that the meek would inherit the earth.

As Canada's century wears on, of course, the confident voices emerge. Canada's west coast poets, Bowering, Davey, Marlatt and others, think of Frye's "stark terror"

Stan Dragland

as quite inapplicable to their experience, sometimes as a joke. Alone, at night, in good company with the rock and the creatures in Elora Gorge, so would Christopher Dewdney. Post-colonialist critics, dropping the shackles of their imperialist "Commonwealth" origins and trying to maintain in their new centrality the spirit of the margin, have little left, in literary terms at least, to apologize for.

If we had learned earlier the limitations of thematic reading, we would earlier have found a way to value our literature(s) and ourselves. I used to hear complaints about the lack of strong female role models in Canadian writing, and I would say look at Alice Munro, Audrey Thomas, Daphne Marlatt; look at *how* these fabulous writers write about failure. *There's* role models, if you want them. It's no victim writing so wittily about failure in *Survival.* And now the anatomist of failure is a huge international success. Unaccustomed to success, do we Canadians like that? Do we enjoy it? We do not. In the last decade of Canada's century, the post-colonialist century, we are still the last to recognize and celebrate our own. As the critical fashion turns from cataloguing victims and flinching from the terrors of nature, the challenge is going to be to remember and hold on to the element of truth in these partial formulations.

Civil Elegies doesn't simply speak for me. That is to say, I have many other feelings about Canada than it expresses. I'm Albertan in origin; perhaps that makes some of the difference. Others, enjoying the indignity of regional marginalization, have pigeonholed Lee, and Anansi Press, as centralist (Ontario) literary phenomena. But Lee didn't undertake to speak for me. At an early stage of thinking about this article, a victim of thematic thinking, I considered detaching myself from Lee's vision of Canada, perhaps with the help of Al Purdy's "Transient," which catches an instinctive feeling of belonging here, not in nor expecting a nation *accompli,* but in a process. But immersion in *Civil Elegies* yielded the realization that it's nowhere imprisoned by the impotence that is part of its subject. So the poem does not perpetuate emasculation, not only because it moves through and beyond that, but also because it is always throwing up those curls of wave which contradict placelessness. The curls make a wave of their own that swells through the poem and crests in the 9th Elegy, confirming the Rilkean attachment to home that is palpable, if often muted, everywhere in it. Lee might agree with Margaret Atwood that "if we do choose [this country] we are still choosing a violent duality" (*Journals* 62) but he would speak in terms of multiple dualities. The themes, the structure, the very cadence of *Civil Elegies* make these complexities inescapable, and thereby Lee earns his determination to be at home here in heart and body and mind. His poem is sinewy and sensuous, an innoculation of fibre into wills inclined to be flaccid.

Works Cited

Atwood, Margaret. *The Journals of Susanna Moodie.* Toronto: Oxford, 1970.
—. *Survival.* Toronto: Anansi, 1972.
Bringhurst, Robert. "At Home in the Difficult World." *Tasks of Passion: Dennis Lee at Mid-Career.* Toronto: Descant Editions, 1982.

Conze, Edward, ed. *Buddhist Scriptures.* Harmondsworth, Middlesex: Penguin, 1959.
—., ed., with I.B. Horner, D. Snellgrove, A. Waley. *Buddhist Texts Through the Ages.* New York: Harper Torchbooks, 1964.
Garneau, Saint-Denys. *Complete Poems.* Trans and ed., John Glassco. Ottawa: Oberon, 1975.
Frye, Northrop. *The Bush Garden.* Toronto: Anansi, 1971.
Grant, George. *Technology and Empire.* Toronto: Anansi, 1969.
—. *Lament for a Nation.* Toronto: McClelland and Stewart, 1970.
Lee, Dennis. *Kingdom of Absence.* Toronto: Anansi, 1967.
—. and Roberta Charlesworth, eds. *Anthology of Verse.* Toronto: Oxford, 1964.
—. *Civil Elegies.* Toronto: Anansi, 1968.
—. *Civil Elegies and Other Poems.* Toronto: Anansi, 1972.
—. "Running and Dwelling: Homage to Al Purdy." *Saturday Night* 87 (July 1972), 14-16.
—. and David Helwig. rev. of *Civil Elegies and Other Poems. Quarry* 21 (Summer 1972), 66-70.
—. and Robin Mathews. "Rejoinder." *Saturday Night* 87 (September 1972), 31-33.
—. *The Gods.* Toronto: McClelland and Stewart, 1979.
—. *Élégies civiles.* Trans. and ed., Marc Lebel. Montreal: L'Hexagone, 1980.
—. "Cadence, Country, Silence: Writing in Colonial Space." *Open Letter* Second Series, 6 (Fall 1973), 34-53.
—. "Polyphony: Enacting a Meditation." *Tasks of Passion: Dennis Lee at Mid-Career.* Toronto: Descant Editions, 1982.
Purdy, A.W., ed. *The New Romans: Candid Opinions of the U.S.* Edmonton: Hurtig, 1968.
Reaney, James. *Colours in the Dark.* Vancouver: Talon, 1969.

AL PURDY'S POETRY: OPENINGS

I am a part of all that I have met;
Yet experience is an arch wherethro'
Gleams that untravelled world whose margin fades
For ever and for ever when I move...
Tennyson, "Ulysses"

a sort of human magic

When I first heard Al Purdy read "The Dead Poet" I was amazed. Here was a poem of beauty and great concentration, obviously a Purdy poem, but with all of the Purdy self-consciousness, the rough-edged Purdy persona, refined out of it. I felt I was hearing not just a gain in technique but something orchestral. The tight nesting structure of "The Dead Poet" gave me visions of a new Purdy volume that would somehow ripple out concentrically from that poem. That didn't happen in *The Stone Bird.* The book opens with "The Dead Poet," but it's the typical Purdy miscellany. Not that "The Dead Poet" is anomalous; I think it *is* a key to reading Purdy, because so much of Purdy fits snugly into it. So everything that follows here, however unlikely that may sometimes seem, is about "The Dead Poet." Call it Purdy's mythic poem in Northrop Frye's sense: the poem all good poets sooner or later compose in which their poetic essence is so concentrated that the rest of the writing falls into place around it. That is too neat, of course. Aphoristic neatness is part of Frye's rhetoric. Finding a key is not the same as finding a solution, but the key may certainly be a talisman—pure energy—to hold onto while you wrestle with the possibilities it suddenly opens up.

Wrestling with *The Collected Poems,* for instance. Here is another Purdy miscellany, a huge one. "Homer's Poem" and "The Dead Poet" frame the book, but otherwise the progression is chronological. There are no signposts for a reader making his way through these poems and, page by page, never knowing what's going to happen next. Hold on to that key. If this world appears as random as life, it's meant to, not being sponsored by an external creator and meaning-maker. This life is not pre-organized. That opens an opportunity for the reader: to create the book, the books, that *The Collected Poems* contains. Purdy's effort has mostly been devoted to making each poem. In fact, negotiating poem after poem through this book, you keep coming on scenes of making. Often you find yourself looking over the shoulder of various witnesses to creation.

Purdy is more and more trying to re-invent the source, to start afresh, in openness and innocence and without arrogance, trying to find the words to shape the spirit that has not one name but many, and those names only to be spoken in words preserving shadows and glints of them. This is romantic; this is religious; this is a quest for "a lost kind of coherence" ("The Darkness" 278 [unless otherwise noted, all references are to *The Collected Poems*]) so vigorous and reverent and irreverent and joyful and *precise* that it doesn't feel in the least nostalgic—though of course it often involves looking back, for meanings resting in the shift of origins already imagined, at records left by other searchers. Looking back to renew the world. Stepping out of scratch, darkness, chaos, into the very first experience. Then and only then, say these poems made out of words, come the words. The voice that most eloquently carries this news is the voice that never did belong to Purdy, the one whose origin is buried in the blood. Dennis Lee's borrowing of the term *"tremendum,"* "meant to honour the mystery, not to straitjacket it," (385) helps to zone the experience of reading Purdy's poetry of the eighties, those "poems of an extraordinary yet often inscrutable clarity" (387) that Lee opens the way to seeing. Purdy has been courting the inscrutable "deep core of the world" ("The Cartography of Myself" *No Other Country* 17) for decades, and talking about it in poetry and prose, but sometimes, more often recently, the discursive voice has fallen silent and a singing has occurred:

> the rare arrival
> of something entirely beyond us,
> beyond the repeated daily dying,
> the singing moment—
> ("Time Past/Time Now" 318)

What a long way the recent "unsigned" masterpieces are from "Home-Made Beer," which I place at the other distant end of the Purdy Spectrum. "Home-Made Beer" and "The Dead Poet": between them a cosmos, but "The Dead Poet" contains it all.

Keep your ass out of my beer!

We got tired of "Home-Made Beer" at Western when Purdy was writer-in-residence, ten years ago. You'd have thought it *the* Purdy poem, it opened so many readings. "At the Quinte Hotel" ("for I am a sensitive man") was usually not far behind, but it wears a bit better than "Home-Made Beer."

Why that same old poem over and over, Al? Don't you get bored with it? I forget what Al said. Something about breaking the ice, maybe, something about variety; nothing convincing. Al, you've got dozens of other poems that could break the ice, if you want it broken. We couldn't figure it out. Al didn't strike us as one of the nervous sort, the kind who create their own formula for surviving public appearances.

Stan Dragland

I remember a reading a year or so later that was different. More than different; it was electric. Not only because Al seemed really interested in reading the poems for a change, but because of the poems he was reading. "The Dead Poet" is the one that hooked deepest in my memory, but there were others, mint-new poems about beginnings, in the womb, in the garden.

The Stone Bird, with the new poems in it, came out in '81 and I invited Al down to Western for a reading on October 7, 1982. I figured I knew Al well enough by now to throw him a curve in the intro., even though, as introducers go, I'm the nervous sort. So I introduced Al as an established poet whose wonderful new poems were exploring such fascinating new/old territory that he couldn't possibly ever again open a reading with "Home-Made Beer."

Al was on the platform with me, but he didn't seem to be listening. He had to arrange his books, he had to straighten the desk. It's important to get those heavy teacher's desks aligned just so for a reading, and they make a wonderful racket when they slide. The first time Al looked up was when I mentioned "Home-Made Beer."

"Whaddya mean? Ya want me to read 'Home-Made Beer'?"

A Pause. In a cold country you have to deal with frozen water a lot. Sometimes you're breaking the ice; sometimes it's getting thin underneath you. I hate it when that happens in front of an audience.

"You do whatever you like, Al," I said. If this story had a hero, it wouldn't be me.

Mine was the nth introduction to a Purdy reading; maybe Al wasn't paying attention. Maybe he mistook my reference to "Home-Made Beer" for a request. But it's equally possible that, keeping "an absolutely straight face" (see "Notes on a Fictional Character" III) Al was saying, "Up yours, Bud." I have never been able to read that occasion; all I know is that for the nth time Al's reading began:

I was justly annoyed 10 years ago
in Vancouver ...

P.S.: Nov. 3, 1990

Purdy finally reads again at Western. The nervous introducer (a sensitive man) is this time a member of the audience. The new introducer reminisces about drinking beer with Al when Al was writer-in-residence, sounding unlikely to have a problem with "Home-Made Beer." Once introduced, Al loses no time in mentioning Stan Dragland as the reason he has decided never again to read "Home-Made Beer." (He has read what I have written on the subject.) To show how firmly his mind is made up, Al repeats his determination a couple more times during the reading, adding once that he'd better not read "At the Quinte Hotel" either. But during the question period someone asks Al if he meant The Quinte Hotel in Trenton or The Quinte Hotel in Belleville, and it seems only polite to read the poem in question. Then someone else, obviously insensitive to Al's wishes, requests "Home-Made Beer." The audience loves both poems. It should never be said that critics are no use to the writers in this country.

Now, having found a way to whet his audience's appetite, Al will be *ending* all his readings with "Home-Made Beer."

the shape of home is under your fingernails

"I'd prefer to be understood with a minimum of mental strain by people as intelligent or more so than myself," says Purdy in "A Sort of Intro." to *Bursting into Song*. If that were all he wanted, if that was the length of his reach, I doubt that his poetry would be cause for celebration, but it's not an unworthy ambition. Realizing that almost keeps me from saying that "Home-Made Beer" doesn't create any mental strain at all. Well, the reputation is not built on it, not for those who find their Purdy on the page, at least. A lot of the reputation *is* based on that unmistakeable Purdy voice, though, on the "I" that gets to be "joyfully and relentlessly Al Purdy" in and after *Poems for All the Annettes*, according to George Bowering in his 1970 book on Purdy (21). With the voice comes the image of the sprawling, brawling, beer-drinking, straight-talking impermanent husband familiar to people who have never met Purdy, just as they feel they know Ameliasburgh and that "watery omphalos" (Woodcock 9), Roblin Lake. What should be said about that voice and the myth of Al Purdy is that, while neither would exactly be contradicted by having a beer with the guy, they were not somehow transferred whole from the life into the work. The "I" in those poems is the painstaking creation of decades and many false starts; that persona is made of words. If it turns out that behind the persona is an artist who now commands a wide range of styles, the capacity to modulate between a vernacular or "low" style ("Home-Made Beer" would be an instance) and a lyrical high style (as in "The Dead Poet"), there is a sense in which the whole concern, including Purdy's social and political conscience, rests on the vernacular base. Knowing this makes me less impatient when, as in "The Horsemen of Agawa," the base sounds more like interference than a modulation of voice, unnecessarily grounding the lyrical flight.

Some god in ourselves buried deep in the dying flesh

Michael Ondaatje's Caravaggio escapes from the penitentiary outside of Kingston by strapping himself to the roof and letting the other two members of the roof-painting detail paint him, blue on blue, invisible. After dark he unstraps himself and shinnies down.

When Caravaggio got loose, he could have fled in any direction, so what pulled him west, towards Trenton, to cross paths with six year old Alfred Purdy? It must have been Ondaatje's reading of the memoir, *Morning and it's Summer,* written by the adult Al Purdy; maybe this passage in it: "Some part of me still remains a child: sitting on a pile of lumber behind Reddick's Sash and Door Factory in 1924, trying to explain to myself how I got here and what I'm going to do about it" (11). At least it's behind Reddick's Sash and Door that Caravaggio finds Al, who scarcely bats an eye when this blue man walks up. There is a movie currently being shot in Trenton, which might somehow explain this dramatic colouring, but Al doesn't need an explanation. He is not much older than the child of "Pre-School" (one of the autobiographical poems "introduced" by the memoir) who is just discovering primary colours, naming them and proving to himself "that I could invent the world" (40). A blue person probably wouldn't stretch him much.

What kind of gesture is this borrowing of the main character of *Morning and it's Summer* to play a minor role in Ondaatje's novel, *In the Skin of a Lion*? Ondaatje is always "deviously" thinking out plots "across the character of his friends" ("Burning Hills," *Rat Jelly* 56) so the gesture is anything but isolated. It should be recognized as part of the network of such references in the discontinuous multi-genre *roman à clef* that Ondaatje is writing, but each one raises its own questions. To judge by the fun it is to recognize Purdy in Ondaatje's novel, the guest spot is a sort of friendly joke: Ondaatje hospitably opening his fiction to another writer's "actual" past. Purdy can't have expected his character to find a second life beyond the covers of his memoir, but I doubt that he'd mind. Privately, he might even be pleased to have been offered a compliment in "trickster skin" ("Uswetakeiyawa," *Trick* 91). Of course he would respond in kind. Ondaatje's interest on the loan of young Al was a copy of *In the Skin of a Lion*. The story goes that Al wrote back to say he couldn't find a trace of himself. (The story goes on, in a later installment: Al got impatient with looking for himself— he'd been warned that he might show up—and wrote to complain about his absence, having given up a couple pages too soon.) If Purdy was pleased, it would probably be because he has said that he feels Ondaatje "writes under the skin." I understand this to mean that you can't catch him at it. He gets under the skin without breaking the surface. Takes one to know one,

> Foregoing the balanced certainty of work,
> And seeking apertures, a loose chink
> In the wall of understanding.
> ("As a Young Man?" *Pressed on Sand* 13)

In all our bones the long history of becoming

There is a passage in a poem called "Wanting" that catches a doubleness typical of the stance in Purdy's poems, at once inside and outside the experience:

> I bow low over a woman's hand and
> suspiciously glance sideways just in case
> some sonuvabitch is grinning
> (*At Marsport Drugstore* 19)

This is actually what it is to be Anglo-Canadian, inhibited from fully living the moment. We've made an art of poking fun at the famous Canadian diffidence. Give it a twist, though, and it turns out to have a shiny side. It's because he feels the drag on taking himself too seriously that Purdy can voice the strength of Canadian hesitancy:

The Bees of the Invisible

Sometimes it seems that people of nations
outside my country's boundaries are dancing
and shouting in the streets for joy
at their great good fortune in being citizens
of whatever it is they are citizens of—
And at other times it seems we are the only
country in the world whose people
do not dance in the streets very much
but sometimes stand looking at each other
in morning or evening as if to see there
something about their neighbors
overlooked by anthropologists
born of the land itself perhaps
what is quietly human and will remain so
when the dancing has ended
                    ("Home Thoughts" 361)

The quiet reflective rhythms, voice of refined simplicity, this resounding understatement is typically Canadian too, and it is a rock on which something can be built. It's "a place to stand on" ("Roblin's Mills [ii]" 133).

these inner rooms / one cannot enter waking ...

The speaker of "Lament for the Dorsets" witnesses the last few moments before silence falls on the last Dorset. Purdy typically names this man and dramatises his finale. As a result, watching Kudluk's quiet death, one *feels* his race disappear. The puzzled Kudluk's last act is the carving of a tiny ivory swan. Meant to speak to a dead person, it's the Dorset's pivot into the future, because the beauty of the carving still speaks to us.

The swan as proof against death is the image the poem looks towards and ends with, but I'm more interested now in another survival, that of Kudluk himself. He is one of the Dorset giants who "lurk behind bone rafters / in the brain of modern hunters." This brain which houses ancestors is a metaphor at the heart of Purdy's perennial preoccupation with the layers, "all condensed like a compacted millennium" (xv), in the individual mind. A variation on the metaphor also helps him focus on the mysterious sources of his poetry. "Where does the song come from," is the question asked in "The Dead Poet." One answer is suggested by the image of a Purdy whose own mind is a muse-occupied dwelling.

There are more Purdy introductions to Purdy books than one might expect, given that he tends on those occasions to undermine the value of introductions. To read these is to swing, in prose, through much of the spectrum of style and approach found in the poems. At the ballsy end I would place the jokey hardboiled "Autobiographical Introduction" to the NCL *Poems of Al Purdy,* and at the poetic end I would place the rather tender "To See the Shore: A Preface" to *The Collected Poems of Al Purdy* (not to

Stan Dragland

mention the lyrical *Morning and It's Summer*). Of course disarming casualness appears in the serious introductions, and mysteries are mentioned in the more offhand ones—like the mystery of that mental warehouse, and how to get into it.

"What each of us writes," Purdy says in the "Introduction" to *A Handful of Earth*, "balances and juggles the whole history of literature, and we are for that moment the 'midland navel-stone' of earth." But, he also says, poems "connect with sources I'm not even aware of, and if I were the poems would be impossible." In "A Sort of Intro." to *Bursting Into Song* this becomes, "I write because I do not know, or know very little." Aimed at non-specialist readers, Purdy's introductions scarcely qualify as poetics. The casual approach would explain a natural enough alternation between confidence and diffidence on the subject of the muse. "To See the Shore" may not get much nearer the truth of what, after all, works only where it hides, but the image for it, a variation on that dwelling metaphor and the technique which brought Kudluk up close, is sustained.

"Inner recesses of the mind are not at your beck and call," Purdy says in "To See the Shore."

Perhaps there are small elves in the head, privileged guests living there and continually busy with their own affairs. The only connection the conscious mind has with them is when they permit a collaboration, which perhaps neither the conscious nor the unconscious was capable of alone (xvi).

This low-key, un-bardic image of the muse, or muses, is typical Purdy. "They are very old," he says about these occupants, "collaborators," custodians of the wisdom of the ages, quite familiar to readers of folktales. "You try to predict their thoughts during the sun by day and the moon by night, then discover they have their own internal moons and suns" (xvii). Something fascinating happens here to the image of the mind as a dwelling. Its walls and roof dissolve to reveal an alternative interior universe, the key to it lost or broken. "It's only when I forget about [the elves] entirely," Purdy says, "that they gently intrude into my thoughts" (xvii).

To look for Al Purdy in his poems, and not only recent ones, is often to find his features, his voice, re-composed into those of another: someone like Menelaus, say, telling his heartbreaking story about Helen, or like an unnamed stone age misfit on the brink of discovering that he was born to follow something "into myself to find / outside myself," about to discover that he is an artist, though his existence predates both the term and the role. Sometimes the voice of the poem is all but unrecognizable as that of the man who wrote "Home-Made Beer." Such poems seem sung, without mediation, by the old ones themselves. If Jay Macpherson's Noah, carefully balancing the golden bubble of his creation-containing head, had a voice it might sound like this gentle powerful singing. "Angel declare: what sways when Noah nods?" is the question of Macpherson's "The Anagogic Man," and the answer returns: "The sun, the stars, the figures of the gods" (*Poems Twice Told* 42).

96

The Bees of the Invisible

It surprises me to be seeing Purdy clearer by the light of Jay Macpherson, whose poetry I also love. I doubt that either poet would be flattered by the connection. Jay Macpherson's Emblem Books published Purdy's 1962 chapbook, *The Blur in Between*, but if the two have something mythopoeic in common now it would be because they have written towards each other from opposite ends of the literary spectrum: the personal and locally particular, in Purdy's case; in Macpherson's, the literary and archetypal.

It's not surprising that, in "To See the Shore," (as in the poem called "Ritual") Purdy endorses Mircea Eliade's "theories about myth and legend: primitive peoples re-enact original events in ritual repetitions, and each time becomes for them the first time. And thus they negate huge areas of time itself" (xv). For years now, the Purdy who is deeply rooted in twentieth century Prince Edward County, Ontario, has been vaulting over centuries, millennia, over the whole globe and bringing back authentic news of remote times and places. "In the poetry of the eighties," Dennis Lee says, "there is a greater willingness to speak of first and last things without jokey or belligerent irony, long his defence against sentimentality and pretentiousness" (386). But I come back to singing. I feel that Purdy doesn't speak, so much as he sings, in some of these new poems. He sings, from inside, the very unfolding of birth, the opening of the world.

Purdy gets antsy in the presence of "the high gods of serious things" (xviii), of course. You can find his own version of himself as Noah at the end of "To See the Shore," "aboard a rowboat floating in the middle of all the beer I've drunk in a lifetime" (xviii). He cherishes the subversive in himself, but he knows there are moments when the trickster hears a compelling voice from inside, or maybe from out there (it hardly matters), and simply stands still to listen.

II

I confess I do not believe in time. I like to fold my magic carpet, after use, in such a way as to superimpose one part of the pattern upon another. Let visitors trip. And the highest enjoyment of timelessness—in a landscape selected at random—is when I stand among rare butterflies and their food plants. This is ecstacy, and behind the ecstacy is something else, which is hard to explain. It is like a momentary vacuum into which rushes all that I love. A sense of oneness with sun and stone. A thrill of gratitude to whom it may concern—to the contrapuntal genius of human fate or to tender ghosts humouring a lucky mortal.

Nabokov, *Speak, Memory*

"Our father which art the earth!"

The poem called "Ritual" is a slightly sardonic meditation on surviving a Winnipeg winter—during which all human systems threaten to shut down—with the aid of some brain-warmth from Mircea Eliade who

Stan Dragland

in uncanny mnemonics
remembers the birth of the world
for me in his books (217)

If the reference to Eliade weren't, so to speak, centred by "To See the Shore," one might let it slide. The ironic context of "Ritual" almost buries its importance. But turning from Purdy to Eliade and back gives a sense of déjà vu. As Eliade says, in *The Myth of the Eternal Return,* "any real act [performed by archaic man], i.e. any repetition of an archetypal gesture, suspends duration, abolishes profane time, and participates in mythical time" (36). You can open Purdy almost anywhere and find something connecting with that. Try "The Nurselog," spoken by a fallen tree tenderly holding its thousand-year history in trust for the seedlings nursed by its decay:

> I remember this in a dream
> when we all dreamed
> as if I were an old repeated story
> once told to me that I retell (274-5)

"An old repeated story"—it almost seems a single story, the story of creation. Eliade sees everything folding back into it; Purdy circles back to tell and tell and—for the sheer joy in it—retell it in shades and tints of its infinite variety.

> There are moments of such elation
> in a man's life it's like being struck
> alive on the street by the first
> god one meets at an intersection
> whom one must believe in a second
> time after twenty years of atheism
> You press the stomach of your business
> suit flat and stride on into the sunset
> pretending to be serious
> ("The Jackhammer Syndrome" 168)

If you draw a mental line between the great many such moments recreated in Purdy's poems, you find a good many of them observing or narrating or dramatising a variation on some First or other, in his own experience, or that of someone else, or of the world.

But why, or rather how, does he escape the predicament of modern man, "the terror of history," Eliade calls it, a life comprised of unrepeatable moments, one following another, that collect into a finite span of years, desacralized and meaningless? The answer is that he doesn't. Whatever magic Purdy can do with time, one of his great strengths as a poet is that he is stuck in his own time and place—rooted in a process, of course, as poems like "Transient" show. His vernacular voice, in "Home-Made Beer" and many serviceable, often serious, variants, issues from the here and now, and Purdy very often takes the here and now for his subject and his theme. He has paid his dues to the present; he *knows* the sensation that linear existence is absurd. You can feel the black thrill of the abyss often enough in his poems; it yawns under so much of contemporary experience a man would have to be blind not to notice. Purdy does more than that. Feeling it, he uses his powers to make others feel it as well. Hiroshima, South Africa, the poor of Mexico, nuclear waste—a monster of meaninglessness looks out of his poems at times; he is often enough "mind-lost in an immense / garbage heap of yesterday's details" ("D.H. Lawrence at Lake Chapala" 261).

But there is also that inner chamber with its dissolving walls, the compensating vistas that open up anywhere in time. This doesn't cancel time, but it does the next best thing—subdivides it multiply, restoring some of the duration of lost eras, refleshing ghosts. Especially in the sense that Purdy's muses conduct him again and again to scenes of first unfolding, first seeing, he is Eliade's archaic or primitive or mythic man, eternally returning to versions of a cosmogonic moment when chaos coalesced into something. His fascination with endings fits; the ending curls round to a new beginning, and folds back into the integral wholeness of a continued present. Of course Purdy does not accept the traditional first term in this system—the creating god outside of all, containing all and making it mean. For this and other reasons, there is a huge unignorable difference between him and the anonymous cave-painter of Nerja or the painter of the Agawa pictographs he writes about. But it's remarkable how vividly, how plausibly and *presently* such figures appear in his poems. His "primitive brain" ("Lost in the Badlands" 291) does draw him, over and over, to create moments of origin "saturated with being" (Eliade 4). He becomes the living paradox Eliade speaks of as a sort of modern primitive, "a modern man with a sensibility less closed to the miracle of life ... " (77).

It's no wonder Purdy celebrates the core of vitalism in the person and the writing of that other primitive modern, D.H. Lawrence. Lawrence is the iconoclast whom Purdy salutes for

> the glowing question mark he wrote
> after every single one
> of the million names of God?
> ("D.H. Lawrence at Lake Chapala" 262)

The sentence is not interrogative, so the question mark is Purdy's way of saying "me too." This independent Lawrence is the one on whose refutation of the New Testament version of creation ("In the beginning was *not* the Word/—but a Chirrup") Purdy builds one of his loveliest cosmogonic poems ("In the Beginning was the Word"). Lawrence is one of those for whom the dismissal of God and transcendent Elsewhere Reality makes the earthly present throb with value. His reverence for life needs no single source to credit. In an unusual gesture, Purdy gives over the conclusion (the consolation) of his elegy, "Death of DHL," to DHL, making this celebration of the miracle of living his own:

> "For me, the vast marvel is to be
> alive. For man, as for flowers or
> beast and bird, the supreme triumph
> is to be most vividly and perfectly
> alive. Whatever the unborn and the dead
> may know, they cannot know the beauty,
> the marvel of being alive in the flesh.
> The dead may look after the afterwards.
> But the magnificent here and now of
> life in the flesh is ours, and ours alone,
> and ours only for a time.
> I am part of the sun as my eye
> is part of me. That I am part of the earth
> my feet know perfectly, and my blood
> is part of the sea—" (323-24)

There is something unPurdy-like in the confidence of this exultation, the centrality in it of the "I," but the faith in the words (such remarkable words to find at the end of *Apocalypse*, Lawrence's prose commentary on Revelation, and his last book) is near the heart of what Purdy's art is about.

Being Alive is the right title for his collected poems; too bad he'd used it before. Into the wholeness of Lawrence's "here and now," Purdy draws the past, reconciling time and space. It all comes together in the figure of earth, analagous to the teeming brain of the writer, itself a containing brain with a language of its own. "The earth is all things," begins a passage in a poem ("Driving the Spanish Coast") that muses on the significance of the palaeolithic caves at Nerja, Spain, with its "20,000 year-old cave paintings,"

> its shapes greater than imagination
> preconceiving all our discoveries
> all artifacts of man duplicated
> in caves and desert places
> (*Stone Bird* 45)

Of the many possible openings into the "primitive" Purdy, then, I choose his reverence for earth—stone, in the first place, and a totemic initiation into kinship with stone that happened in the arctic.

The Bees of the Invisible

The arctic visit is quite famous. It produced *North of Summer* and other poems in which Purdy explores the arctic, with its people, as a highly distinctive "region" of the country. The surest proof that Purdy became something more than a tourist in the north, though, is an experience that was not recorded in *North of Summer*. Purdy puts it this way in "The Cartography of Myself," the essay which opens *No Other Country*:

I lay with my ear flat against the monstrous stone silence of [Kikastan] island, listening to the deep core of the world—silence unending and elemental, leaked from a billion-year period before and after the season of man (17).

"After?" Human existence is parenthesized, a short-lived "season," by the eons of time compacted into this stone that speaks—a silence. The passage is brief, but it obeys some of the stresses in the stone it describes, and it's one of those passages in Purdy one returns to, because *he* circles back to the experience, renewing it in the title poem of *The Stone Bird*.

This poem is addressed to a woman in pain. She is recoiling from the "terror of horror of being / alive in this sewer world." The obverse of the coin of Lawrence's "marvel of being alive" is a dark reality Purdy never denies, or his essential optimism would carry less force. In "The Stone Bird" he reminds the suffering woman of her own faith (lapsed, but perhaps temporarily) in the way things are, a primitive vision of wholeness, then goes on to share with her his own. Founded on that arctic stone.

> once on an arctic island
> at Kikastan in Cumberland Sound
> in a moment of desolation
> I laid my head flat against the island
> a mountaintop of gneiss and granite
> with ice floes silent nearby
> and heard the heart of the world
> beating
> It was a singing sound
> steady and with no discernible pauses
> a song with only one note
> like some stone bird with such a beautiful voice
> any change of pitch would destroy it
> (*Stone Bird* 107)

"Earth sound" this is, a heart song that Purdy hears because he believes he does, his primitive self quelling the modern awareness that science could offer a demystified account of his experience. (Reminding me of an aside in Eliade: "If miracles have been so rare since the appearance of Christianity, the blame rests not on Christianity but on Christians" 160n). Reminding me of the speaker of a section of "No Second Spring" (*Stone Bird* 78) "listening" to a voice of reality that, like Purdy, he carries in his head—

> a different one
> whose voice spoke in my head
> and who still had something called sight
> instead of this knowing we have
> whether a thing is round or square
> whether it is good to eat or not
> friendly or unfriendly ...

What is the song of the stone bird? It is "all that beginning earth / singing still," singing all that was and is in time and space.

> those geologic ages
> convulsions of history and pre-history
> all those dawn murders rapes and cruelties
> are condensed into one symphony
> are singing in my ears
> —a wind-song a sun-song
> an earth song and a song of the sea (108)

"Listen," the poem insists ("listen" is a key word in Purdy; it's the first word of the first poem in the *Collected*), listen to this "song of life;" you can hear it anywhere. Listening is not necessarily a pleasure, since the song is of ill as well as of good, but it all returns to that core of origin, made simultaneous (intelligible) to the ear, if not to the mind.

Perhaps because "The Stone Bird" is a little talky and diffuse it was omitted from the *Collected Poems*. But it interests me greatly as the record of an actual, concrete, "historical" experience of return to origins. It has helped me to notice the many other responses to "earth power" ("Transvestite" 212) which ripple through Purdy's poems. (It is not as though he hears earth's voice for the first time ever in the north, though that instance sounds freer of the static that interferes with the song in settled and developed areas.) The mythic poem in this stone lineage is "Gondwanaland." It ends with the image of a "Cairn on an arctic island" that pays homage to the stone bird, but it's a lament for lost geological unity, the earth as single land mass which, in theory, broke up into "stone islands," "stone galleons." In the poem the history of everything, animal, vegetable and mineral is

> riding ships of floating stone
> without meaning or purpose

The Bees of the Invisible

> for there never was any purpose
> and there never was any meaning—

After the dash, and a stanza break, there is an oblique leap away from the nihilistic view into the receiving senses (hearing first) as registers of ... let's say meaning, though the word seems too blunt because the meaning is happening and will not be abstracted from its performance. This is far from the only Purdy poem that embodies meaning as fragile, resistant to the direct approach, to be taken, if at all, by surprise, and purest when pre-verbal:

> Only that one listened to the birds
> or saw how the sun coloured the sky
> and were thoughtful in quiet moments
> Sometimes in these short lives
> when our minds drifted off alone
> moving in the space vacated by leaves
> to allow sunlight to pass thru
> at the wind's soft prompting
> there was reasonable content
> that we were aware of only afterwards
> and clapping our hands together like children
> we broke the spell (320)

The second person plural in this poem means that one is speaking for many, and this happens in other strong creation poems like "In the Garden" and "In the Beginning was the Word." It's more usual for Purdy to imagine his beginnings in singular and particular terms, but he has more than one string to his fiddle, and these plurals (like his dramatised personae) are signs of his escape from a single self. No one who can't change shape has any claim to being a voice of the tribe.

As the myth of the eternal return is to the creation, so is the "monomyth" (Joseph Campbell's term) to the story of the hero—the same story discernible through the countless variations of plot and all the name changes of the hero. In a lower case way this sort of return is always happening in Purdy's poems. When he changes shape he never ceases to be himself. By probing what is most intensely important to him, he finds out how to understand (and create) the primitive figures in his poems. For example, traces of Purdy's connection with arctic stone appear in the poem called "Meeting" as it follows the first entrance into the caves of Nerja:

> the earth possessed a womb
> old as earth is old
> cream-coloured smooth stone

Stan Dragland

hidden in blood darkness
with a surrounding network
of creamy ganglions and nerves
in which light flickered and danced
leading away from the glowing centre
to join the body of the earth
(*Stone Bird* 48)

Three entrances are made to this cave in the one poem: the primary one is that of a persona (whose "name was Man"), but this is shadowed by Purdy's own, centuries later, and also by the entry of writing, which carries from other poems a context for addressing stone. Once again, though the terms for it are different, there is a birth, an awakening to a new spiral of awareness

—something awakened inside the man
as if he had just been born
and looked at the new world
outside himself
with a vast surprise
(*Stone Bird* 48)

Purdy often returns to such pivotal moments, of ending or (especially) beginning; and these moments of birth (of world, of consciousness) stack up as versions of each other, the same and not the same, so one feels them opening and widening, approaching anagogy. There are several other poems I might follow on this track, but the obvious step from the poem I've just glanced at is to another (very different) version of the same experience, an earlier (1973) and parallel poem called "In the Caves" that I'd like to linger with.

"Meeting," to isolate one parallel, leaves the man at a point where he has been charged with the magic of stone whose centre he has touched, whose voice spoke inside him, leaving him with an ambiguous "strength / which some would think weakness," "knowledge that could be ignorance." Such "gifts" are also given to the speaker of "In the Caves" (181-184) a young stumblebum, marginal to his primitive community, unvalued even by himself, because he's no good at hunting (see the "inept hunter"/pictographer of "The Horsemen of Agawa" 176). Typically, in the recent hunt for a "grey mountain," a mammoth, that the hunters of his tribe brought down, his spear went astray. In other ways that hunt was not the same experience for him as it was for the others. For them it happened and was over; to him it keeps happening— and in more ways than one. He has no idea why, but the spears that struck the mammoth now strike him, again and again, and repeatedly the mountain's dying shriek escapes his body.

The Bees of the Invisible

So-called primitive peoples do not draw lines of demarcation between themselves and the earth, other creatures, the dead. This commonplace of anthropology would suggest that primitives (who are *other*, not inferior, to "civilized" people) have unity of being without dissociation of sensibility, to borrow phrases from Yeats and Eliot intended to express what moderns desire and do without. Perhaps the lives of, say, the Bushmen *are* as harmonious as modern anthropologists claim, though it's interesting how smoothly such visions of unity slide into myths of lost Edens. Coherence interests Purdy, but his stories of primitives don't vanish into the archetype of an organic existence. That idea of primitive harmony in group consciousness and activity would be a joke to the misfit of "In the Caves," and the unity that he *does* feel—identity with the mammoth—is anything but benign. The others have danced and chanted "to the mountain spirit that it might forgive them," and the ritual has drained their culpability into metaphor. They are blissfully limited men, not visceral junctures of blood bone and stone like the misfit. If you are the mammoth and they kill the mammoth, that unity hurts. This man is a flesh-and-blood demonstration of what, besides awe and expectancy, an encounter with *mysterium tremendum* (holy otherness) means: disorientation, bewilderment, fear. He is undergoing an initiation, a preparation, but the world is so new that no one else, not even the shaman, can explain what's happening. How is he going to find an outlet for the shriek?

By trial and error he finds out what he can do, what he was meant to be. What he discovers reveals that the poem is a portrait of the artist, another of Purdy's self-portraits. First, with a stick, in the earth, and then in "caves at the edge of the higher mountains / where my people fear to come," he scratches the image of that shriek.

> there is something here I must follow
> into myself to find
> outside myself in the mammoth (183)

he says as he haltingly discovers a pictorial power analogous to the power of words to carry being. But the power of making and the power of comprehending are not, alas, vouchsafed to the same person.

> The shriek flows back into the mammoth
> returning from sky and stars
> finds the cave and its dark entrance
> brushes by where I stand on tip-toes
> to scratch the mountain body on stone
> moves past me into the body itself
> toward a meaning I do not know
> and perhaps should not (183)

Neither will any interrogation by Purdy of the old ones, his muse-elves, induce them to address him directly. The conduit of the power does not question the power; the brain relaxes and lets the hand write what it will.

By a circuitous route, with many backward loops, we have returned to the question that Purdy worries at in his introductions and in many of his poems ("What it Was" [64] is one of the earliest), realizing that it must be framed as a series of unanswerable questions that nestle one inside each other like Russian dolls: where does the song come from? where does meaning live? and so on. Purdy doesn't write of any single origin, first cause, except to say why the search for such is futile:

> —and if there was anywhere
> a First Cause
> it had hidden itself perfectly
> by remaining in plain sight
> without intention or design
> ("Journey to the Sea" 258)

I doubt that Purdy is interested in a philosophical Primary; it's the sacred spirit source he's after, and he taps it in a large variety of poems that are different and the same. His beginnings are multiple, and they are not points but processes. In the beginning was the earth; in the beginning were the beavers; in the beginning was black; in the beginning was a mountain's shriek; in the beginning was a brother writing words on the wall of a womb: such openings Purdy invents out of a direct primitive feeling of basics like primary colours, sun and moon, the four elements, the senses. His myth-making draws from no authority outside of world in time; it begins at the moment a wave of being begins the motion of a poem. His contribution to dramatising events that must in some sense have happened is to speed them up and particularize them minutely (the first view of the first flower "must have been around 7 A.M." according to "In the Early Cretaceous" 348; the arrival of the "Great Dying" of dinosaurs was the morning after the evening "the sun went down at 5:30 / P.M." in "Lost in the Badlands" 296) and to supply a finely-tuned set of human senses to register them. The authority of these poems is not that of writ, but of the senses; not retrospection but observation.

Originals are not divisible

> I was altered in the placenta
> by the dead brother before me
> who built a place in the womb
> knowing I was coming:
> he wrote words on the walls of flesh
> painting a woman inside a woman

The Bees of the Invisible

whispering a faint lullaby
that sings in my blind heart still

The others were lumberjacks
backwoods wrestlers and farmers
their women were meek and mild
nothing of them survives
but an image inside an image
of a cookstove and the kettle boiling
—how else explain myself to myself
where does the song come from?

Now on my wanderings:
at the Alhambra's lyric dazzle
where the Moors built stone poems
a wan white face peering out
and the shadow in Plato's cave
remembers the small dead one
—at Samarcand in pale blue light
the words came slowly from him
—I recall the music of blood
on the Street of the Silversmiths

Sleep softly spirit of earth
as the days and nights join hands
when everything becomes one thing
wait softly brother
but do not expect it to happen
that great whoop announcing resurrection
expect only a small whisper
of birds nesting and green things growing
and a brief saying of them
and know where the words came from (369)

"The Dead Poet" is tightly woven of the various materials Purdy has used to make his poetry as a whole—conjunctions and disagreements of native and exotic, female and male, life and art. The practical and the poetic, dream and reality, repetition and variation, then and now—in parentheses of first and last things—and it is the right poem to end Purdy's *Collected.* There, isolated by a blank page and italic typeface, it holds Purdy's whole career, near enough, in four shapely stanzas. I sensed this largeness when the poem first thrilled me in 1980—the active suspension of so many elements, separate words incandescing in the energy of their association.

The scope of this small poem is large, but its intensity is owing to its stress on a single subject, the relationship of the speaker and a fictional dead brother who is projected as an answer to the riddle of the speaker's existence, the reason why, despite his practical pioneering heritage, he should have become a poet. Perhaps the dead brother of this poem has a foundation in reality—a miscarriage, or even the wish of an only child. A dead brother is unurgently referred to in at least two other poems.

But Purdy could never have been as close to a flesh and blood brother as his speaker is to a spirit-brother, maker, who fashioned him, in his own image, a poet. The dead one is the forerunner. Knowing that being alive (we are remembering what this means to Purdy/Lawrence) is to be denied him, he makes sure that a brother will live in his place. There is almost a sense that the one who got born is an impostor, living moments of greatest intensity in words he does not own. The dead poet, being family, is a blood version of those estranged muse/elves. He is the only kindred spirit in the family at large. The poem's elegiac sadness is for this soul who never lived in the flesh, except vicariously, and for the poet's loss of a companion who might have made him less lonely. (See "Night Summer" 228: "a music / that is complete forgiveness / for being" is "not to be known unless the lost self / aches.") "The Dead Poet" turns A.M. Klein's wonderful "Portrait of the Poet as Landscape" inside out, since the question it asks is "where do the words come from?" not "where do they go?"

The last stanza of "The Dead Poet" is a lullaby, sung to the brother in return for his "faint lullaby / that sings in my blind heart still." "Sleep," it says, and "wait," not words addressed to one without a future. The last stanza is the consolation of the elegy, looking towards another birth, a waking, as a brother once again prepares a place into which his brother may be born.

This mirroring of the first and last stanzas is one of many teasing near-symmetries in the poem. Of course, the dead brother's preparation of the womb is purposeful and shaman-like. He makes the womb a nest for a poet in a ritual combining three arts that join in poetry: writing "words on the walls of flesh / painting a woman inside a woman," whispering his lullaby-song. The dead brother is related to Purdy's primitive cave-painters, especially the one whose canvas is a womb of stone. The picture of the brother at his work being so concrete and substantial, one tends to forget that he has only the substance of words. He is a fiction who stands for a mystery that can only be guessed at—so the question at the end of stanza two tells us—the source of the words. He is real and unreal, a living ghost, an ubiquitous absence. Inside and outside! The ritual in the womb must have been to prepare a brother to greet his other self in every experience so moving as to call forth words of poetry. Vastly different though they are, the traces or glimpses or whispers of the dead one in stanza three are not random. The mournfulness of the trim they give to monuments of the soul's magnificence reminds me of another amazing Purdy poem, "Spinning," uncannily written in the exact manner of Canada's least-known important poet, Colleen Thibaudeau. In "Spinning," every loved thing is always whirling away and it's necessary to turn at a desperate rate just to catch a glimpse of them going.

As a whole, "The Dead Poet" is more difficult to catch than its simplicity might suggest, and the third stanza is the most elusive. It shifts rapidly from image to image through dislocations of syntax, punctuation and tense, a protean unit attached by a colon to the word "wanderings" and subdivided by dashes signalling remarkable metamorphoses. This is a Grand Tour conducted at lightning speed and featuring some unusual stops. One of these, Plato's cave, is a metaphor for life lived entirely as in a cave, parallel to and remote from Reality. This cave is found only in *The Republic*, and the Ephesus Street of the Silversmiths appears only (Acts 19:24) in *The Bible*. Purdy has actually wandered in these realms of gold, as, literally, he visited Spain (The Alhambra) and Russia (Samarkand). There are Samarkand poems in the small volume called *Moths in the Iron Curtain*. There is a certain sense that the wanderer is meeting versions (different and the same) of images his Canadian past in and out of the womb had prepared him for. Wherever he goes in stanza four, the poet is reverently visiting works of the imagination, monuments to being; wherever he goes, his dead brother precedes him—always powerless, always dependent on the living voice, but nevertheless a seam running through everything worth seeing and doing. No wonder he is called "spirit of earth" (read "spirit of being") in stanza four.

All of the nesting images in the poem, one thing inside the other—not only the obvious ones in the first stanza, but the citizens in the dim cave, the music in the blood—create a feeling of concealment, and seem to acknowledge the interiority of essence. These are buried things. To reach them you have to peel off a layer—of flesh, of appearance. They are inside the poet's skull, in his bloodstream, living a life of their own just under the skin. The nesting images are ambiguous, though. Concealment and imprisonment are the dark faces of protection and nurturing. And this ambiguous custodianship is performed by a collaboration of the senses. The dead brother opens the poem for rhetorically dramatic reasons, but, as I have said, the second stanza is set in an earlier time, and might be discussed first.

Among the poet's ancestors, the sexes fall into their customary positions in the patriarchal order. The men are active, the women passive, submissive, "meek and mild." Their pioneering is domestic, interior; its emblem is the "cookstove and the kettle boiling." This is an image within the larger image of pioneering in which the women fuel with food the "backwoods wrestlers," their men. Wrestling *in* the backwoods, perhaps, but more likely wrestling with it. Pioneering was a combat, and these pioneers were victorious—so they thought—in clearing the trees (as lumberjacks), planting the crops (as farmers). The process of domesticating this country is caught in just two words, nouns made active by a verb—"wrestling." I said that the poet has been plucked from the path represented by all of this muscular, outward-looking pioneering, but it's nearer the mark, as the layers of this poem peel back, to say that he is a poet because his womb-initiation was androgynous. Inside the female womb a masculine spirit creates the totemic image of a woman while whispering a motherly lullaby. This complex portrait of Purdy's muse is not of the male's poet's conventionally female muse, but of a male strongly marked, perhaps even dominated, by the fem-

Stan Dragland

inine. A surprising thing to be saying about Purdy? One large book that might be assembled from *The Collected Poems* is an anthology of male attitudes to the dance, or battle, of the sexes. But the Purdy I have been following is a male poet highly responsive to an other in his nature that is, if not feminine, at least ambiguous in gender. "Spinning" must originate somewhere near the feminine end of that continuum. And "The Dead Poet" feels very reminiscent of the telescoping poems in Jay Macpherson's *Boatman.* It was James Reaney who named the "myth of things within things" (30) that holds *The Boatman* together. Noah's head contains all of humanity; the ark holds both Noah and his originary pairs of beasts; at the last judgement the ark sails back into the eye of God. A précis hardly does justice to the exercise of emotion and imagination these poems ask of a reader, but might suggest why the nesting structure of "The Dead Poet" would call *The Boatman* to mind when I first heard it read.

There is such a gentle vision of the restoration of unity between all things in the last stanza of "The Dead Poet" that one might not notice how radically it rewrites traditional eschatology. It's wholly characteristic of Purdy's undermining of the humanistic God and his Word that he forgoes all of the apocalyptic fooferaw of *Revelation.* That is the western world's most familiar telos, though there are others equally dramatic. Ragnarök—any Norse or Germanic Götterdammerung—makes great theatre, as long as you aren't in the cast, and none of it is a patch on the nuclear finale we have prepared for ourselves. Sometimes it's hard not to think of ourselves as people of the last days:

> In the darkness is no certitude
> that morning will ever come
> in dawn spreading pink from the east
> is no guarantee that light will follow
> nor that human justice is more than a name
> or the guilty will ever acknowledge guilt
> All these opinions arrived at in years past
> by men whose wisdom consisted of saying things
> they knew might be admired but not practised
> arrived at by others whose wisdom was silence
> And yet I expect the morning
> always I expect the sunlight … .
>   ("Remembering Hiroshima" 161)

It's not by evasion but with determined faith that writers keep writing in such terrible times. I'm thankful that a writer like Purdy can still authentically imagine a completion to the patterns of things that is not apocalyptic, that foresees a tender evolution, into some new/old Garden state. Purdy's version, in "The Dead Poet," feels like a correction of T.S. Eliot's "The Hollow Men," with its equally unattractive alternative endings, the bang and the whimper. Purdy substitutes the whoop and the whisper. But, he says, don't expect the whoop—a sound you might hear in the sort of blast that is a party—just listen; carefully. You'll hear the same sounds you hear now, and they will be totally transformed, everything singing itself and its harmony with every other thing.

Now what's going on? No big deal. The riddle of existence is merely solving itself. Only a Canadian could pull off such affirmation deep in the twentieth century, in quiet words cleaned, as they are uttered, by their very unpretentiousness. And here is another respect in which "The Dead Poet" is at the core of Purdy. It is written in the same key as the poem addressed to the man who thought Canada was no nation, and that poem stands in turn for all those in which Purdy expresses his no-nonsense confidence in the value of rootedness in his own country.

One more thing. The diction and the rhythms of this poem are heightened as part of the tightness of the ensemble. I have spoken of singing. This lyrical Purdy is at the other end of the gamut of sound and substance from the Purdy of "Home-Made Beer" (whose colloquialism and rhetoric of understatement, to be fair, are not completely unlyrical). The sound of "The Dead Poet" carries as much of its sad intensity as the sense. There must have been some temptation to fly this voice, to ride it right away into that other country where the dead poet is at home. As it is, the voice of the poem is largely his. But, astonishingly, this *is* a Purdy poem. What makes it so is a certain angular irregularity to the rhythm and, especially, an awkwardness in the last stanza:

> do not expect it to happen
> that great whoop announcing resurrection

An editing reflex, entranced by the general lift of the music, might "polish" this unit:

> do not expect that great whoop
> announcing resurrection

But this poem, like all of Purdy's poems, is a product of earth. It must not lift free. The resurrection, such as it is, will happen here. It was easy for Browning's Fra Lippo Lippi to see how to improve Raphael's line, impossible for him to reproduce the *life* in those paintings. Al, I withdraw my objection to "Home-Made Beer." There could be no "Dead Poet" without it.

ಌ

As the best directions have it, you must cling to Proteus with arms like the jaws of a pit bull. What a fantastic ride this is, thrashing in tandem through his whole anthology of changes! Some readers lose their hold, but those who hang on through all that torque of transformation, the ones who demonstrate that if necessary this embrace is till death do us part, they say that those ones are granted a wish.

You were perhaps expecting a conclusion to my remarks on Purdy, but his poems keep opening up and swallowing the last word.

Works Cited

Bowering, George. *Al Purdy.* Toronto: Copp Clark, 1970.

Eliade, Mircea. *The Myth of the Eternal Return: Cosmos and History.* Princeton, N.J.: Princeton University Press, 1974.

Macpherson, Jay. *Poems Twice Told.* Toronto: Oxford University Press, 1981.

Lawrence, D.H. *Apocalypse and the Writings on Revelation.* Ed. Mark Kalnins. Cambridge: Cambridge University Press, 1980.

Ondaatje, Michael. *Rat Jelly.* Toronto: Coach House, 1973.

—. *There's a Trick With a Knife I'm Learning to Do.* Toronto: McClelland and Stewart, 1978.

—. *In the Skin of a Lion.* Toronto: McClelland and Stewart, 1987.

Purdy, Al. *Pressed on Sand.* Toronto: Ryerson, 1955.

—. *Selected Poems* (Introduction by George Woodcock). Toronto: McClelland and Stewart, 1972.

—. *The Poems of Al Purdy: A New Canadian Library Selection.* Toronto: McClelland and Stewart, 1976.

—. *A Handful of Earth.* Coatsworth, Ont.: Black Moss, 1977.

—. *At Marsport Drugstore* (with an appreciation by Charles Bukowski). Sutton West, Ont.: Paget, 1977.

—. *Moths in the Iron Curtain* (Illustrated by Eurithe Purdy). Sutton West, Ont.: Paget, 1977.

—. *No Other Country.* Toronto: McClelland and Stewart, 1977.

—. *The Stone Bird.* Toronto: McClelland and Stewart, 1981.

—. *Bursting into Song: an Al Purdy Omnibus.* Windsor, Ont.: Black Moss, 1982.

—. *Morning and It's Summer.* Dunvegan, Ont.: Quadrant, 1983.

—. *Piling Blood.* Toronto: McClelland and Stewart, 1984.

—. *The Collected Poems of Al Purdy.* Ed. Russell Brown (Afterword by Dennis Lee). Toronto: McClelland and Stewart, 1986.

Reaney, James. "The "Third Eye: Jay Macpherson's *The Boatman*." *Canadian Literature* 3 (Winter 1960), 23-34.

ও

The section titles are lines from Purdy Poems:

a sort of human magic: "Method for Calling Up Ghosts" 74

"Keep your ass out of my beer!": "Home-Made Beer" 56

the shape of home is under your fingernails: "Transient" 79

some god in ourselves buried deep in the dying flesh: "My Grandfather's Country (Upper Hastings County)": 148

in all our bones the long history of becoming: "Man Without a Country" 314

those inner rooms / one cannot enter waking … : "'—Great Flowers Bar the Roads'": 354

"Our father which art the earth!": "Driving the Spanish Coast" *Stone Bird* 45.

originals are not divisible: "The Son of Someone Loved" 340

THE BEES OF THE INVISIBLE:

KERRISDALE ELEGIES

> things that could never be told,
> so we gave words instead.

A friend of mine opened *Kerrisdale Elegies* in a bookstore, read a few pages, replaced it. Maybe he noticed the reference to Rilke in Robert Kroetsch's blurb on the back of the book; anyway, he detected Bowering poaching on *Duino Elegies* and it put him off. Like any good browser he was looking to fall in love at first sight. Which is how *Kerrisdale Elegies* took me. What I liked first was the voice, curiously unRilkean, unless we were to imagine how a Rilke reborn and settled in present-day Vancouver might sound. That voice has its modulations, but one very important thing it does is swallow all influences. Therefore *Kerrisdale Elegies* is not like, say, *Burning Water* or *Allophanes*, into which Bowering introduces undigested chunks of other books. In the novel, shifts of style are the only signals that the ground has changed. Of course that's for fun. Nobody whoops it up in an elegy. *Duino Elegies* and *Kerrisdale Elegies* are really like night and day—caught at the same hour on the same globe. Despite the powerful presence of another powerful poem in it, I still read *Kerrisdale Elegies* every time with admiration for its originality.

We are not talking about *Duino Elegies* as a general influence or model, as for Dennis Lee's *Civil Elegies*, Jan Zwicky's *Wittgenstein Elegies*, Stephen Scobie's *Dunino*—Rilke has certainly had his effect in Canada—or Jack Spicer's unfinished group of elegies. *Kerrisdale Elegies* is actually, in part, a free translation of *Duino Elegies*. At times the two poems go along together almost line for line, though Bowering makes changes no translator would be permitted. A translator doesn't substitute a baseball team for a family of acrobats, as Bowering does in "Elegy 5." A translator doesn't all but throw out Rilke's angels, dispersing their function among humans, as Bowering does. Amazing but true, the spirit of *Duino Elegies* doesn't evaporate as Bowering writes his own time and place, his own life across it.

It's impossible to show all the sorts of difference between the Rilke and the Bowering in a short parallel passage from each, but the opening of each poem might illustrate some of the things I've been saying. The Rilke is in Stephen Mitchell's translation:

Who, if I cried out, would hear me among the angels'
hierarchies? and even if one of them pressed me
suddenly against his heart: I would be consumed
in that overwhelming existence. For beauty is nothing
but the beginning of terror, which we still are just able to endure,
and we are so awed because it serenely disdains
to annihilate us. Every angel is terrifying.
        (Rilke, "The First Elegy")

If I did complain, who among my friends
would hear?
            If one of them
amazed me with an embrace
he would find his arms empty, his own face
staring from a mirror.

Beauty is the first prod of fear,
                    we must
live our lives in.
            We reach for her,
we think we love her, because she holds the knife
a knife-edge from our throat.
                   Every fair heart
is frightful.
             Every rose petal
exudes poison in bright sunlight.
        (Bowering, "Elegy 1")

We recognize the Rilke in the Bowering here, though a divergence has already begun. Bowering's personified beauty is more concrete, more secular, his generalization therefore less sweeping than Rilke's, to mention only one thing. *Duino Elegies* is a sort of core text which Bowering courts in a rhythm of departure and return. Sometimes he is quite near; sometimes he moves off where there is no Rilke to follow. Since there is always something more than translation going on, Bowering is always in dialogue with Rilke. Sometimes he explicitly interrogates his source. But always there is this sense of vindication of the essential vision of Rilke, always the feeling of homage being paid, and ultimately of two powerful voices contrapuntally celebrating life lived in the shadow of death.

    Bowering's poem is full of his own versions of Rilke's "Things" to be valued and praised for themselves, and also as part of the rich ensemble of life so loved that the prospect of leaving it is agonizing—until pain is recognized as a principle of that life.

The Bees of the Invisible

> How we squander our hours of pain.
> How we gaze beyond them into the bitter duration
> to see if they have an end. Though they are really
> our winter-enduring foliage, our dark evergreen,
> *one* season in our inner year—, not only a season
> in time—, but are place and settlement, foundation and soil and home.
>
> (Rilke, "The Tenth Elegy")

> Precious
>
> agony.
>
> How we threw away half our lives
> waiting like cows for better weather.
>
> Suffering
>
> is our winter of bare branches,
>
> our secret abode.
>
> (Bowering, "Elegy 10")

Bowering sparely endorses Rilke's conviction that the world is recreated and sustained in the eyes of the committed beholder. That is their answer to mutability. It takes hold, as these passages from "The Tenth Elegy" and "Elegy 10" begin to say, when we stop trying to leave our home in suffering.

Bowering's type of this committed individual, more explicitly than Rilke's, is the poet, and the poet at the centre of the poem is quite like Bowering himself. *Kerrisdale Elegies* is an unchronological portrait of the artist in formation, but Bowering manages to handle the autobiographical element impersonally and with self-irony. He doesn't grandstand. If he did, the reader would not feel invited to share the immensely difficult task of sustaining the spirit of the things that are.

So what is Bowering in *Kerrisdale Elegies*—an audacious pirate or a self-effacing participant in tradition? He is surely both, and if I stress the latter mask it's to argue for the seriousness of his wonderful poem. The fact that it *matters* could easily be lost as critics move in on the question of influence. A reader needs to be relaxed about what Bowering is doing, and that means first simply responding to his words. Then one can safely enter the labyrinth of influences. Holding on to what the words actually do, wherever they came from, one never gets lost.

Am I the only reader who almost prefers to get his Rilke in Bowering's words? I don't read German and it's unsettling to go from translation to translation. Something of great poetry comes through and the something is probably Rilke's, but there's no definitive Rilke in English, whatever various publishers and reviewers claim. This is Bowering's opportunity. Released from the impossible demands of exact fidelity to the German he can make real poetry in English.

Stan Dragland

Anyone who studies the intertextuality (presence of one text in another, by quotation, paraphrase, allusion, echo and so on) of *Kerrisdale Elegies* needs to delight in seeing double. Such a person will also want to remember the context of Bowering's other writing—like *Allophanes*, whose playful intertextuality throws out this mani-festo-like unattributed line from Yeats: "Talk to me of originality / and I will turn on you with rage." Why not take Bowering at Yeats' words?—which might mean reading *Kerrisdale Elegies* alongside *Duino Elegies* the way scholars read Malory's *Morte Darthur* as both an original text and an edited translation of French originals, an origin Malory doesn't hide. Even the idea of offering under one's own name a text borrowed from a writer in another language is far from new, and there are modern precedents like Pound's "Chinese" poems.

Kerrisdale Elegies sounds nothing like *Duino Elegies*. The two poems look com-pletely different too, and at one level the arrangement of the poem on the page controls how it sounds, but this is not so much in the way Bowering effortlessly catches the idiom of his time and place. He never speaks "poetically," in fact he never raises his voice, and yet he comes across with authority, speaking levelly and conversationally to his peers, with confidence that people will listen. His language is bare of artificial ornament, there is no straining at figures of speech; quiet conversational rhythms carry much of the effect, while avoiding the banal or monotonous. In everything from the brief burst to the drawn-out periodic sentence (see the last page of "Elegy 5"), in tones from jaunty to hushed, diction from correct to slangy, *Kerrisdale Elegies* strikes the ear in an authentic North American accent. The lines are as natural as speech, if you imagine speech that is everywhere active, like a chord augmented with a fifth or a seventh note—on its way somewhere else. There are examples on most pages. One of my favourite active colloquialisms (oxymoronic, in this case) is from "Elegy 9" and is an attempt to persuade the reader to make his or her own joyful noise.

> The ghastly dead will never applaud your imitation of them,
> your beautiful silence.

> They wrote the book on silence.

Bowering's voice could not be colloquial in the same way as Rilke's, given the gap between their time and place and language, but there is an even greater disparity in the deeper principles of sound and sense caused by Bowering's distinctive notation, with alternation between full lines and stepped half lines and shorter units. Bowering makes the page a unit of composition and his page might show a number of opened-up couplets or tercets or longer staves. Visually there is a lot more open space than there is in *Duino Elegies*. The amount and disposition of space is not constant; it depends on the words it surrounds. These are all arranged along the traditional horizontal axis, though the stepping introduces a degree of verticality into the wordscape, but they do sometimes seem to rise and float on a white ground. There is almost the feeling that if the page weren't opaque you could see past the words to something else. Writing or typing out the lines makes you feel their physicality, their almost sculptural interaction with white space. That is also an interaction between sound and silence. Variations in these, together with subtleties in the use of traditional schemes of sound arrangement like repetition and refrain, give an improvisational feel to the music of the poem. It never settles into a predictable pattern.

∽

Rilke is the most important literary presence in *Kerrisdale Elegies*, but by no means the only one. In all of Bowering's elegies but the third, adding up to the "magic number" of nine, there suddenly appear a few untranslated and unattributed lines of French poetry. None of the passages sounds like Bowering (and none of them reads like any other) but the French lines are not out of place in terms of content. Sometimes the lines follow the sense of what Bowering has just been doing, so that a bilingual reader will feel only an enharmonic change of language; sometimes the lines are not locally related but pick up or point ahead to something elsewhere in the poem. Occasionally, freely translated phrases from the French passages appear in Bowering's text proper (though the more we look into this matter, the fewer words we find that seem to be merely Bowering *propre*). A further advance in understanding the French presence in *Kerrisdale Elegies* requires finding out where the passages come from. There are orthodox ways of doing this, with concordances and so on, if you know the authors' names, but it doesn't hurt to get lucky.

I was reading *Kerrisdale Elegies* on the plane to Winnipeg where I spent some time with other readers and it occurred to me to ask if any of them knew anything about the French in Bowering's poem. Yes, said Smaro Kamboureli, she'd asked Bowering about it for an article she was writing on the *Elegies* and Dennis Cooley's *Bloody Jack*. Bowering might appreciate this "chance" encounter because in *Burning Water* he tells the reader how infallibly his choice of apparently unlikely writing venues produced "something for his book" (192).

But I wonder how Bowering, this burier of things he's not sure he wants his readers to find, liked his critic's direct approach. "For me to know and you to find out," might he not have whispered to himself? The peekaboo poet bearded by the audacious critic. Sic 'im, Smaro!

Who generously shared with me all she worried out of the poet. We still haven't located the Rimbaud-sounding lines in "Elegy 10," but here are the sources of the other passages:

"Elegy 1": Baudelaire, "La prière d'un paien."
"Elegy 2": Villon, *Le Testament*.
"Elegy 4": Hébert, "Le Tombeau des Rois."
"Elegy 5": Apollinaire, "L'Ermite."
"Elegy 6": Beaulieu, "Rémission du corps enamouré."
"Elegy 7": Mallarmé, "Petit air."

"Elegy 8": Nerval, "Vers dorés."
"Elegy 9": Laforgue, "Complainte de l'oubli des morts."

This is a sampler of French poetry; fragments from a whole tradition of "dead poets" implicitly acknowledged as Bowering's ancestors by their mere presence in a poem saturated with literary tradition. A reader bridges two languages in coming to terms with them, and two Canadian cultures as well, because Anne Hébert is a Québecois poet, as was the late Michel Beaulieu.

Searching for Bowering's French sources and finding them often in literary territory new to me was a pleasure in itself (finding not only Mallarmé's "Petit air," for example, but the holograph version illustrated by Maurice Denis) and I often felt like lingering there whether or not it would help me with Bowering. But questions remain about their place in *Kerrisdale Elegies*. How far do we push the relevance of each whole poem from which Bowering selects? Is the volume it appeared in relevant? The writer's other work? His/her literary milieu? The answer is probably "It depends." Take the Villon:

> Si me soubmectz, leur serviteur
> En tout ce que puis faire et dire,
> A les honnorer de bon cuer.
> ("Elegy 2")

This works beautifully as a comment that could easily be Bowering's on the lovers he has observed "on each other in a lamplit Chevrolet." He is their servant. He submits himself in all that he may do or say to honour them with open heart. The lines are wrenched from their context in *Le Testament*, and that might seem to rule the context out, but the forms of testament and elegy are joined through their inspiration by death. That helps me to notice Bowering actually verging on the testament form in "Elegy 9," where the explicit homage to Rilke appears:

> On my dresser upstairs you'll find a limestone pebble
> I brought across the sky from a cliffside path
> at Duino.
>
> I'll leave it here when I go,
> along with
> everything else.

Of *Le Testament* and (stretching a point) of *Kerrisdale Elegies* it could be said that each is both testament and bequest. Bowering actually addresses "Dear children to come" in "Elegy 7." And the work of all the writers Bowering draws by various means into his text is both cultural inheritance and reassurance to him of the enduring value of a trade which calls out loving acts of response to forebears:

>Dead poets' voices I have heard in my head
>are not terrifying.
>   They tell me like lovers
>we are worth speaking to,
>   I am a branch
>a singing bird will stand on for a moment.
>
>Like a singing branch I call out in return. How
>do otherwise?
>   ("Elegy 2")

Whatever one makes of the French poets, adding their presence to that of Rilke, both sorts of source make sense as part of an intricate web of conscious intertextuality that includes the epigraph stanza from Emily Dickinson, reference to H.D., quotation of Margaret Avison, dedication of "Elegy 8" to Michael Ondaatje, general references to famous dead poets in "that great anthology," allusions to and echoes of all sorts of specific poets, vestiges of Bowering's other work, even the poem's doubling back on itself as it reconfigures certain clusters of thought and feeling in refrain and self-quotation. The self-reference works us back towards the central figure of "Bowering" and his poem as the container of all that tradition. A highly self-conscious poem, at times about itself. So the reader is entertained with a view of the writer writing—discovering the poem—and is shown certain pressures of the passage of time on the very lines being read. In the postmodern way, then, the reader is shown the process of poem-making. In the case of *Kerrisdale Elegies* that means watching the tip of a living tradition unfold.

It isn't easy to summarize what happens in *Duino Elegies* because the writing is so volatile, to borrow Robert Hass's term for it in his lovely introduction to Stephen Mitchell's *Selected Poetry of Rainer Maria Rilke*. It's even harder to offer a general account of *Kerrisdale Elegies* because, as Borges might say, Bowering's elegies contaminate each other. We aren't reading a general "argument" punctuated by elegy-examples so much as a metamorphosing field of images that roll, not without hesitations and detours, towards a hard-won and convincing affirmation. *Kerrisdale Elegies* has the mitigated coherence of the long poem, its structure interwoven, partly, of repeated motifs. The line, "Beauty is the first prod of fear," for instance, appears as the poem opens then reappears in subsequent elegies, prodding the reader with new faces for beauty and fear, becoming a cluster of associations. Let's be bold and call this cluster a symbol. There are other refrains too: "Being dead is no bed of roses," "Lightning and love," "Half the beautiful ones I have known are gone." And there are other sorts of gathering through the poem. (See what is done with "glistening with creation" in "Elegy 2," "Elegy

Stan Dragland

7" and "Elegy 10.") The poem doesn't shake out into stiff categories, but once the sense of shift in it has been remarked it seems worthwhile to offer an overview of its shape.

It's tempting to see "Elegy 5" as pivotal because of its middle position and since it's the most uniform of all the elegies, being about baseball from beginning to end. About doomed physical grace and beauty. "Elegy 5" is the home, as it were, of all the references to baseball elsewhere in the poem. Baseball is the "game of boyhood." The ballpark is "the fancied green of our wishes," and watching the game in such pastoral surroundings creates a moment of equilibrium that transcends the game.

> I sit in section nine and sometimes wonder why,
> but know I am at ground zero
> where art is made,
>
>   where there is no profit,
> no loss.
>
>   The planet lies perfect in its orbit.

This moment of peace (and potential, "ground zero" being the point of explosion) almost divides two movements of the *Elegies*. The first plays over childhood and youth, the nurturing of a poet by parents and ancestors under the open skies of all time and space. The voice is that of an adult, of course, and his perspective is that of one who has lived half his life, much of it as a poet. Therefore he can look back on his work in lyric forms as juvenilia, as a stage outlived, presumably on the way to inhabiting a form with an amplitude and seriousness capable of containing more mature thoughts on love and time and death. A long poem composed of elegies might qualify. ("Elegy 7" picks up the outgrown lyric and plays it in a different key, a farewell to love songs; elegies are paired in certain ways.) The most traditionally elegiac material in *Kerrisdale Elegies* appears in "Elegy 4," in Bowering's moving lament for his father (the theme of two earlier longish and deeply felt elegies, "The Descent" and "Desert Elm").

To regard the first four or five elegies as a single movement is to register an awareness of certain matters present in them which don't really slip into fine focus until "Elegy 10" has been read. Quiet intimations of immortality prepare for the dramatization of entry into the afterlife in "Elegy 10." Retrospectively, then, one understands a certain blurring of identity between the dead and the living in early elegies, as well as the serious side of an amusing deadpan picture of spooks with deadlines ("Being dead is no bed of roses, / you have so much work piled up in front of you / before the long weekend"). Why death is not the release it's cracked up to be we have to read on to discover.

Beyond the "Elegy 5" watershed, "Elegy 6" is an extended treatment of a figure whose presence is felt throughout the poem—the "bright flash," the hero who dies young but leaves his name behind as he blazes into a star (looking towards a more

The Bees of the Invisible

sedate and mournful transformation of the heavens in "Elegy 10"). And then the turn of the sequence is reached in "Elegy 7." This is not consolation, in any traditional terms, because it doesn't reaffirm a pre-existing truth, such as that those lost to us find a home in God or in some other welcoming bosom. Rather it begins to show, and "Elegy 9" and "Elegy 10" continue to reveal, that we make our own consolation and that there is no harder work. This requires an extraordinary devotion to loving, praising the world, a superhuman direction of attention to what will pass if not rebuilt, piece by piece, inside, by people become poets, in thought if not in word. "Elegy 8" is a relapse of sorts, an upswelling of the feeling of foreignness on the planet that raises its head in other elegies, a feeling, here, of inferiority to dumb animals. Even a robin

> will eat and fly and die,
>   and reach eternity
> without naming it.

Nothing in *Kerrisdale Elegies* is easy. Naming is a curse, like the consciousness it serves, but refined to hair-trigger sensitivity it's also the only blessing that can repay the gift of being. Readers will recognize Rilke in all this, but it should be clear by now that there is more than Rilke here. It certainly isn't the usual contemporary poet's stance and address, is it?

જી

The least Rilkean lines of *Kerrisdale Elegies* appear in "Elegy 8":

> Oh oh, says the anxious reviewer,
> this poet is not in control of his materials.

This one-time break with decorum is actually much more jarring than any of the French passages. The lines that precede it, about the difference between the way humans and animals meet the world, are unlikely to create much anxiety. The "materials" in them seem controlled enough. So what do we do with this brief taunt? It almost seems snipped out of one of those other Bowering poems that take a consistently provocative/challenging stance towards the reader. "Uncle Louis," the long poem about Louis St. Laurent, has a running gloss written in the point of view of a debunker of the poem; *Allophanes* has a string of self-reflexive passages, including this one:

> (Shit, shore up the fragments
> for yourself, don't expect
> a fullness here, I'm only
> one pair of ears)
> (xxiv)

The question of what belongs in a poem was always less complicated for a loving reader than for the critic who theorizes reading, but in recent years it has become critical "policy" not to risk homogenizing a heterogeneous poem by presupposing that everything in it, however hard to connect, was tailored to round out a whole. That saves us all sorts of stretching and squashing in the service of an obligatory organic view. Now critics are allowed to delight in strays and anomalies. Some like such passages best and use them as keys to wind up an argument aimed at undermining the whole poetic edifice. But you have to get up very early to catch a postmodernist poet in full stride.

The passage in question can be annotated with the help of sources elsewhere in Bowering's work, all right, but it's just as interesting to think of it as a mild slap of the reader's face which might ("I needed that") jar him or her out of an illusory feeling of following everything that has been going on in the *Elegies*. There is certainly a forward thrust of an almost narrative sort (a multiple story is being told, with "Bowering" at its core; an accommodation with mortality is being negotiated); we can almost make a map of the cosmos the poem assumes, and almost paraphrase an argument, particularly in the last half of the poem. But look more closely at the poem's small units—half lines, lines, stanzas, sections. "I'm always quoting Mailer who quoted Gide, who probably quoted somebody else," Alden Nowlan once said, indirectly addressing his own readers in an interview, " 'please do not understand me too quickly' " (16-17). One can too quickly bridge the spaces in *Kerrisdale Elegies*, join the units too facilely, ignoring leaps and dislocations that in fact are more of its energy-source than what makes immediate sense. The weave is visually and otherwise extremely open ("refusing / a closing couplet," to adapt something Bowering says about the immortals in "Elegy 10") and the spaces are packed with mystery. Why not think of that odd reflection on the reviewer as merely the most overt of the signals that poetic not logical sense will be made here? This poem will not work unless it pitches the reader into mystery, into the "open" on the road between the stars where the immortals are. It won't work unless it makes the reader believe in busy ghosts. Argument alone can't do that; technique must. Linger with the smallest units of the poem, then, and see if their relatedness doesn't swim in and out of focus, like the identity of the "speaker" which metamorphoses through "I," "he" and "you," offering a subject-object gamut where we normally find a stable identity. This slide happens to various other characters in the poem too, most obviously the women, who are both many and one. The poem is full of small exciting bewilderments of easy meaning, though the units themselves are crystal. This adds up to a palpable presence greater than anything that greets the eye or ear—something huge between the lines, just out of range.

So much for the oblique approach to that little assault on the reviewer. A reader gets various other passes at it, since Bowering likes to recycle some of his nuggets (a quotation from Heraclitus—"Men who love wisdom should acquaint themselves with a great many particulars"—appears unacknowledged in "Desert Elm," in *Autobiology IX*, and then, identified, as epigraph to *Curious*), and I linger on this one because it turns out to touch much of what Bowering feels poetry and his relationship to it are. One other pass, in a fairly early poem called "Single World West," doesn't help much: "Right now / are you wishing I had more control / over my material?" Others, in Bowering's *Open Letter* interview of Frank Davey and in the *Outposts/Avant-postes* interview of Bowering by Caroline Bayard and Jack David, do:

> I know that the main danger to that [energy source] is my trying to control the material, me trying to tell it what to do. You know that old thing, that newspaper reviewers always say, "He doesn't exhibit enough control over his materials," right? Well that's what I don't want to happen (*Outposts* 93).

The last sentence is ambiguous. Bowering is talking about "capital D dictation." "I just get into that space and the writing comes through from somewhere else." So there's an irony: the obtuse reviewer inadvertently damns the poet's very aesthetic. This reviewer seemed to me like a straw person until I read Keith Richardson's book on Tish and Terry Whalen's article on Bowering's *West Window*. Both, participating in the irony unawares, chastise the poet for his lack of control over his materials. Shirley Neuman, by no means an anxious reviewer, approaching *Kerrisdale Elegies* profitably with the "concept of meaning residing in the relation of words to other words and not in the relation of words to referents" (16) finds Bowering's breach of decorum "silly," and says that "the poet is not living up to his materials" (20). Maybe not. But he hasn't just suddenly lost it either.

"If there is a place in poetry for discipline and control," Bowering says, "they are to be applied to the poet by himself and not to the poem or its subject material" (*Craft Slices* 84). Relaxing control means submitting to a deeper discipline, to something— Bowering calls it language—larger than yourself.

> No artist can really create. He gathers and arranges materials found at hand— pebbles on a beach, song from the boughs, bright colours from the veins of the earth, those materials that Nature shares with Herselves. The artist excels as he enters, not as he controls. He arranges himself among the particulars (*Craft Slices* 126-127).

"There was a discipline," Frank Lewis says, thinking back on the art of his colleague Buddy Bolden, in Michael Ondaatje's *Coming Through Slaughter* ("There was no control except the *mood* of his power"), "it was just that we didn't understand" (37).

Bowering says himself that there's no point in trying to take dictation before the poet is ready with craft. That is a precondition for receiving, or at least for doing something with what you get. Control in that sense is important. And then after you've got something it will probably need to be reworked. There's nothing very wild about all this. It is mysterious but it needn't be mystified, and Bowering doesn't want to do that. It just means that intuition not reason moves the words into place; the poet shunts his daily self out of the way of the self with antennae. Bowering's breezy comments about the process in the interview are nowhere near as convincing as a passage in "Elegy 4" that comes in after the elegiac words for his father:

> I am staring at this sound
> coming out blue, so hard,
> another voice
> must mix with its own,
> a dead poet or father.

What is it about those words "blue" and "hard," as gnomic as they are simple, that seems so right? Some focussed flame, something anthracite. Something is missing from the interview: mixing voices is not like mixing drinks; it costs to be the conduit. Bowering draws back from the subject of his father into a related subject, the poem he's writing. There's no relaxation of intensity as he reveals his lack of control over his materials. What is being dictated, here, has to do with dictation. The sharing of astonishment at what is coming through reminds us that the writer is the first reader of his/her own work, a fact Daphne Marlatt makes much of. For her, writing *is* reading. There would be no point in doing it if you knew what was coming.

The poet is not always passively surprised as he watches the words appear; he also questions, comments, exclaims, in a range of response to the influence of Rilke, the most important dead poet in the mix. "Is this true?" he asks (do dogs have memories?). Or later, "Is this possible?" (that things want "to disappear / and live again in me"). "Am I going mad in Kerrisdale?" Or, about these lines: "Those lovers in the car / are seduced not by each other but by secret earth / filled with proper desire for transfiguration": "That I should say such a word in a poem." Or

> Corny, isn't it?
> The world turns with us,
> while we transform it,
> fancy words but true,
> sweetheart.
> ("Elegy 7")

These various tones, from the awed to the laconic (Bogart at the end of that last bit?) are responses not only to the words that emerge. We are also hearing something like "My god, look what I turn out to believe!"

"I?" I slides into other persons in the poem, as I said, and at one point the I darkens its own identity in a way that seems like a more cynical take on the mixture of voices:

> I am not I here,

The Bees of the Invisible

> but the burglar
>
> of your past.
>
> ("Elegy 4")

"You?" The most obvious victim of theft is Rilke, but the reader seems implicated too—our common past is being plagiarized and the theft disguised? At any rate, between this passage and the one about the hard blue words lies a range of moods in which the writer catches himself thinking about making the poem—is it collaboration or ripoff? And that sentence about the reviewer is not as isolated as it first appears.

ℰℛ

Kerrisdale Elegies radiates from a house at West 37th and Larch streets in the Kerrisdale neighbourhood of Vancouver, where Bowering lives; it issues from the study of that house where, with his "toys—a pen, some lined paper, / my books open around me" ("Elegy 4"), he writes. The physical place, with its particular streets, trees, bushes, its human and animal denizens, is effortlessly established in brief strokes.

This sense of locus is necessary to set up one of the surprises for the speaker/poet near the end of the poem: the Vancouver neighbourhood which seemed so independent of him (and he—communing with dead heroes—aloof from it) actually needs him. That's not how it seems in "Elegy 4":

> These high chestnut branches along Larch Street
> fade above the streetlights,
>
> live without me.

Through much of the poem the speaker wonders intermittently about his relationship with the world he lives in. At times he feels implicated with the alienated human exploiters of the earth, "late in the machine age," those with too much consciousness and too little conscience. Always looking for something better, never getting it, wasting valuable time out of the now.

> Stupid fate,
> to be nothing more than this,
>
> a foreign timetable,
> an unwanted designer trampling the woods.
>
> ("Elegy 8")

But this is the ironic stance, only one way of looking at it. By "Elegy 9" that mood has given way to the realization that a poet, an ephemeral human being, has a function in the world:

> Because here this once I can be bound to

125

meaning,
> because it looks as if the world wanted me,

this disappearing neighbourhood needs my step.
> ("Elegy 9")

One chance—one life, one blank page to fill—and it's over so quickly. But at least there is the once chance. So one speaks, names things.

> To count them and bind them to life,
>> to praise
> them and energize the earth.
> ("Elegy 9")

Now the chestnut trees are like the ash trees along Larch Street, like the whole neighbourhood, they

> turn to me for their life,
>> to this ephemeron in running shoes.
> ("Elegy 9")

"Death is the side of life that is turned away from us and not illuminated," Rilke says in a letter, and he elaborates in another, written to his Polish translator about his *Elegies*.

> Affirmation of *life-AND-death* turns out to be one in the Elegies. ... We of the here-and-now are not for a moment satisfied in the world of time, nor are we bound in it; we are continually overflowing toward those who preceded us, toward our origin, and toward those who seemingly come after us. In that vast "open" world, all beings *are*—one cannot say "contemporaneous," for the very fact that time has ceased determines that they all *are*. Everywhere transience is plunging into the depths of Being. ... It is our task to imprint this temporary, perishable earth into ourselves so deeply, so painfully and passionately, that its essence can rise again, "invisibly," inside us. We are the bees of the invisible. We wildly collect the honey of the visible, to store it in the great golden hive of the invisible. The *Elegies* show us at this work, the work of the continual conversion of the beloved visible and tangible world into the invisible vibrations and agitation of our own nature ... (Mitchell 316).

This is the argument of *Duino Elegies*, beautifully paraphrased. Reading *Kerrisdale Elegies*, you feel some understandable resistance to Rilke's certainty, some space of irony between Bowering and his forebear, but "Elegy 9" comes around in amazement to accepting it, the view of life lived *with* death (but not as a dead end) in the lure of the open.

For the dead as for the living the open is perpetually out of range. We feel near it making love, in dream sometimes, sometimes in writing. Dream returns us to a home prior to our earthly home, among the "gruesome gone" who in Bowering's poem are located among the stars. Perhaps everyone invents his or her open, those at least who feel its pull. The pattern is Rilke's; Bowering illustrates it with a small sector of the open, the road between the stars made of dead poets' voices.

In "Elegy 10," in a bar on Hastings Street, there is a woman who has appeared in different form in other elegies—a mysterious young woman clad in a "diaphanous comet tail dress." Earlier she has been mother, lover, reader, muse, *Deèse*. She has been the world. In "Elegy 10" she is too good for this cheap bar, and a Dad who's been drinking the golden stuff they serve there considers trying to pick her up. She's not for taking, though. Her home is on the road between the stars, as becomes clear when she begins to shed her earthly guise just as mythological goddesses used to. She is a goddess who enters Bowering's poem through Rilke's, Bowering's version of Rilke's "Sisterhood of Laments," and she leads a "newly dead" "young visitor" into the afterlife, showing him a very familiar neighbourhood—Kerrisdale—turning spectral. It seems he might spend his death there, where he and the other dead would rub elbows with the living if there were any tangible substance to them. This departure/arrival happens, in an atmosphere of poignantly beautiful melancholy, in both Rilke and Bowering, but Bowering uses a metaphor whose effect is opposite to Rilke's—an erasure of life as it slips into death, the unwriting of a poem. This is "decreation," possibly attended by a shade of Robert Kroetsch, though the word is Simone Weil's for the absurdly generous act of love that imitates God's absence, "the death of the thing within us that says 'I'" (156). The Guide offers the young man

> a short poem of unwelcome comfort,
>   a direction
> to read where reading erases the words
> line by line,
>   street by street.
>
> Till the last page opens onto the earth
> beyond his darkened acres,
>   above invisible branches.
>
> Every star becomes a coal as he reads it,
>   figures
> turning to ashes:
>   the Archer, the Scribe,
> the one he's always called the Infielder, to the south

the Triestino,
    quickly followed by the Coyote,
the Wine Glass, Erato, the three-armed Saguaro.

Last to go,
    drawing his reluctant gaze,
the clear white diamonds of the Number Nine.
    ("Elegy 10")

Rilke makes his own quite different list of stars, but his are "the new stars of the land of grief" that the Laments conduct one to, not the symbols of a life that blink off as they're bid goodbye. (Not for good. They "come on again inside the committed dead" ["Elegy 10"], and this seems to fulfill a promise made to the one who fills his or her single page in "Elegy 9": "No eraser can undo your visit.")

Who is that dead youth? He has no name, but he is perhaps becoming a "ghost of the dying young," the hero of "Elegy 6," one of those

    few who sprout flames in the dark before morning,
lighting the air we've only learned to breathe,
    their godlike voices singing from their still skinny bodies.

The dead youth can't exactly be Bowering, who has lasted into middle age, admiring movie heroes like James Dean, Marilyn Monroe, Fred Astaire and Ginger Rogers, besides his baseball players and poets, long enough to need the music of lament that the young can't hear, except when the theme is love. But the dead youth is looking at Bowering's stars, a sort of constellation of Bowering's life and work, so he is a mask of the writer after all.

∽

The list of stars is interesting for the image-shapes and for the sounds of the words and for the traces of the *Elegies* that gather in them—the appearance they offer of summarizing what has gone before in the poem. So they have a function and a resonance beyond the merely private. At the same time, as will be clear, it isn't easy (for me) to speculate further about them without straying into the arbitrary.

The Archer, the centaur Chiron, might be found in the Greek skies and in the zodiac. He is Sagittarius, Bowering's sign. The Greek background with heroes-become-stars that both Rilke and Bowering inherit is most often touched in Bowering's "Elegy 3," as in the allusion to Mt. Cyllene, where Hermes was born and where, to shorten a long story, he made the first lyre by stretching the intestines of sacrificial bulls over the shell of a tortoise. A scribe is one who writes down the words of another, a poet taking dictation, like Yeats, Spicer, Bowering. Saguaro is one of those huge armed cacti that have become cartoon shorthand for American desert.

The Bees of the Invisible

Quite exotic to most of us; not to Bowering, who has some poems about the Southern U.S. and Mexico in which Saguaro appears—by name in "American Cops." The Triestino? I'm not sure. Bowering went to Trieste to begin writing *Burning Water*, rather perversely travelling about as far east as he could to begin his novel about George Vancouver's far-western exploration. There is a polyglot Triestino, Everyday Luigi, in Bowering's *Caprice*. But maybe it's more important that Duino Castle, where Rilke began the Elegies, is near Trieste. There is a wine glass in a Bowering poem called "The House," but that's a weak guess at the source of the Wine Glass. Mt. Cyllene was one of the mountains Pan particularly liked to wander, but I doubt that he bothered with a glass.

Of Coyote, Bowering says in "The smooth loper":

> He was my favourite animal
> but I didn't know
> I imitated him
> till recent years.
> (*Smoking Mirror* 42)

Bowering doesn't imitate the lope, as far as I know. He would be thinking of the coyote's sly resourcefulness, and beyond that of Coyote in Indian legend and of Coyote's place in Sheila Watson's *The Double Hook*. Essays on this novel, especially those by Kroetsch and Bowering, have turned Coyote into a figure of the postmodernist writer as ambiguous shapeshifter and trickster whose pranks sometimes rebound on him. "Do you know I am keeping secrets from you," Bowering says to his reader in *Allophanes*, "& I want you to discover them & I will be disappointed with myself if you do." *Kerrisdale Elegies*, as already mentioned, is full of the metamorphosing or disappearing I. The poem opens with it, in fact, and one remembers, reading an enigmatic play with persona in "Elegy 2," that Bowering's collection of essays on fiction is called *The Mask in Place*, after Roland Barthes' observation about writing in the novel: "Its task is to put the mask in place and at the same time to point it out" (30).

> Does a mask
> feel the touch of a mask;
> does the face
> beneath the mask feel the mask?

The Infielder and the Number Nine pick up threads from the baseball elegy and, very indirectly, so does Erato (who also recalls the "team of womanly figures" in "Elegy 7"). Bowering's passion for baseball is no secret to his readers. In *Baseball: a Poem in the Magic Number 9*, he names, under "today's lineup," his ideal team:

Stan Dragland

lf Terpsichore
2b Polyhymnia
rf Clio
ib Erato
3b Urania
cf Euterpe
ss Thalia
c Melpomene
p Calliope

Playing First and batting cleanup, the muse of erotic poetry. She is chosen for the All-Star Team of *Kerrisdale Elegies* to represent the metamorphosing selves of the Desire who's not for taking home, not for keeping.

From contemplating the stars one always returns, the writer who is alive, and his reader, to the dear surroundings we desire to perpetuate, saying

> chestnut tree, laurel bush, cherry, front porch, eyes
> open,
> to tell bird, window, lover, determined insect
> happily burrowed in the earth round these gladiola.
> ("Elegy 9")

These are Kerrisdale Things, modelled on Rilke's different ones, that Bowering praises to bind them to life. We have met each of them elsewhere in the *Elegies*, so the list is an earthly gathering to parallel the heavenly bodies in "Elegy 10." The poem compacts a cosmos of flowers and stars—a double cosmos, because homely flowers and exotic stars do not cease to matter to the dead. In "Elegy 10" there is that amazing shadow-Kerrisdale held together by sorrow.

☙

Borges's Pierre Menard duplicates in the twentieth century, from scratch, part of the *Quixote*, and Menard's biographer (the narrator of the story) prints side by side a passage from the original and one from the new version. The two excerpts are identical, but the biographer claims that the latter is infinitely richer, given the complex circumstances (including all the history between the seventeenth and twentieth centuries) it sprang from. The idea is hilarious, but the story still teases the mind to see double in a way whose ramifications somehow exceed the humour. Bowering is hardly Menard to Rilke's Cervantes, but he has achieved a not dissimilar doubleness. Bowering's complicated but unqualified affirmations are in a way more remarkable than those of Rilke. We don't want to underestimate the opportunities for despair in Rilke's age, but he was not writing in the shadow of nuclear annihilation. Bowering is, and the understanding is there between the lines of his poem. For

The Bees of the Invisible

Bowering, though, despair bottomed out among the literary modernists, and his own age is—*has* to be—on the rebound. He says this about fiction in "Sheila Watson: Trickster", but it fits *Kerrisdale Elegies*: " ... the post-modernists live in a second stage of twentieth-century irony, and they are interested in some kind of reconstruction beyond despair—that is why their fictions are characterized by both laughter and non-realistic treatment" (*Mask* 109).

Laughter and comic endings, accommodations with existence, are nowhere in a bland text, of course. The consolation of the traditional elegy had to be wrested out of the pain of loss made palpable in words, or no one would care. Bowering still has to earn his consolation, his affirmation. So he wraps the commonplace of impermanence in the new words needed to make us feel it. Here he makes a grab at a couple of moments, and misses:

> What happened
> to that smile that was on your face
> a minute ago?
> God, there goes another breath,
> and I go with it,
> I was further from my grave
> two stanzas back, I'm human.
> ("Elegy 2")

O Heraclitus! Suddenly time is racing by. Yes, beauty is the first prod of fear. We never love anything that isn't disappearing. No wonder we generally ignore the seconds and pay attention to the hours and days that can actually seem like solid blocks of time. No wonder we panic noticing that whole years have slipped away, and search the past and the future for meaning. Both Rilke and Bowering reconcentrate the attention on the here and now to bring the beauty of it burningly home. Both poets offer the vision of existence as a continuum joining life and death, past and future, but in the poems of both everything intensely crucial is now. There is unpatronizing pity in both poems for those Bowering calls "poor *insensatti*," the ones who see nothing of life as it passes. "The optic heart must venture," says Margaret Avison in words that Bowering folds into his poem.

> Dear children to come,
> remember this word above all else:
> what you live all your live to be,
> you are now.
> ("Elegy 7")

"These are the good old days," as the song says. We need reminding.

Stan Dragland

                  It is lovely to be here.
Even you know that,
                you women lost in your familiar
dirty coats in front of a broken door,
                    a pissy hotel
on East Hastings,
             rain on passing cop cars, somewhere
you know it.
            For each of you there was an hour,
there was a long minute,
            a time I can measure
with half a line,
            when your eyes were wide enough
for your soul to leap out,
            stand and say
yes,
    here I am,
        I am.
            Entire.
                  You felt it beating
against your nerve-ends.
("Elegy 7")

Grief is the sharpest reminder and we shun grief like passing time. Rilke and Bowering practise a discipline of grief that dilates the optic heart, that imprints the here and now, transforming it inside, preserving it "where it will never be razed, invisible." This is a communal work carried out in individual cells by those who care, and the results are shared. Each observed death, like that of the youth in "Elegy 10," makes a difference.

    as he goes,
        his going lifts our eyes;
            we see
a little more from time to time.

   …

each quick appearance is a farewell.

The single events that raise our eyes and stop our time
are saying goodbye, lover,
        goodbye.
("Elegy 10")

The Bees of the Invisible

Kerrisdale Elegies ends in a paradox of stopped time and farewell.

ɘ

Yes, I'm going to die; no it's not out of my hands. You have been reading words written on my "one page." I wrote them not for money or fame but because *Kerrisdale Elegies* moved me and raised my eyes. How could I help but sing in return? It makes a thin sort of melody, spinning the poem out like this, but everybody ought to do a little something around the hive.

Works Cited

Bayard, Caroline and Jack David, eds. *Outposts/Avant-postes. Interviews, Poetry, Bibliographies & Critical Introduction to 8 Major Modern Poets.* Erin, Ontario: Press Porcepic, 1978.

Barthes, Roland. *Writing Degree Zero and Elements of Semiology.* London: Jonathan Cape, 1984.

Borges, Jorge Luis. *Labyrinths: Selected Stories & Other Writings.* New York: New Directions, 1962.

Bowering, George: *Baseball: a Poem in the Magic Number 9.* Toronto: Coach House, 1967.

—. *Allophanes.* Toronto: Coach House, 1977.

—. "Interview with Frank Davey." *Open Letter* Fourth Series, 3 (Spring 1979), 89-181.

—. *Burning Water.* Toronto: Musson, 1980.

—. *Smoking Mirror.* Edmonton: Longspoon, 1982.

—. *The Mask in Place: Essays on Fiction in North America.* Winnipeg: Turnstone, 1982.

—. *Kerrisdale Elegies* Toronto: Coach House, 1984.

—. *Craft Slices.* Ottawa: Oberon, 1985.

Kamboureli, Smaro. "Stealing the Text: George Bowering's *Kerrisdale Elegies* and Dennis Cooley's *Bloody Jack.*" *Canadian Literature* 115 (Winter 1987), 9-23.

Metcalf, John. "Interview with Alden Nowlan." *Canadian Literature* 63 (Winter 1975), 8-17.

Neuman, Shirley. Rev. of *Kerrisdale Elegies. Journal of Canadian Poetry* 1 (1984), 12-20.

Ondaatje, Michael. *Coming Through Slaughter.* Toronto: Anansi, 1976.

Richardson, Keith. *Poetry and the Colonized Mind: Tish.* Oakville/Ottawa: Mosaic/Valley Editions, 1976.

Rilke, Rainer Maria. *The Selected Poetry.* Stephen Mitchell, ed. and trans. Intro. Robert Hass. New York: Vintage, 1984.

Weil, Simone. *On Science, Necessity, and the Love of God.* Richard Rees, ed. and trans. London: Oxford University Press, 1968.

Whalen, Terry. "Discourse and Method: Narrative Strategy in George Bowering's *West Window. Canadian Poetry* 22 (Spring/Summer 1988), 32-39.

CHRISTOPHER DEWDNEY'S WRITING:
BEYOND SCIENCE AND MADNESS

In the "Author's Preface" to *Predators of the Adoration*, Christopher Dewdney writes warmly of his childhood at the forest end of Erie Avenue in London, Ontario. He says he got his education in the woods, and from books that extended what he found there. He also recalls the excitement he felt when his father told him, inadvertently planting a seed that bloomed into *A Paleozoic Geology of London, Ontario*, that the limestone underlying Southwestern Ontario had been a prehistoric sea. What the preface does not touch is the question of how Dewdney became a poet, rather than the scientist his passion for natural history might have seemed likely to produce. Of course his father Selwyn Dewdney was a novelist as well as an expert on Indian pictographs and Ojibway sacred scrolls. And Chris Dewdney was very close to Bob Fones, another London writer and visual artist, who seems quite early to have encouraged his friend in his own artistic vocation (McFadden 88). The two shared an interest in poetry which, for Dewdney, focussed on the likes of Olson, Dorn, Eliot, Spicer, Rimbaud, and Baudelaire. But identifying a few of the many strands of influence that get woven into Dewdney's writing can only hint at the amazing fabric it becomes.

As early as *Golders Green* (the chapbook published before *A Palaeozoic Geology of London, Ontario*), Dewdney's imaginative territory was a much larger chunk of planetary history (about 550 million years) than most writers bite off. All those years, he points out in the preface to *Predators*, were frozen under his feet. For a reader who follows Dewdney into some of his scientific sources (an encyclopaedia, even a dictionary, are helpful for starters), or visits Byron Botanical Bog in London, or the oxbow lakes called The Coves that were once a meander of London's Thames River (Askunessippi, Antler River, the Neutral Indians called it), his work becomes a key that opens up the geology and natural history of Southwestern Ontario. The raised regional consciousness is transferable to other locales too, because it involves a way of looking at surface features in terms of a millennial palimpsest that exists everywhere. But that much Dewdney might have accomplished as a popularizing scientist, a reverse Midas with a flair for touching rock into life in the layperson's imagination— as a geologist accustomed to thinking of humans as latecomers to the earth, say, or an astronomer used to seeing the earth as a miniscule body in limitless space. Dewdney's work subsumes such vast perspectives and throws humans off centre stage to give other creatures their moment in the limelight. Dewdney has lived so intensely in prehistory, for example, that he has come to see it, with extinct and fabulous creatures, as alive and patiently waiting to be released into association with future mutations of present life. This vision of the future is a new simultaneity of collapsed time in which there is no qualitative hierarchy of creatures (though Dewdney does have personal favourites), no subordination of past to present. The identity of everything is in continual flux. Dewdney's writing is firmly based in present knowledge, both commonplace and arcane, but his visionary imagination has grown a thoroughly realized alternative cosmos out of certain dormant seeds in our own.

As the vision I've briefly sketched will probably suggest, the reader who goes with Dewdney is privileged to travel with fear and wonder outside the human enterprise that is normally considered the biggest deal in the universe. I sometimes feel profoundly lost in Dewdney's writing, as if everything I ever thought I knew were sliding away. At other times, more often since I began to give it careful attention, I feel as if I'm finding my way around in it, and that it supplies nearly all the directions a reader needs. More than that. I feel that I get lost only to wake from what Dewdney calls "the profound sleep of the faithless" (158 [unless otherwise noted, all references are to *Predators of the Adoration*]) (dead to the evolving miracle of life) into a territory more like dream than anything else I now know. "Thou losest here," says the faithful France to Cordelia, "a better where to find." For the reader of Dewdney, the better where turns out to be a new and independent vision of "the secret harmony of all things" that humans have been seeking ever since the Fall. "There is a path for you here if you see it," Dewdney says in *Spring Trances in the Control Emerald Night*. I am accepting that invitation as though it were offered by all of Dewdney's writing so far. The path I will be following (not the only one available) leads eventually to *Spring Trances* and *The Cenozoic Asylum*, his first two natural histories of Southwestern Ontario. These are the twin jewels of his work insofar as they bring together almost everything else that goes on in it.

℘

Among other probes of the operation of language in his 1980 volume *Alter Sublime*, Dewdney included an essay on the relationship of language and the brain called "Parasite Maintenance." In it he accepts the Whorf/Sapir hypothesis that language is normally a closed field of ready-made patterns, a filtering system impossible to transcend (Wolfson 45-46), certainly by those who assume the language we share to be ample for all we would want to think. If Dewdney's poetry lacks the common touch, it's because much of it tests the limits of this enclosure. "Parasite Maintenance" theorizes about what in the poet's neurological constitution makes breakthroughs possible. Science is in the service of poetics here, though support for the argument is found in other poetics as well, most importantly Jack Spicer's approach to the "outside" as a source of his poems in a sort of Yeatsian daemon-dictation ("Vancouver Lecture I" 175-186).

Stan Dragland

The stripped-down summary of "Parasite Maintenance" I offer is no substitute for the essay in all its exciting complexity (and its extension into *The Immaculate Perception*, a book of "bits, aphorisms, essays and verbal 'takes' ... constellated around a larger theme, which is, roughly, the spectacle of consciousness embracing its own materiality" 1), but it should help me to explain why Dewdney's practice of language and form is not arbitrarily radical. In his view, language has evolved with the human species in such a way as to become "animated," "much like a model of artificial intelligence, or a robot," and has "taken on a life of its own." He detects in the English language a "'Governor' (in a mechanistic sense) with which the 'animated' language acts on the individual, restricting the limits of conceptualization" (75). The poet wants outside this barrier. To get there, he depends on "a special neural system singular to the ontogeny of the writer" (75) which Dewdney calls, using a biological analogy, "the Parasite" (76). The writer's brain, then, is the field of a complex battle between the Parasite-hero and the Governor-villain, "and the spoils are those bits of information from beyond the limits of science and madness. This is privileged information. It places the poet in the same vanguard of research as physics, molecular chemistry and pure mathematics" (78). It shouldn't be surprising that the language which brings such spoils to the page, and constructs a new universe of them, will not be what a reader is used to:

> The writer, particularly the poet, places an unusual demand on the speech centre [of the brain], and this demand is for *novel configurations*. Novel configuration is not to be confused with 'novelty for the sake of.' All writers resist the feedback tendencies of perseverance in phrasing, if not recurrent words. Thus, the writer, and most particularly the poet, requires novel configurations in order to create a forward motion idealized by its transcendence over unconscious entropy [the loss of energy that comes of habitual usage within the supervision of the Governor] (89-90).

Novel configurations are not rare in the poems of other writers, but in Dewdney the novelty is often extreme. The path through a particular poem or prose-poem is likely to follow a series of leaps or shifts or dislocations, and the sorts of shift will not always be the same. So a reader wants to keep loose, cultivate a taste for the unexpected. It helps to bring to this writing some reading of other contemporary poetry that creates a passage through experience, rather than a shapely ordering of it. But then it's good to read any poetry for the bounce of its surprise, the tickle of irresolution even in seeming closure, rather than trying to assimilate the poem to some more comfortable discourse.

Dewdney's work unfolds, often in the clean dreamlike mode of apparent non sequitur. It often proceeds with an hallucinatory authenticity that persuades of its authority. Even when the procession of a poem seems alien to the understanding, it tends to spark an excitement in the feeling that there is a logic just out of range in it, creating what Margaret Avison calls "the chasm of creation." "Probably that is the core of being alive," she says (64). Perhaps a path is not exactly what one looks for, though Dewdney uses that metaphor. Rather, a reader is offered a field of images which gathers, from line to line, poem to poem, book to book to make a total serial "poem with no hard corners" (Spicer, "Billy the Kid" 79). This gathering field is like Dewdney's favourite geological artifacts, the concretions. These are actual globes of mineral matter which have grown between strata of rock around a nucleus—a grain of sand or a fossil—over thousands of years. Dewdney makes these curiosities into a mystery, saying that they build up around an unknown core and, "however perfectly dissected, never yield theiyr identity" (25). Form gathers, then; it enacts a process, a mystery. "It is," as Robin Blaser says of Jack Spicer's poetry, "a proposal of the wildness of meaning—a lost and found, a coming and going" (281).

How does one follow a poem like "The Memory Table I," which opens Dewdney's first full-length book?

> Lime, calcium, silica, pyrites,
> THESE came to remember.
>
> As there is
> a water table
> there is also
> a memory table.
> The shafts
> by which we remember
> are called
> "wishing wells" by some,
> and the children
> of the memory table
> are Baudelaire's
> somnambulistic chairs.
> Which goes to show
> some radio stations
> are so flexible
> you can pick them up
> with a dime. (19)

This poem is syntactically conventional. It doesn't offer the sort of unexpectedness of other Dewdney poems with scrambled syntax, absent parts of speech, or sentences which swivel curiously one into another. But the logical sentence structure is not matched by a similar logic of content. Initially I think a reader follows this sort of poem, admiring the deft shifts from image to image, like Alice through Wonderland (though unattended by a reassuring narrator who reminds us how dream reality differs from reality outside it). Or perhaps one first holds on to the horizontal/vertical shape in the simile which compares well shafts and water table to memory equivalents. Remembering, then, would be sinking a shaft through mind-strata. But it's something more than that, as the epigraph suggests.

The remembering minerals mentioned in the epigraph are the components of limestone, rock made of fossils, and that recalls the aphorism which ended the "Author's Preface" to *Palaeozoic Geology*: "THE FOSSIL IS PURE MEMORY." The limestone is given an attribute of mind, memory, that metaphorically contains the "compressed millennia" (7) Dewdney speaks of in his preface to *Predators*. The idea becomes one of the commonplaces of *Palaeozoic Geology*, space being a recurrent metaphor for time, as in the vertical history of layers, systems and subsystems of rock whose structure influences that of the book. "The Memory Table I" is not completed by accretions to it. Rather it expands in the mind of the reader as Dewdney folds in more and more related matter—again like the concretion, which itself is obeying "the evolutionary mind of form" ("Preface, *Palaeozoic Geology*). This is an early introduction of the unknown other (sometimes others), the secular deity whose presence Dewdney intuits from its operations and which assumes in his cosmos a position something like that occupied by God in the cosmos of the past, as is suggested by certain displaced echoes of language once applied to a divine absolute and the religion, especially Catholicism, dependent on belief in it. Of the evolutionary mind of form we hear, in "Gas Port," that "Men are powerless but to obey its command and build palaces and cathedrals which to the FORM are tiny distorted lenses of a mirror in which it can satiate its eternal narcissism" (23). The FORM is not an absolute, but an otherness of intelligence, often predatory, which itself evolves in Dewdney's work.

But we aren't reduced to putting "The Memory Table" into its context to find something to say about it. The poem simply draws normally discrete items into a new relationship. Prehistoric rocks can be cored and read by geologists, as we know, but the shafts of memory here are more magical and dreamlike than scientific. This is suggested by the folktale "wishing wells" and the allusion to Baudelaire's "La chambre double" (in *Petits poèmes en prose*). In one of Baudelaire's chambers, the room of dream, "les meubles ont l'air de rêver; on les dirait doués d'une vie somnambulique … " (41). This is "une chambre véritablement *spirituelle*" (41), a visionary one. Even if the allusion is not traced to its source, though, the image is obviously dreamlike and helps to create an atmosphere hospitable to associations and animations that waking life resists. The freak radio station reception doesn't seem foreign in that climate.

What is typical of Dewdney's poetry in "The Memory Table" is the slide from one element to another through a zone of association that combines known things in a new and magical way. Sometimes this happens within a sentence, or even a single word. The word "theiyr," for example, appears in *Palaeozoic Geology* and then regularly thereafter. What is it? A combination of "they" and "their," I suppose. I once heard Dewdney answer a question about "theiyr" by saying it was a typo that kept appearing until he just accepted it. More recently he has simply called it a diphthong word, because of the double or sliding vowel in it. But neither explanation (unless we recognize the fairly banal side of a serious source of dictation behind the first) covers the foreign look of the word, the uncertainty of its existence between two pronouns and its accommodation of a range of sound.

I wouldn't make so much of a single word if it didn't seem to catch something of Dewdney's excitingly unstable and hazardous cosmos. (In the poem called "United" there is a characteristically subversive pun, "manifold destiny" (159), which substitutes a multiple future for the simpleminded and dangerous "manifest destiny" of American social Darwinism.) One can trace words or phrases through his work and watch them change as it grows. Certain key words or phrases, becoming titles of volumes, burn a little brighter in retrospect. The "altar sublime," or communion table, introduced in *Palaeozoic Geology*, becomes "alter sublime" in *Fovea Centralis*, a pun which suggests a metamorphosis of the sacral, and links up with "predators of the adoration." This phrase is drawn from the title poem of *Alter Sublime*, and points to the most obvious of the ways Dewdney connects his books to each other. A fragment from *The Cenozoic Asylum* ("As if paradise renewed a tangible & immaculate perception" 144) is chosen from the company to be the title of the collection of theoretical probes which, among other things, is a manual for reading the natural histories— something of "a covert ars poetica" (194) Bruce Whiteman calls it. "Limestone" becomes "line storm" (a weather front) in *Spring Trances*, then "lime storm" in *Alter Sublime*. To take a larger conception, the real but magical concretions, "sacraments of the memory table" in *Palaeozoic Geology*, are discovered in *Fovea Centralis* to be "remote control mechanisms" (I'll say more about remote control later), a development consistent with the fact that, earlier, they were said to receive and transmit the dreams of living individuals. Later, in *Alter Sublime*, the concretions at Kettle Point on Lake Huron are claimed to generate such a powerful energy-field that it's impossible to set up any other transmitting device within a 400-metre radius. Conceptions or images like this are evolving symbols. They are introduced, then altered and extended without any entropic redundancy. To borrow a line from "Intent," one might say that the design of Dewdney's work, like the design of the moon in that poem, is "to reduce a certain / inevitability into dance..." (121). That fits the operation of the language as it evolves Dewdney's vision: a dance of meanings in relativity.

What to do with a sentence like "There be shall mutt natching of teat" (40), which is the playful "explanation" of a log entry in *Palaeozoic Geology*? Well, the "gnashing of teeth" that shadows the "natching" runs through the biblical book of Matthew to describe how the unredeemed are going to behave when Heaven becomes permanent and they aren't in it. But I sometimes think there be shall mutt natching of teat when Dewdney's alternative to the New Jerusalem arrives. There's already some natching going on:

Stan Dragland

The subject, a continuity consultant in his late fifties, exhibited inordinate fear of commonplace objects and complained of spastic hair-trigger orgasms. After two hours of consultation we recommended a four month term in Hamilton. Sentence to be served consecutively (167).

Continuity consultants will be in low demand in the universe where "accidents are almost predatory" (65). There's no reason why a new order has to be heralded only with portentous seriousness. Sometimes Dewdney's subversion of the language and assumptions of the past and present is funny as hell. Nonsense, as Edward Lear and Lewis Carroll used it, is not gobbledygook. It is sense on holiday, in the saturnalian tradition of misrule, and of course it sometimes pushes laughter to the border of madness.

Lewis Carroll is parenthesized in a section of one of Dewdney's more radical fiddles with prose technique, "The Parenthetical." The starting point of the sequence is conventional enough in its use of the sentence, though it begins with an unattached simile, but not in terms of subject:

Like sticking your arm through the dry plaster wall of your bedroom and having it emerge out the other side. The next room is dark and filled with warm water. Your arm is immersed to the elbow and slippery creatures brush your skin. This is the dike of your mind. You are a Dutch boy and the only person *this* ocean belongs to is *you*. And you can't stand there forever (95).

Before I say something about how parentheses begin to insinuate themselves between these words, I should mention that we quite often find in Dewdney's work various punctures of the apparently solid compartments of the physical world and the mind—models of successful skirmishes with the Governor mentioned above, and passages into Dewdney's own dreamlike cosmos. In the sequence which begins with the poem "Alter Sublime," for instance, someone looks through a mirror at a "human in the other room." The meeting of their symmetry, through the glass, breaks the room "into flashing white fragments. The room reduced to smooth glowing shards" (153). This is going through the looking glass the hard way, and with no return. It happens also in *Spring Trances*, where "the room breaks into flashing white shards of interstellar nothingness" (69). In Dewdney, the shattering of the mirror, and by projection the collapse of the dike, is an entry to a new otherness painful to minds subject to an "opaque logos" (146) because there is no firm place to stand in it. Quantum physicists have already entered the possibility that nothing in existence is ever fixed, and much contemporary philosophic/literary thinking builds on the theory that meaning is infinitely deferred in language, that reference is ultimately empty.

It is the, it is

140

The Bees of the Invisible

like a hole
that runs through everything.
Seen
it is altered.
Grasped
it is broken,
Strange herald,
predator of the adoration,
it is the mind
eating itself. (150)

The conventional sentences which open "The Parenthetical" are varied in the next two sections, before giving way to completely different ones. Parentheses begin to appear in the second piece, as Dewdney pries apart the words of the string of sentences that thread the sequence, and inserts into the holes thus opened words or phrases that at first may appear to be arbitrary and unrelated, but are actually associated opposites or extensions, many of which are easy enough to pursue on their own. Multiplied as they are, though, the openings are richly labyrinthine. The tangents to the connecting thread they keep throwing up remind us how few of the possible wrinkles of thought are caught up by a conventionally linear sentence. And "The Parenthetical" is not the only place where Dewdney attends to the show that goes on between the words.

One of the prose pieces of the "Alter Sublime" sequence is another "parenthetical" whose parentheses metaphorically mimic electronic feedback. It contains this astonishing claim of hitherto unsuspected life in silence: "a pregnant silence caesarean with lingual foetuses" (155). A related image appears later in the same volume: "There are words that are standing waves between the words. Interference nodes virtually stationary in the regular emission of morphotactics. There are poems that are the standing waves between the words. Standing waves fabricated by words vibrating within the resonance memory gives them" (*Alter Sublime* 39). The parenthesized words in "The Parenthetical" certainly resonate in the spaces opened between the others. They vibrate with an energy of opposition or variation which suggests that between every word is a road not taken. (Standing waves, by the way, are not exactly still. They are interference waves produced by the intersection of waves moving towards each other from opposite ends of, for example, a ripple tank. They remind me of the sort of wave known as a haystack, a violent curl thrown up when a rapids suddenly hits calm water. Expert kayakers can lodge atop that paradox of stationary rush. See also "Mind as Standing Wave" in *The Immaculate Perception* 14, with later variations, 88 and 95.)

An interesting thing about "The Parenthetical" is that it's both hypnotic and hilarious read aloud. This is always worth remembering—how Dewdney is often directly pleasurable to the listener or reader who relaxes and expects the writing to be what it turns out to be, rather than a fiendish disguise for conventional discourse. If

141

the strain of relaxing takes its toll, try reading "The Dialectical Criminal" aloud—that novel configuration of clichés—and see if your voice doesn't automatically fall into the rhythms of the hard-nosed murder mystery detective/narrator.

A little after the middle of "The Parenthetical," the parenthesized interruptions are suddenly suspended and a voice speaks "with a note of disquiet" in an oblique comment on the experience a listener or reader may well have been having:

"I'm glad you noticed the way I used that particular word because what you felt, that it was kind of 'hollow' and 'non-sentient,' is merely an instinctive reaction to the truly alien. I can, using certain colloquialisms with correct intonation, create a hole in your morphemic conception of the language. I truly *say* nothing, and yet a faint echo is heard, with distinct clarity, tiny. The quality of the sound in the echo allows you to reconstruct with absolute clarity, the dimensional qualities of this limit. A black velvet meniscus in space itself" (99).

Here is another hole in language which, by the breathtaking leap at the end of the passage, is associated with a presumably huge "emptiness" in space. The language suddenly seems very roomy with interstices no more empty than the room reached through the hole in the dike of the mind. What to do with fright at what is on the other side, or between the words? One possibility is to withdraw,

> Mind's known factors assembled together
> small & huddled in the corner
> of the enlarging room (157).

The other is to bake a cake, set the table.

Who is speaking between the quotation marks in "The Parenthetical"? Who is the speaker of the whole sequence? In the title of one of his stories, Rudy Wiebe raises a good question that has to be asked of Dewdney's writing as a whole: "Where Is the Voice Coming From?" We won't ignore the obvious; it comes from Dewdney. But it feels more like it comes *through* Dewdney from some other source ("beyond science and madness"), the price for being attuned to which is pre-critical acceptance of what it says. In "Parasite Maintenance" Dewdney says that the Parasite reaches nirvana, "though the mind does not follow it (there have been exceptions). It is this process which makes a Galahad out of the poet, able to reveal the Grail to others, but not to himself" (91). This is the opposite of egotism, as Dewdney's claim in the "Author's Preface" to *Predators* that he is "merely a scribe" (8) for the plants and animals is the opposite of false modesty. He means what he says, and his writing supports him. There are "voices" in it, but no single voice anchored in a lyric or narrative centre that draws the work to a univocal core of sound and sense.

Perhaps Dewdney is furthest from his source when he is most " 'pataphysical," most pseudo-scientific, in the term that Steve McCaffery borrows from Alfred Jarry as an approximation of Dewdney's methodology (189). Often he parodies the voice of an authoritative scientist (or serious "continuity consultant") who uses the language of measurement, or cool observation—in the ironically fragmentary "Log Entries," for instance—to record details of an unfamiliar universe whose rules appear to change from entry to entry. We get a similar sort of voice in such pieces as "The Memory Table II" and "From a Handbook of Remote Control," those very plausible-sounding propositions of unusual "facts." And perhaps he is closest to his source in the heightened, shamanistic voice that makes a beautiful, predatory music in many of the poems, and in the prose poems of *Spring Trances* and *Cenozoic Asylum*.

Readers of "Parasite Maintenance" would not expect a single voice to reflect an organism as complex as human personality or the brain that animates it.

It's not as if the outside world is funnelled through a homunculus in the centre of the brain & then displayed on the neo-cortex in some kind of phrenological cinema. There are sub-stations & relays so profuse they confound the neuro-anatomists of today.

Remember always that there is no homunculus. 'I' is an illusion
(*Alter Sublime* 76).

The decentralizing of ego is analogous to the attack on anthropomorphism that in turn reflects the dwindling importance of earth-centred thinking. Such shifts in modern thought filter out into open-form poetry like Charles Olson's (quite frequently alluded to in Dewdney) which is partly energized by the de-humanizing, re-inspiriting belief that man has little more claim to being at the centre than any other object.

Dewdney understands how contemporary physicists are extending relativity theory in ways which make Einstein's hope of a single, unifying law look unrealizable. Everything seems more and more relative to the observing, measuring eye, and physics meets poetry in the hypothesis that we dream a world and then make it come true, à la Borges. Existence may be no solid fact, but a series of notations from which we infer a continuum.

Being stretches from thought to thought in much the same way as the main thread of the wasp's waist connects thorax and abdomen. In much the same way as the siphuncle of the chambered nautilus winds through the spirals of its growth. This being is perceived as soul and threads the phenomena of mind in a special sequence known as personality. The beginning and end of each thought is marked by a gap. Existence implicates a thread through the gap which cannot be proven (87).

Dewdney accepts the gap and actually tries to widen it—the gap between thoughts, between words—to seek a way of existing that does not depend on the unprovable connecting thread. It's possible to live, he might say, under "the voice of the cicada,"

> ...an indeterminate philosophy
> in a court where the evidence
> neither confirms nor denies
> its testimony (75).

This would be to live in a sort of free fall, or free flotation, a new possibility that Dewdney is not only facing up to, but inviting:

> (...O that somehow in the vertigo of knowledge
> the equation for a pure random will raise itself
> like braille on the bark of these blind elms.) (103)

This oxymoron of a pure random somehow codified by an equation seems (though mathematicians, chaos theorists, are in fact seeking it), to pass the limits of rational thought. It speaks of an order or way of the random, the unconnected.

It's good to have *Spring Trances* and *Cenozoic Asylum* collected with much of Dewdney's other writing to 1982, in *Predators of the Adoration*, for those interested in the basis on which these two prose poems are built. In fact they fit quite naturally into the sequence of *Predators*, separated by selections from *Fovea Centralis*, though they have been published as a single volume (and, combined, in the "recombinant text," *Permugenesis*) and I'll eventually be treating them as a continuous unit. I think that the natural histories are the most complete realization of Dewdney's search for "a pure random" in which "the secret harmony of all life unfolds." The writing creates this unconventional paradise regained with an extraordinarily alien naturalness. Neither *Spring Trances* nor *Cenozoic Asylum* conducts the reader into this cosmos, though; they open inside it. So one useful entry is through material drawn from the more open-weave structures of the other three volumes.

The shafts of "The Memory Table I" reach down to fossils in suspended animation. In this and various other ways a subterranean past with the potential for reification communicates with the surface/present. The white elms in *Spring Trances* "that flowered all of beneath into above & translated it perfectly" (58) are present in this lovely passage from "Gas Port I":

When a deciduous tree draws its nourishment from limestone instead of glacial till, its intrinsic form is substantially different from others of the same species. At a carefully chosen angel and on particular winter days, the vaulting and altar plans for Chartres, Rheims, Orléans, and Amiens can be seen in theiyr branches. These designs are fixed, like a mathematical constant, from forest to forest. The trees, however, are living entirely in the age they tap. They can exist in this dreamlike state obliviously (23).

Somnambulistic chairs, remembering fossils, dreaming trees. Certainly Dewdney is the voice of creatures vulnerable to man in their inarticulateness. He frees them into language, even the moths "pressed between the layers of [lime]stone" in "Out of Control: the Quarry" which opens *Predators* and reappears as the first segment of *Spring Trances* proper. The same thing happens on a larger scale in *Cenozoic Asylum,* as "the limestone heaves up & dissolves in an awesome rumbling giving up all of time trapped in its layers. Legions of extinct creatures crawl up through the rubble, transparent with age" (139-140).

If Dewdney were writing a Hollywood "B" horror flick, it might be called "Revenge of the Fossil." To put it mildly, he is not enchanted with the way the human race has managed the planet, the "divine technology of nature" (*Immaculate Perception* 11), so he pulls the rug out from under its "victory" over the inarticulate ones.

The continued use of fossil fuels has released countless side-effects unknown to mankind. The highways are actually arteries carrying the lifeblood to an unarticulated primaeval form using cities, oil refineries, jet and auto engines, factories, and any form of fossil fuel consumption to slowly replace the present composition of the atmosphere with the chemical composition of the atmosphere some 200 million years ago. After a certain critical point this atmosphere will become capable of generating the life-forms essential to this ancient form (38).

Spring Trances and *Cenozoic Asylum* take place under a "fossil-fuel atmosphere" (132) and that explains the "unlikely appearance of Cenozoic bi-valves" (142), smilodons and other creatures recovered from extinction to neighbour in Southwestern Ontario. Automobiles have not disappeared, but "night siphons mirror & chrome into itself" (60), feeding from them. In the natural histories the future has arrived and it is partly composed of the past. The "glass machinery" that keeps appearing, though, feels ethereally futuristic.

As the products of technological progress feed "an unarticulated primaeval form" so are human beings "a catalyst freeing information into the cosmos ... unknowingly perpetuating higher forms of intelligence" ("Control Data" 167). Whether primaeval or futuristically interstellar in nature, or a combination, "there are conferences" in *Spring Trances* "to which we are interminably drawn over which forces other than human preside" (65). We are "out of control."

On a mechanistic level remote control is a familiar technology. Kids run radio-controlled cars with it; scientists correct the orbit of a satellite with commands from earth. Dewdney first evolves the concept into a mysterious secret society insidiously controlling other humans by mental processes, inducing paranoia and mental derangement in its subjects.

> Remote control was discovered by
> a Japanese secret society near the end
> of the second world war. The secret
> society was minimally aware of this war.
> (*Fovea Centralis* 27)

In the first item of "From a Handbook of Remote Control" we hear of "dark zones" of ignorance in the human mind in which there is

> room for almost infinite distortion. Using this area as a starting point the remote control agent can slowly erode a particular person's concept & perception of the universe. Unthought-of possibilities, suddenly hostile and chaotic, appear in the once peaceful universe of the attacked mind" (109).

So remote control is a threat to the normal mind, oblivious to its operations and vulnerable to insanity in terms of the so-called norm. But I've tried to show that breakdown in Dewdney is also, or may be, a breakout from the confines of a narrowly defined universe/mind. A further evolution of remote control, then, pushes it through madness into a realm where the concept of insanity seems irrelevant. The Parasite makes its escape into a new omniscience by taking dictation from remote control. "The poem is written within the jurisdiction / of remote control" (103).

So what sometimes seems to be the amphibious stance of poet as double agent ("under— / out of— / remote control" in "Permanent Trust—Huron & Erie" 119) is more accurately sorted out into two phases of remote control's evolution. There is a darkly humorous edge to much of Dewdney's conception of remote control, even in its sinister early phase, but one might identify modern analogues of the initial stage that are not funny. Mind control experiments are not unknown to psychology, nor to advertising and politics. Since one of the functions of Dewdney's remote control agents is to "replace reality with fiction" (104) so smoothly that no one notices, they seem to be working in the Czechoslovakia of Milan Kundera's *Book of Laughter and Forgetting*, which shows history being replaced with lies. Dewdney is not amused about the effect on John Koegler, a friend who committed suicide. In his moving elegy, "I am the Lord and these are my flies," he says that Koegler "ate the insect under instructions / from a meteoroid circling outside of Mercury" (77). The possible tragedy of mind-bending is registered, then, and the early manifestations of remote control are endorsed only insofar as they lead to further developments.

What is human in Dewdney's new universe is first contaminated, then almost beatified, by the drawing out of alien possibilities from the dark peripheries of consciousness, the areas of the mind least controlled by the conservative elements of the brain and the language it sanctions. In the long run, remote control coaxes out a transformed, beautiful and vertiginously edgeless consciousness; it serves a benevolent transcendence. And so does Dewdney. This is why he seems rather oriental in his mountain-top perspective on mental disruptions that are opening the way to a more inclusive, ecstatic existence. I can still hear him chuckling, during a reading, about the obvious dementia of Alexander Haig. I envision him in 1990 cocking a knowing eye at Saddam Hussein and George Bush while most of us were fearing another Vietnam or worse. Perhaps it seems odd, considering that he's about half on the side of the paranoia-mongers, but Dewdney seems to approach contemporary life more sanely than anyone else I know. From where I stand, the opening of "True Heart, Cruel Heart," the last entry in *The Immaculate Perception*, almost seems like a self-portrait: "Only the ultra-sane can afford reality. Only the sane, with that manic edge that depressives would insist on calling psychopathological, can withstand, while maintaining a position of pure faith, determinate reality" (116). In this piece consciousness is "at root composed of the same infinite energy & light which fuels the heart;" the book as a whole explores ways of achieving a perception so intense and complete that, in one analogy, it would be as if "the fovea centralis, the point of attention in the retina, is slowly expanded to sensitize the entire retina" (38). Is the sanity that I attribute to Dewdney owing to his detection in the chaos of contemporary times the approach of an incomparably enriched inner life, a stance towards existence flexible to the nth degree? Anyway, that is what we find in *Spring Trances* and *Cenozoic Asylum*, the dovetailing first two natural histories of a series in progress. (The "Bibliography of Creatures" in *Spring Trances* is annotated, though not in sequence, by *Cenozoic Asylum's* "Grid Erectile.") In *Spring Trances*, along Wharncliffe Road in London, Ontario, "everything is working by remote control" (65).

Let's call the source of the voice in the natural histories "cosmic consciousness," after the title of the most famous book by Richard Maurice Bucke, another Londoner, an "alienist," who broke through science into an intuition of the unified "life and order of the universe" (3). Or let's call it "celestial consciousness," as Dewdney does in *The Immaculate Perception*, linking it to "Pascal's definition of Nature, 'an infinite sphere, whose center is everywhere and whose circumference is nowhere'" (52). The consciousness, or narrative stance, of the natural histories is impossible to pinpoint. It always speaks in the present tense (except in "Grid Erectile"), but sometimes as "I," more often as "we." Occasionally there is an address to "you." There is designedly no single witness to what is going on. Everything is looking ("the forest is filled with eyes" 58) or nothing is. "The secret harmony of all life unfolds itself in silence and without witness" (59). Or presence and absence fade in and out. But the field of sensation ("rain of sensorium" 138) is continuous within a de-selved source of observation. "There can be no highlights if there is no point of view" (141). "Yes, we are alone. Alone being totally lonely, totally lovely, totally omniscient" (69). The consciousness of the two sequences is a compound of animal, vegetable, and mineral, human and extra-human, though it occasionally coalesces in an unnamed "she" who appears and reappears as the spirit of it all, one not easily labelled as earth mother, though there's a lot of that in her. It's a consciousness raised to an almost painfully rich receptivity. "The air inebriates the eyes never quite open enough for the detail" (59). "Events occur linearly so densely they are viewed as simultaneous" (60). Here is a clue to the workings of the form and language. Everything is simultaneous, so there is no narrative progression. One could in principle read the pieces in different sequence. In fact there's much less disruption than one might expect when parts of sentences from *Spring Trances* and *Cenozoic Asylum* are shuffled together to produce *Permugenesis*, "Book Three of A Natural History of Southwestern Ontario." The sentences often lack verbs, as though it would be stretching things to speak in terms of action through time and space, which are themselves collapsed so that creatures of many eras cohabit, and "Distance is not perspective here, is merely out of reach" (67). ("A translucent saturn, large as the moon, ascends behind the vacant observatory" 134).

Some of the verbal units are incredibly dense concretions of metaphor built on bunched adjectives: "The lynx padded forest floor bathed in monsoon stained glass northern mineshaft star cathedral" (69). "Stars drip out of the cutaneous erectile velvet blue bandshell night" (65). It would take an essay to analyze the associations compacted in a few such units, and to trace their resonances with Dewdney's other work. I want to quote only one other loaded passage, an epitome of Dewdney's occasionally thorny verbal arcana which almost reaches self-parody level here: "Deity being the manifold ontogenetic synthesis display-herald for the intrinsic & implacable technocracy of homeomorphic evolution" (137). I won't take the time to untie that knot (except to mention that homeomorphism is the close similarity of crystalline forms between substances of different chemical composition, and points to nodes of harmony between them), feeling that it might already have been loosened by my discussion above of "manifold destiny" and of the evolutionary secular deity which presides over it. In any case, the abstract definition is unusual in the context of writing that is sensually concrete.

Dewdney uses synaesthesia (speaking of one sense in terms of another) in the natural histories with the effect Benjamin Whorf claims for it, and for metaphorical usage generally, in a passage quoted in "Parasite Maintenance." It reaches "a deeper aesthetic sense leading toward a more direct apprehension of underlying unity behind the phenomena so variously reported by our sense channels" (79). Synaesthesia is in fact mentioned in *Cenozoic Asylum* (137), though more obliquely as to function. The important point is that this unusual prose does hold keys to its behaviour inside itself. So it's to help establish an "underlying unity" or "secret harmony," an "alien wholeness" (61) that we get synaesthetic conceits like "blue megahertz evening stars" (138) "sun vibrato" (142), "magneto purples" (61) and "silver mist audio-fog" (144).

In *Spring Trances* and *Cenozoic Asylum*, the "outside," to which access is normally blocked by the Governor, is more interior. What are we inside? A brain, a womb, an eye, a sub-aquatic room, an incredibly colourful night forest. We are in a maze, a dream, a "hyper-personal theatre" (143), a processional and celebration of the erotics of all nature. In a redeemed universe, "As if paradise renewed a tangible & immaculate perception" (144). The Governor has lost control, the mind, like the forest, runs "omnidirectional" (143). Why does everything present itself with such hallucinatory clarity? "Everything [is] / interpenetrating, extensile, / at once continuous and discrete" says the title poem of *The Radiant Inventory* (11). "[T]hat which is most completely out of control most clearly reveals the workings of the unseen machinations" (138). As in the other work discussed above, nothing is stable or static. There are multiple interfaces of creatures in this universe where "what we consider uncanny here occurs almost ten times as frequently" (65), where "the evidence constantly re-assembles itself" (60). But, and this is as true for a reasonably persistent reader as it is for those inside this uncanny cosmos, "one soon loses the sensation of falling" (58).

Spring Trances and *Cenozoic Asylum* are among the most erotic pieces of writing I've ever encountered, but the eroticism is seldom localized in human sex, which in any case is sometimes hermaphroditic here. Everything has its openings of flesh and spirit. This writing is what results when Dewdney opens up to full throttle the prose that is idling (very attractively) over similar subject matter in the "Author's Preface" to *Predators*.

e/s

If this essay persuades you to enter Dewdney's writing for the first time, perhaps your passage will be eased. Perhaps readers who have already sampled Dewdney will have a rudimentary map to take with them through it again. That's fine with me. I love maps, and so does Dewdney—maps and diagrams—but he also loves to parody them, to subvert the locating and classifying mentality. He believes in lostness. It might be best to take my words as testimonial, rather than guide. I do stand behind my map, but with some misgivings, remembering Steve McCaffery chiding Barry Alpert for his "co-opting of the poems [of *A Paleozoic Geology*] to a poetics of place" (188). I've done that myself, though there's much more support for the position now than there was in 1976 when McCaffery wrote his article. "Dewdney's work," he goes on to say, "is a highly successful evasion of experience that underscores the hiatus between word and thing" (190). That gives me greater pause. If it were the whole case, if it weren't accurate to say that Dewdney transforms experience as much as he evades it, I doubt I would always be reminded, driving through rural Southwestern Ontario, of Dewdney's "definition" of silos: "parachutes / with a reinforced concrete flight-plan" (155). I doubt that this section of "Elora Gorge" would seem so true to me:

The canyons are interlaced with thousands of paths, most of them are invisible. There are even aerial paths, the regular tunnels through the air used by birds and flying insects. Insect paths are mathematical vectors, high-speed routes between feeding territories. Bird paths are almost as baroque as the paths of bats. There are ant trails though the grass and the routes of certain small mammals which

149

Stan Dragland

alternately surface and plunge beneath the forest floor. The human paths are the largest here, though they are interlocked within the larger necessitites of the gorge as surely as all paths.

It is as if the gorge, its three-dimensional continuum, was full, totally composed of such an interplay of paths that there was no empty space left. The components of this world are both constituents of, and a means of propulsion in, the total network of necessity (*Radiant Inventory* 97).

Still, McCaffery has his finger on a strain of Dewdney that, as a non-referentialist writer himself, he is well-placed to emphasize. Myself, I've been finding it hard to avoid acting like one of those "hopeless paranoids with delusions of reference" who can't help "reading sense into any sequence of words due to the referential bias of language" (*The Immaculate Perception* 74). I'll give this wheel just one more spin, with the help of Don McKay, and then let go: "Freeing words from the necessity to refer is equivalent to freeing Tundra Swans from the necessity to migrate or, getting down to it, freeing any creature from its longing for an other" (208).

∽

I might as well admit that I've been writing under the influence of remote control, which has no sense of humour. I've been plodding down a path I should have flown over, and I blame remote control. So I want to say that I remember, from before I was taken in, the first time I looked through *Palaeozoic Geology* and was tickled by the witty playfulness of the collages with their crazy captions, and by the wildly original writing. Now I find it impossible to fix the edge between the play and seriousness in Dewdney's cosmos, but I don't retract my belief in it. It may be possible for other readers to enjoy it simply as a grand design of great wit and obliquity.

Works Cited

Avison, Margaret. "Voluptuaries and Others." *Winter Sun.* Toronto: Oxford, 1960.
Blaser, Robin. "The Practice of Outside," in *The Collected Books of Jack Spicer.* Los Angeles: Black Sparrow, 1975.
Baudelaire, Charles. *Petits poemes en prose (le spleen de Paris).* Chronologie et introduction par Marcel A. Ruff. Paris: Garnier-Flammarion, 1967.
Bucke, William Maurice. *Cosmic Consciousness.* New York: Dutton, 1969.
Dewdney, Christopher. *Alter Sublime.* Toronto: Coach House, 1980.
—. *Fovea Centralis.* Toronto: Coach House, 1975.
—. *Predators of the Adoration.* Toronto: McClelland and Stewart, 1983.
—. *The Immaculate Perception.* Toronto: Anansi, 1986.
—. *Permugenesis.* London, Ontario: Nightwood, 1987.
—. *Radiant Inventory.* Toronto: McClelland and Stewart, 1988.
McCaffery, Steve. "Strata and Strategy: 'Pataphysics in the Poetry of Christopher Dewdney." *Open Letter* Third Series 4 (Winter 1976), 45-56.

McFadden, David. "The Twilight of Self-Consciousness." *The Human Elements: Critical Essays*. First Series. Ed. David Helwig. Ottawa: Oberon, 1978.

McKay, Don. "Notes on Poetic Attention." John Metcalf and Leon Rooke, eds. *The Second MacMillan Anthology*. Toronto: MacMillan, 1989.

Spicer, Jack. "Vancouver Lecture I." *Caterpillar* 12 (July 1970), 175-186.

—. "Billy the Kid." *The Collected Books of Jack Spicer*. Los Angeles: Black Sparrow: 1975.

Whiteman, Bruce. "As If Paradise Renewed a Tangible and Immaculate Perception: Dewdney's Textbook." *Sagetrieb* 7, 1 (Spring 1988), 193-199.

Wolfson, Peter. "Language, Thought and Culture." *Language: Introductory Readings*. Virginia P. Clark, Paul A. Eschholz and Alfred F. Rosa, eds. New York: St. Martin's, 1981.

CREATURES OF ECSTACY

The Review

To begin with the end of *Touch to My Tongue*—with part of the note by Cheryl Sourkes about her six photographs (including the one on the cover), selected from a series called *Memory Room*, that counterpoint the poems by Daphne Marlatt:

Memory Room grows out of two related concerns.

First, a perception that our culture has its sexuality and gender behaviour out of balance. To value the feminine is the revolution of our times. It implies reshaping our care for each other and the earth. This work emphasizes psyche and the dream, rather than ego and rationality.

Second, a sense of the insecurity and fear at the bottom of the strutting forces of oppression. We live with media images of horrible death and global annihilation. The political energy in *Memory Room* is a kind of teasing of the monster. Death is a transition here rather than an enemy (53).

"About the photographs" clarifies the relationship of the Sourkes to the Marlatt in *Touch*. The connection is closest between Sourkes' statement and Marlatt's "musing with mothertongue," an essay on feminist aesthetics written for the Women and Words/Les femmes et les mots conference, and first published in *Tessera*. Neither the photographs nor the poems depend on the texts that set them in feminist context (though the poems are overtly feminist while the photographs are not), nor do they depend on each other. But Sourkes and Marlatt must have been struck by the similar drive behind their work in different media. The pictures are made up of layered images whose logic is as associational and archaeological as Marlatt's poetry. Marlatt sees language, in fact, as a kind of "memory room," where words are stacked with meanings and both sound and sense units pull towards each other: "we know from dreams and schizophrenic speech how deeply association works in our psyches, a form of thought that is not rational but erotic because it works by attraction, a drawing, a pulling toward, a 'liking' "(45).

This review was published in 1986.

Both Sourkes and Marlatt have patriarchal values and structures to subvert, and both do that by being themselves, undefensive about their feminism, their art. No man can agree with them about the indisputable value of the feminine without feeling a touch lonely, implicated by maleness in the oppressive system, shut out of sisterhood. So it's good to feel the restraint in the fact that Sourkes does not sex the monster, and it's good to hear, beyond attack, the joyousness in Marlatt's vision of the "new woman writer":

> inhabitant of language, not master, not even mistress, this new woman writer ... in having is had, is held by it, what she is given to say, in giving it away is given herself, on that double edge where she has always lived, between the already spoken and the unspeakable, sense and nonsense, only now she writes it, risking nonsense, chaotic language leafings, unspeakable breaches of usage, intuitive leaps, inside language she leaps for joy, shoving out the walls of taboo and propriety, kicking syntax, discovering life in old roots (48-49).

Beyond the first flush of exhilaration following the flow of Marlatt's line, there is pleasure in beginning to find out what the words contain, what shapes the poems make. These are ample poems with no excess verbiage, no unnecessary explanation. What is *not* said is very important. Marlatt lets her reader spin a narrative out of her lyric rushes. So the words are seeds with the power of seeds; they sprout with reading and they grow. What grows in a reader is a sense of the relationship of all the words in a particular poem, and then of how the poems join in family. Also, *Touch to My Tongue* comes to seem intimately related to two other texts: "In the Month of Hungry Ghosts" and *How Hug a Stone*.

Formally these three texts are very different from each other, and retrospectively that seems significant. One can look at the three in terms of the words one might use to guide a searcher to a known goal; cold, warmer, hot! So the formal diversity of "Hungry Ghosts"—journal entries, pictures, letters, poems, "stories"—is quite as inconclusive as the content, the journey to Malaysia where Marlatt begins to look for herself in the circumstances of her upbringing. *How Hug a Stone* records Marlatt's trip to England with her son Kit. Here she penetrates deeper into her personal past, and beyond that into an identification of the origin of the feminine, the Great Mother, in the stone circles at Avebury. This volume is quite heterogeneous as regards materials (journal, maps, poems), but it is thoroughly refined as a whole. It identifies certain personal sources of repression, tied up with the mother whom she comes increasingly to understand, and it beautifully alters Robert Graves's catalogue of goddess-muses (*The White Goddess* 347) to show how the matriarchal story got supplanted by a patriarchal line:

> earth word (home again), seed word (safe again),

Stan Dragland

>   that bears us in this *kiel,* to *ku-*, to,
> a hollow space or place, enclosing object, round object, a lump. mound in
> the surrounding sea of grass. *ku-*, *kunte*, to, wave-breaking womb: Bride
> who comes unsung in the muse-ship shared with Mary Gypsy, Mary of
> Egypt, Miriam, Marianne suppressed, become / Mary of the Blue Veil, Sea
> Lamb sifting sand & dust, dust & bone, whose Son ... (72)

The ellipsis is Marlatt's own, her economical way of saying "You know the rest": his story from here on in.

Increasingly, Marlatt's personal search becomes identified with the quest of Woman, and the closer she comes to the centre of everything feminine, the more vaginal are the images that describe it. She looks for her mother and finds the Great Mother ("not a person, she is what we come out of, ground & source" *How Hug* 73), on the way to finding herself in another woman, which finding, foundness, is the subject of *Touch to My Tongue. Touch* is formally various only in containing photographs and prose statements, as well as poems. But the poems themselves, none of them over a page in length, are a close, complex weave. No supporting documentary material except Marlatt's notes on her mythological and etymological allusions. The form echoes what the words say in so many ways: the lost is found. The search was partly for ways to assert the feminine values of relatedness and wholeness over the usurping patriarchal drive to power and control. (In that nutshell, feminism is common sense.) Marlatt's particular search brought her to Betsy Warland, to whom all the love poems in *Touch* are addressed.

The opening of *Touch* finds Marlatt already "flush with being" in the new relationship (perfectly aligned with being—no alienation—and filled up with it, ablush) but the earliest point in the "narrative" is probably located in "yes," the third poem, where there is the recollection of a marriage in which something always had to be held back. The poem then pivots into the realization of the false turned true in the discovery of the right sort of other: "lost daughter, other mother and lover" (27).

> perverse in that, having to defend myself from attack, encroachment on that
> soft abyss, that tidal place I knew as mine, know now is the place I find with
> you. not perverse but turned the *right* way round, redefined, it signals us
> beyond limits in a new tongue our connection runs along (21).

In the new foundness there is an astonishing release, "all that weight of heartlocked years let loose" (25). In what one might call the story of the book, Marlatt first explores her nurturing relationship in six poems focusing on various particular situations. Then there is a series of poems of separation, as Marlatt drives east while her heart tends west to British Columbia and her lover. A poem of reconciliation is then followed by two others having to do with temporary separation, one from sickness, one caused by an operation. Fourteen poems to make a constellation. One reason why these poems never seem self-indulgent, though they are highly personal and frankly erotic, is the breadth of the net they cast. Marlatt uses everything she knows about language to draw the wide world into the field whose centre is the lover, "heart-of-the world."

Here is the theory, from "musing with mothertongue":

> like the atomic particles of our bodies, phonemes and syllables gravitate toward each other. they attract each other in movements we call assonance, euphony, alliteration, rhyme. they are drawn together and echo each other in rhythms we identify as feet—lines run on, phrases patter like speaking feet. on a macroscopic level, words evoke each other in movements we know as puns and figures of speech (these endless similes, this continuing fascination with making one out of two, a new one, a similitude.) meaning moves us deepest the more of the whole it puts together, and so we get sense where it borders on nonsense ("what is the sense of it all?") as what we sense our way into. the sentence ("life") making our multiplicity whole and even intelligible by the end-point. intelligible: logos there in the gathering hand, the reading eye (46).

Marlatt is a postmodernist who brings a new feminist energy to an old desire: to harmonize the world.

Theory is general; practice is particular, or else frozen. Marlatt would not want her individual experience to disappear into the feminist generality, and there is little danger of that happening. Her poems are full of sensuous images that localize and make concrete her experience, while the sentences that carry them flow in sound and sense patterns of subtle responsiveness to nuance of feeling. So the line enacts the love, because being found is not a finality. Being found is to be freer more flowing than before, beyond "the need for limits" that is so often run up against in *How Hug a Stone*:

> our territory we found (we inhabit together), not *terra firma*, not dry land, owned, along the highway, cleared for use, but that other, lowlying, moist and undefined, hidden ground, wild and running everywhere along the outer edges. lost, *losti*, lust-y one, who calls my untamed answering one to sally forth ... (27).

Patriarchal colonization, in the words "owned" and "cleared for use," is subtly disowned. The lovers have penetrated to something more primitively free than that. "Wild" is a word for it that recurs. And images of pool, river, tide, estuary, geyser, recur in the fluid dynamic of a relationship in continual rearrangement and discovery. The metaphors for it shift, too. Each moment, to take a line out of context, is "just one of the houses we pass through in the endless constellation of our being" (30). "House" holds both dwelling and astrological sign, and "constellation" involves making. In

Stan Dragland

Touch the layered language and the wild line round up an identity between two lovers that contains not only them, but women of myth, landscape, other creatures and objects—everything they see and hear and touch and taste. "kore" and "eating" are next to each other in the book. Their subjects—love-making—are similar; technically, they are totally different. A few words about them might suggest how technique conveys the multiplicity of experience that is central to the book's content. "kore" is heavily notated with commas and periods, and it contains three parentheses, each longer than the other. It ends in ellipsis. "eating" has no punctuation except a single virgule, though it shapes a circle by opening and ending with an image of kiwi fruit. The first poem goes digressively, slyly, in exploratory stages to a sharp, dramatic peak; "*yu!* cry jubilant excess … (23)." The second winds an uninterrupted quiet way to climax. The technique speaks, saying that two acts of love might be as different as night and day.

The foregoing paragraph is to Marlatt's poetry as the explanation to the joke; it's like taking a shower with your clothes on. But, after all, there is *some* danger of invading privacy here. Please go to the original, gentle reader.

I want to offer my favourite poem intact, the first one, "this place full of contradiction." It weaves four or so different times and places, different experiences of "you and i" into one. They happened sequentially in time, but they elide and overlap in memory.

a confusion of times if not of place, though you understood when i said no not the Danish Tearoom—the Indonesian or Indian, was in fact that place of warm walls, a comfortable tarot deck even the lamps pick up your glow, a cabin of going, fjords in there, a clear and pristine look the winds weave through your eyes i'm watching you talk of a different birth, blonde hair on my tongue, of numbers, nine aflush with cappuccino and brandy and rain outside on that street we flash down, laughing with no umbrella, i see your face because i don't see mine equally flush with being, co-incidence being together we meet in these far places we find in each other, it's Sappho i said, on the radio, always we meet original, blind of direction, astonished your hand covers mine walking lowtide strands of Colaba, the lighthouse, Mumbai meaning great mother, you wearing your irish drover's cap and waiting alive in the glow while i come up worrying danish and curry, this place full of contradiction—you know, you knew, it was the one place i meant (19).

It takes a line sensitive as a divining rod to slip from time to time and to contain each one in a single present of perfect clarity, a single portmanteau "sentence." It takes some reading to see what's going on here, and in the other poems, but then recognition causes a lingering explosion of warmth in the heart. How appropriate to be able to say that about a book addressed to a lover who is an "excessive and radiant storehouse of sun" (23). Any reader at all advanced in years who finds her/himself still or again east of eden in matters of the heart should *take* heart from this passionate celebration of relatively late fulfilment. But these are hardly poems for older folk. They are written in the spirit of spring (a leap and a fountain), a season, in the last words of the book, of "beginning all over again."

The Review, Re-vision

For the most part I stand behind what I originally wrote about *Touch to My Tongue*, but I've had second thoughts and counter thoughts that qualify or question or extend rather than cancel. Much of what follows is a freestanding interlinear, or a dialogue with the review. I could have started from scratch, but I think there's value in letting the process of rethinking show—even, perhaps especially, when it exposes some embarrassment. The reading and thinking goes on: what follows is where it got to by 1991.

స

No man can agree with them about the indisputable value of the feminine without feeling a touch lonely, implicated by maleness in the oppressive system, shut out of sisterhood. So it's good to feel the restraint in the fact that Sourkes does not sex the monster, and it's good to hear, beyond attack, the joyousness in Marlatt's vision of the "new woman writer."

To his own male anxiety, reviewing Shirley Neuman and Smaro Kamboureli's *A Mazing Space*, Robert Kroetsch adds that of three of the male critics included in the book: "Vaguely uneasy," he calls them, "apologetic, about their use of the fragment" (199). Well, obviously I have my anxious moments too. *Touch to My Tongue* itself causes me no unease, but tendrils of thought reaching out from the text into the changing world of women sometimes bring back danger signals. Signals of exclusion and increased uncertainty. The issue of attack could be raised, in connection with the love poems of *Touch to My Tongue*, only by a man on the run. Who could blame a woman if she smiled a little to see the marginalizer on edge.

I'll tell you about The Queen. Sometimes in London, Ontario, a woman dressed as the classic Queen Elizabeth and speaking in that poshest of all possible accents performs for local women. As far as I can tell, because I've only heard brief accounts of her monologues, their content would be consistent with the occupation and character of the Monarch herself—nothing ideological, that is, nothing feminist. But in that men are excluded from these events, they are political statements. I only know a few bits of these routines, like the one in which The Queen comments deadpan on images of herself in her own stamp collection. At second hand, this sounded so hilarious that five years later it still makes me grin.

There's something brilliantly demented about the lady in the Queen suit. I'm purely glad she exists so that somebody gets to see her. I know where she works. If I asked I could find out her name, but that's a secret I like to keep from myself. I don't feel defensive about her exclusion of men. In her performances I sense healing of the pain that is implicit in their having to *be* for women only. I want that healing. I want this undefensiveness growing in me.

"*Shut* out"? As I cast around to find a subject for that verb, I keep coming back, uncomfortably, to myself. This reminds me of a passage in *Peter Pan and Wendy*, J.M. Barrie's postmodernist metafiction disguised as a children's book. One emotion the novel harnesses with humor is the sadness of being on the outside looking in. The feeling can instantly transform an adult into a child, but would you expect it to happen to the narrator of a novel? "For all the use we are to her," says *Peter Pan's* narrator about Mrs. Darling's complete readiness for the return of her innocent and heartless runaway children, "we might as well go back to the [pirate] ship. However, as we are here we may as well stay and look on. That is all we are, lookers on. Nobody really wants us. So let us watch and say jaggy things, in the hope that some of them will hurt" (285). Yes, these readjustments in the relationships between the sexes can be painful. Best to admit that, laugh at ourselves if possible—then leave it out of discussions where it's irrelevant.

ல

Touch to my Tongue *comes to seem intimately related to two other texts: "In the Month of Hungry Ghosts" and* How Hug a Stone. … *Cold, warmer, hot!*

This seems too simple to me now, attentive enough neither to the varieties of continuity nor the differences between *Touch* and the other texts. There may well be a gap between the successful search for the mother ("the struggle with her fear which i suspected of being so strong it could actually shape what happened to me. coming to meet it, I see what i've been struggling with here" *How Hug* 76) and the discovery of a natural lesbian sexuality. Perhaps these are successive results of the same search, or perhaps they're merely analogous. (It's not the actual Marlatt I speak of, but the real woman Marlatt has made out of words. The two are not identical but intimately related, like the "i" of certain Marlatt texts to the autobiographical "she" of others.)

It's not as though Marlatt's search for the mother has ended, at least, when the lost child is found in wholehearted love. *Ana Historic* combs again through the story of the mother and the daughter at odds, telling the terribly sad Canadian part of it in some detail for the first time, making more palpable than ever how coffin-like a traditionally patriarchal marriage can feel to a woman with wings. This is the Master Tale of woman taming. Marlatt's mother, Edrys (the textual Edrys, fictionalized as Ina in *Ana Historic*), was not tamed without a struggle. But she swallowed the struggle for control, and the longer it raged inside her the more static it generated. The static was frightening because it could be felt but not articulated by the child it was enveloping. It helps to read *Touch to My Tongue* remembering the child thus bewildered; aspects of the book come clearer, as does its place in Marlatt's continuing life-text.

In Marlatt's writing the mother's intense suppressed emotion often appears in images of sub-verbal or pre-verbal communication, as here in "The Month of Hungry

Ghosts": "Swirling currents through the house [in the Penang of Marlatt's childhood], ... unexpected storms & penance & strange tension (always 'incomprehensible')" (81). The quotation marks double the meaning: the child intuitively realizes that daily domestic emergencies and discomfitures are insufficient explanation for mental disturbances that charge the very atmosphere of the house, but she can't read the sub"text". It can't be read until many years later, not until well after Marlatt's formative years are over, perhaps not even until her mother dies.

Here is another version of the swirling current, in *How Hug a Stone*, a memory of a tense family automobile trip in 1948 seen from the perspective of a four year old Marlatt:

> inside our moveable & too-close room, the aftermath of a rebuke, watching
> the flasher lift its signal colour for me alone in the dark out there, to go,
> beyond my father's back erect & in control, my mother's body soft & angry
> in its hum, & warm, walls that hold, to go back, but the wheels go on, in
> the dark of the dials & gears & the hum ... (18).

That hum is generated by a "torrent" of rage dammed, to use one of the key terms for Edrys/Ina's enclosure in *Ana Historic*. The hum moves inside the child and stays there while the child grows an adult body. "Who mothers me?" Marlatt asks in one of the most moving sections of *How Hug a Stone*, with her son Kit sick and she humming with concern for him, worried (she is her mother in this) that she has put him "at risk."

Two childhood memories in *How Hug a Stone* resonate with this present fear: on Wild Pear beach, almost caught by the rising tide: "if we don't go now we won't get back & i could hear it in her, panic, pan-ic (terror of the wild), shouldn't have brought you here, all three, & the wind rising—risk. to meet it" (55); and in Bombay, aborting a taxi trip to the zoo for fear of abduction during a two-hour ship-leave: "this thrum way back in the tunnel rocketing forward, fear, rocketing through my whole being" (77). At this point, in the last poem of *How Hug*, the fear is structurally a reprise, but dramatically it's a surprise plunge into a reopened (omnipresent) abyss of terror, a memory repressed until now. Seeing "what i've been struggling with here" is no guarantee that it won't have to be faced again and again as it forms in particular vivid memories:

> welcome to Bombay madam
> three small girls ah very pretty   to the zoo she said
> knowing it at Parel Road   Victoria & Albert   untouchable
> scream in the air tearing like fine silk   how does she know
> Hindi know this isn't the way stiffening you will die insane
> in a foreign country
> yes yes this is the way   to contact shrinking inside
> her jewellery

> Maha Amba   stop stop i say   beating on the glass
> with rupees   right here   but mem this is not the
> zoo   right now it's Mumbai
>   every cab back a possible abduction off unknown
> streets to bring us back   do you speak English? do you know
> the way to the pier?   unbearable loss don't take them from me (77-78).

The line between mother and daughter is dissolving in the memory, in the writing. You understand the mother when you become the mother.

To "be" Edrys, subject to such abrupt plummets into terror and self-reproach, must at times be a heavy burden for her daughter. But at least, written into consciousness, the weight may be shared. With a reader, a listener. A sharing is mentioned in the first poem of *Touch*, and it presumably alludes to the Bombay trauma. When the connection with *How Hug a Stone* is registered and the explanatory note at the end of *Touch* is factored in, it's clear that experience in "this place full of contradiction" is layering up very thickly. The intensity of the joyful communing of lovers leaves little room for terror, but a reader of *How Hug* knows something of what is being communicated, and comfort given for it, when "astonished your hand covers mine walking lowtide strands of Colaba, the lighthouse, Mumbai meaning great mother" (19). Marlatt's note confirms and extends the connection, glossing *How Hug* in the process:

> Mumbai is the vernacular name for Bombay, after the Koli goddess Mumbai (derived from Maha Amba, Great Mother). According to L.F. Rushbrook Williams in *A Handbook for Travellers in India, Pakistan, Nepal, Bangladesh and Sri Lanka*, she is the tutelary deity of this island, once seven islands separated at high tide, drained and reclaimed by the British. The southernmost tip is the site of the Colaba lighthouse (35).

The connection extends back to the escape from the tide, a danger caused in the first place by fascinated attraction to the Mother in caves: "darkness gathers in cracks, slits, tidal caverns, gathering us up" (*How Hug* 55).

When Marlatt's imagination begins to exfoliate, to swarm, in her writing, what energy is being harnessed? In the constellation of otherness of which she (like each person) is her own centre, the power of love may be as great as that of fear, but there should be no underestimating the component of the push that is swirling current, panic thrum: "you taught me fear but not how to fight," Marlatt says to her dead mother in "Hungry Ghosts." "you, misspelled, gave yourself to the dark of some other light, leaving me here with the words, with fear, love, & a need to keep speaking" (95).

The paradox involved here is poignant, if not unusual: efforts to heal the affliction drive much other valuable exploration as well. Marlatt's work might be private therapy if she didn't draw the contemporary world through the eye of her particular needle. Lorraine Weir is right to say that Marlatt's "feminist ecological poetics gradually came together" over two decades. "The revolutionary energy of such recent texts as *Touch to My Tongue* and *Ana Historic* is no greater than that of *Steveston*; rather, it is part of a consistent pattern of critique and resistance reaching its logical outcome" (63). All of this has personal sources but it isn't merely confessional or egocentric because Marlatt has always been telling "one passage, or one story, or one version of a common story" (*What Matters* 7).

Touch to my Tongue feels primarily like a relief, a release from the pressure, the tension, that hum of be-wildering anxiety. But there is continuity between *Touch* and the mother-texts: Marlatt is still humming in (diminished) concern in two of the poems, and fear returns powerfully in another.

"this place full of contradiction," orchestrating a multiple synchronicity of different times and places, feels full of movement, even hurry, towards a rendezvous. Why the rush? It's explained by the word "worrying" (wondering did she make it clear where they were to meet?) in the arrival. The worry-wart rhythm established in childhood persists, but a resistor (another person, intuitive, for whom meanings, directions, don't have to be spelled out) has been spliced into the circuit. Here is the hurry/worry in another "travel" poem, "coming to you"

> through traffic, honking and off-course, direction veering, presently up your
> street, car slam, soon enough on my feet, eager and hesitant, peering with
> the rush of coming to you, late, through hydrangeas nodding out with
> season's age, and roses open outline still the edge of summer gone in
> grounding rain. elsewhere, or from it, i brush by, impatient, bending to
> your window to surprise you in that place i never know, you alone with
> yourself there, one leg on your knee, you with boots, with headphones on,
> grave, rapt with inaudible music. the day surrounds you: you point where
> everything listens. and i slow down, learning how to enter—implicate and
> unspoken (still) heart-of-the-world (22).

To feel this poem it's only necessary to hear its hectic rhythms slow and pause when the long rushing sentence arrives at the refuge inhabited by the still woman at one with herself, but the release is more moving to a reader who comes to *Touch* from Marlatt's other work, knowing what systemic pain is being soothed here—in this belonging, this home. "having tasted hunting," Marlatt says in "Hungry Ghosts," "i see i've spent most of my life trying to live somewhere. Which perhaps means nothing more than being at home. Or some such notion of a public space as Hannah Arendt describes … where one's life takes place in a web of relations held *in common*" (77).

There's more eagerness and delight and wonder than inherited interference in the two poems I've glanced at, but Marlatt has not for nothing been working all these years "to get the whole field of consciousness (*not* linear logic) of any given 'i' or 'he'" (*What Matters* 74). So a reader hears undertones in this complex music. At one point in *Touch*, in the poem called "houseless," there is a buzz of outright fear that temporary separation might become permanent. Is this the old panic thrum intensified? It certainly feels related:

> and now it's dark in here, deep, my cave a house, you on the other side of
> the country, our country of sea with the wind blowing, our country of reeds
> and grasses under unfathomed sky. i huddle small, i call you up, a tiny point
> of light, memory small like a far-off hole—are you there? (20).

This is a temporary regression; it's framed by passages of joy and strength, eased by the exhilarated feeling that love might make it possible to face anything, to live right out in the open where we're all obliged to live these days.

The fear in "houseless" is vibrating in tune with the fear expressed in other Marlatt books that the world is a house under seige by its own inhabitants. "i huddle small" recalls the dormouse, of the poem in *How Hug a Stone* called "delphiniums blue & geraniums red," "paws to eyes, small creature at the heart of dreaming some blue otherwhere" (69). In A.A. Milne's "The Dormouse and the Doctor" the dormouse is the victim of a authoritative quack who finds him in bed—perfectly happy in a bed of his favourite "geraniums (red) and delphiniums (blue)" (68)—and decides that he is sick. The prescription, chrysanthemums, would have destroyed the small one's world if he hadn't been able to close his eyes and dream. Milne's poem is very complexly worked into Marlatt's, but the basic intense feeling she carries out of it, into her own world of nuclear bombs, is of total powerlessness and vulnerability:

> & if The Common Good, pointing its nineteenth century hand,
> has tyrannized all sense of me, small voice essential to
> life? so that we falls apart, gone mad at the mask of Reason
> which still is quoting Good in the face of annihilation:
> tactical advantage, counterforce capability, stockpiling.
> *the first few weapons arriving do almost all the damage*
> *conceivable to the fabric of the country.* have done so,
> without ever arriving, the nest we live in full of holes these days (70).

In *Ana Historic* the dormouse is Ina, "the you that was you curled up like a small animal inside" (148), reduced to minimal selfhood by electro-shock therapy. "They said you were disturbed, Ina, as if you were a nest whose eggs had been removed (they had), or as if our nest, the house, had been fingered over, picked through by some strange force from outside" (135).

There are continuities between *Touch to My Tongue* and other texts, before and after, then, but they're complex. Some support for knitting all of the books in a single mother-tale comes from Marlatt's own repeated insistence that writing (making narrative) is how she renders the world (where we've been, where we might be going) intelligible to herself. But the movement is not simply linear. It unfolds in a "plot-line," a "drift, which circles back on itself while still moving towards some recognition— this rather than a plotted crescendo of conflict & resolution" (*What Matters* 71). We may think of the work(s) as having a progressive dimension, carrying forward in each instance a vast field of phenomena in waves of recognition. Not towards an end, not "trying to freeze meaning (that transformational current!)" ("Correspondances" 10). Rather, the spiral again, coming round again with fresh eyes, re-covering the same ground with new/old questions.

ຕ໑

The formal diversity of "Hungry Ghosts" is quite as inconclusive as the content. …
How Hug a Stone *is thoroughly refined as a whole.*

There are two problems with this:

1) "Hungry Ghosts" actually edges towards, if not a conclusion, at least a recognition of that devastating hum in two late prose poems about Marlatt's mother, "As the Cup Fills Itself in the Stream" and "Getting Here." "Hungry Ghosts" moves through accounts of a physically, aurally and "humanly dense world" (61)—describing Penang, Marlatt might be describing the thick texture of her poems—in a typical descent pattern. This time there is a sharp dip towards the end. "As the Cup Fills Itself in the Stream" recalls "the mad wind of your anger suppressed," the "wild hysteria & the signals change, erratic" (83). "Getting Here" is a plunge into "fear, love" of the source of alienation: "one cloud of thought, one word of no earthly use, 'mother'"—(95).

2) "Hungry Ghosts" certainly is quite various, with short and long line poems, journal sections, letters and photographs, but it's neither linear nor random; rather, the parts are inter-woven and talk to each other. For example, a small gnomic poem called "Res publica," about the "great cantata" (51) of bird-song, appears before the prose passage which puts it in context: "that wet noise dense with a thicket of birdsong, jubilant, joyous, in the wet, & the falling rain transformed into falling notes, falling & ascending, crossing the rain in darts of melody—wooden shuttle of the Thai silk weaver—running across & through the warp of the rain" (54). Another poem, "mem sahib," whose metamorphosing m/mother words compact the whole story of Marlatt's mother, Edrys Buckle, housewife, anticipates the more overt painful recognitions of the later prose poems. And those recognitions retrospectively annotate the poem.

An essay on *Touch to My Tongue* may seem to call for no clarification of the structural complexity of "In the Month of Hungry Ghosts," though anything clarifying Marlatt's experience of her mother contributes to an understanding of the place of *Touch* in Marlatt's wordfield, and sometimes therefore of *Touch* itself. "leaving the need for limits at your place" (21), you "who calls my untamed answering one to sally forth" (27)—these are signs in *Touch* of the shriving of that lost mother, her liberation in her daughter's release.

Stan Dragland

৩

Marlatt is a postmodernist who brings a new feminist energy to an old desire: to harmonize the world.

A postmodernist? But there is a drive towards meaning in Marlatt's work, a desire to put things together, a movement even towards the logos monster, enemy of most declared postmodernists. Also, Marlatt is not, any more, a poet of the fragment (her poems are extremely spare, but whole and often circular in form). She never toys with a reader, like her contemporaries Bowering and Kroetsch. She is not cool. Her muse of indefiniteness and undependability is not the trickster but, now at least, The Mother. On the other hand, her style is process; her sentences don't respect sense as dictated by grammar with its sources in logos-as-logic. Also, she plays the border between genres (fiction/poetry/autobiography) metafictionally: her work is about itself while it's about *her*self and the world. Postmodernist? Yes and no.

Lately critics have been struggling to redefine what Marlatt does. In a pregnant footnote, Lorraine Weir questions one commonplace of Marlatt definition: "Marlatt's theory of communication is primarily semiotic, not phenomenological" (63); Dennis Cooley accepts the phenomenological basis that Doug Barbour first outlined, but adds that "to a degree few have acknowledged she has worked in a continuance of a liberal-humanist tradition, one which assumes language resides in the individual in expression of herself" (71). Marlatt's conception of the self is trickier than this, or was in 1975 when she wrote to Warren Tallman that "the self is *not* what is written about though it *is* what is written out of. Subjective insofar as it *is* proprioceptive & the body is ground, yes, self transmits—... one cannot ever escape self because there is no other ground, & yet seek always what is 'other' than self that frighteningly small dominion ... " ("Correspondances" 14-15). But Marlatt does seem to be carrying forward something of a humanist stance and aesthetic that many of her mentors and colleagues have discarded totally. Would it be a rift of this sort that causes Frank Davey to find *How Hug a Stone*, sentence by sentence, "complex and plurisignative," but, "on a structural level," offering "meanings that are heavily systematized and through repeated foregrounding overdetermined" (41). I have my problems with each of these recent critical assertions, but they tell me that Marlatt's texts are speaking quite differently to different readers; they tell me that, as a writer, she is elusive.

"Postmodernist," like the "modernist" it contains, tends to be used as a label, misused as a handy bag to dump all sorts of writers in, for ideological or temporal or formal reasons. We might be better off with "avant garde," though we would still have to listen to what it means to each person who uses it. George Bowering and Daphne Marlatt both use it to define a basis for postmodernism they share in the dialogue between them called "Given This Body": GB: "the *avant garde* ... I take simply to mean that we have to work out our own forms for things, that we don't use an inherited line, etc." DM: "*avant garde* is simply writing as close as you can to what you're actually experiencing at any given point. That's where the new forms arise" (33). The word "simply" will stick out for readers unaware of how much so-called Black Mountain poetics the two writers take (or, in 1973, took) as given, and for readers who feel that art, who *cares* if it's avant-garde or not, may be made out of quite other impulses and theories.

બ

The layered landscape and the wild line round up an identity between two lovers that contains not only them, but women of myth, landscape, other creatures and objects - everything they see and hear and touch and taste.

This can be pushed further—virtually the total field of the poem is feminine—with some impetus from Marlatt's second epigraph to *Touch*. "Une femme inscrite en exterritorialité du langage. Elle expose le sujet comme on s'expose à la mort. Car il est question qu'elle vive." In Barbara Godard's translation, here is the passage in its context in Louise Cotnoir's essay, "Writing Ourselves With, In and Against Language," which preceded Marlatt's "musing with mothertongue" in the first *Tessera*:

Arrested vigour, detoured, today she disseminates the interruption of codes. She begins to say what she is feeling without having the words. The feminine enters representation, the symbolic, names herself. A woman inscribed in the extraterritoriality of language. She expounds the subject just as you expose youself to death. Because it's a matter of her life. She gives a reading of her skin & sees trembling there (51-52).

One can see how Marlatt would have been attracted to that "extraterritoriality of language." It rimes, in the *Touch* poem called "hidden ground," with

our territory we found (we inhabit together), not *terra firma*, not dry land, owned, along the highway, cleared for use, but that other, lowlying, moist and undefined, hidden ground, wild and running everywhere along the outer edges (27).

This is a "place" the Mother presides over, this "place," being "what we come through to & what we come out of, ground & source. the space after the colon, the pause (between the words) of all possible relation" (*How Hug* 73).

The question is, how much of Cotnoir's militant thought does the epigraph draw in along with that life-and-death image? Perhaps Marlatt's feminist voice is always moderate because so much of her ground, her context, has in the past been established by male poets. But there is another context now, one that drives at times towards a separatism of the sexes. Marlatt is one of the editors of *Tessera*, of course. She will be aware of the questions asked by Cotnoir in a later *Tessera* (*CV* II 1988):

Is it necessary to remain in enemy territory and produce "neutral criticism" or to join up with the feminist ghetto where it is becoming even easier to "eliminate" the difference outright? As for me, I align myself with feminist criticism because it is conscience, commitment and politics (115).

You don't pussyfoot your way into a revolution. It's not hard to see how eliminating the difference would have its attractions, and not only as tit for tat (the female context or perspective having been ignored for so long); the sparks often fly from the energy generated in a lot of the go-for-broke feminist writing in *Tessera* and elsewhere.

Is Touch to My Tongue addressed to women only? That's another way of asking the question about how much of Cotnoir's toughness (or Betsy Warland's, for that matter) *Touch* draws in. If *Touch* is about "that tongue our bodies utter, woman tongue, speaking in and of and for each other" (27), if it feminizes everything from haystack and hill to the binaries of creation/destruction, where does a male reader find purchase? The answer is so obvious that I can't resist postponing it, even if my question is thus exposed as rhetorical.

The few signs of the masculine in the poem are negatively weighted: "that space between the last rib and the hipbone, that place i couldn't bear the weight of his sleeping hand upon" (21); "the guy in the red shirt, metal flashing, is not Hades but only the latest technician in a long line of measurers" (26); male territory is "owned" and "cleared for use" (27). Not very inviting to the male reader, *if one assumes that the text is supposed to be a mirror reflecting the reader's reality, or a near enough approximation of it not to cause any discomfort or require any adjustment.* I believe that most of us unconsciously hold some shade of that disabling assumption. The pressure for women to buy it is intense these days (as it is for men who want the feminist revolution to work), since so much militancy is needed to root out one-sided assumptions in sexist language and thought.

The answer to my question is that there is no question. No argument needs to be mounted for the validity of a text foreign to the experience of a certain class or sex or creed of readers. True foreignness (the spirit of the other—the one we can *never* know) is a joy. It's what we seek in reading—to be carried somewhere else, sometimes into otherness *within* the perfectly familiar. But this goes for all writing. The argument that simply grants Marlatt her lesbian ground, and asks questions only about how (well) she explores it supports also the true writing of, in Cotnoir's phrase, "the enemy."

Emotionally, though, not everyone finds it easy to grant that ground. Teaching *Touch to My Tongue*, I've found that a shudder of homophobia falls between the text and some readers, heterosexual women as well as men. I think it's one of Marlatt's achievements simply to have occupied her ground undefensively, writing from inside it in the unexplanatory way her readers have come to expect. The joy of her relationship saturates the whole poem. The colouring of all perception by that joy all but excludes from depiction certain harsh realities of membership in a persecuted minority. These come home to a reader less clearly in *Touch* than they do in a parallel text dedicated to Daphne Marlatt, Betsy Warland's *Open is Broken.*

Before reading *Open is Broken* I hadn't realized that Marlatt's poem "where we went" is about a marriage. It follows the lovers as they go to examine rings,

> silver, moon metal engraved in the shape of wild eyes by kwakiutl and haida hands, raven and wolf and whale and unknown birds not seen in the light city. creatures of unorganized territory we become, a *physical impulse* moving from me to you (the poem is), us *dancing in animal skins* in the unmapped part of our world" (28).

Now I see that this is a ceremony of initiation into a relationship presided over as by totems of wolf and whale, fitting symbols of otherness (both native and animal) for a ceremony that Betsy Warland renders as a breaking of taboo:

> in the year 1982 on the sixth day of the eighth month we put on the silver curve of each other's presence with rings of wilderness wolf & whale and committed *exogamy:*

> "The custom of marrying outside the tribe, family, clan or or social unit" (17).

Warland's version is intensely conscious of the social norms being defied. It appropriates the language of the oppressor to satirize it. ("Exogamy" is a neutral anthropological term until linked with the verb "committed;" then it becomes an offense.) "What do you do," says the narrator of *Ana Historic,* "when the true you feel inside sounds different from the standard" (18)? What is it like when your deepest, truest instincts are unacceptable, even repulsive, to the dominant culture you have no choice but to live in? "city that houses stares, city that houses eyes, electricity writing the dark of so many heads figuring where we were" (28): thus "where we went" obliquely registers what homophobia feels like, what it's like to *be* the persecuted other. *Touch to My Tongue* is not a system created to exclude male readers, and maybe there's no need even to see it as a system designed to circulate almost entirely within a female economy. Why not just assume that these love poems were written without designs on the reader, with no external agenda, that they are merely bathed, drenched, in the light of the lover? Love is notorious for its transformative effect on perception.

&

After all, there is some danger of invading privacy here. Please go to the original, gentle reader.

This reminds me of the finale to an uplifting story, the one that Wendy tells to her brothers and the lost boys in the Never Land, of Mr. and Mrs. Darling's reunion with her three children: "So up they flew to their mummy and daddy; and pen cannot

Stan Dragland

describe the happy scene, over which we draw a veil" (*Peter Pan* 206-207). When the
pen shows up in an oral story it signifies that the young narrator is unconsciously in
the grip of her written model. I may have had more control than Wendy but I sound
to myself not much less Victorian.

Beyond the point where I dropped the veil there is a fork in the critical path, a
choice of styles or relationships with the text. Two articles in the special issue of *Line*
devoted to Marlatt may serve to illustrate the possibilites. Lorraine Weir's "Daphne
Marlatt's 'Ecology of Language'" begins in Marlatt's manner, with long loping
sentences notated by commas, with parentheses, fragments. You draw a deep breath
and plunge in, to be rewarded in this case for a persistence not unlike that required
for reading the original texts. Partly because she relaxes after a sort of imitative
prologue, Weir makes the embracing method work. The method has no particular
virtue beyond its effectiveness; in a purer form, its hazard would be the limitation of
its audience to Marlatt enthusiasts, those who know her work inside out.

An opposite method is Frank Davey's semiotic analysis, "Words and Stones in *How
Hug a Stone*." Davey keeps the text at arm's length; he doesn't get involved. His
method, like that involved in abstract thinking, has its appeal; neutralizing the
emotional content of signs (which I assume he intended to do) you can trace more
objectively their interaction in a text. With more scrupulous attention to the shadings
and overlappings of male-female binaries which he finds "overdetermined" in *How
Hug a Stone*, Davey might have been, from my perspective, truer to the poem. As it
is, his analysis accounts for nothing of why the poem moves me so deeply.

The choices of critical way don't divide neatly along male-female lines; Dennis
Cooley's article in the same magazine is both personal and stylistically volatile.
Anyway, neither method—the arms-length nor the at-one-with—have lent themselves
to my own writing about *Touch to My Tongue*. The former is too cool; attempting the
latter would be tantamount to inviting myself inside. I want it both ways.

Perhaps you realized when I introduced the idea of a fork in the critical path that
the split actually opens, if it's going to, before the critical writing begins, and that it
opens the way a river becomes a delta rather than as two paths diverge in a wood. There
are the same number of ways to the sea as there are windows in the house of fiction.
Any path I chose would respect privacy, but not for reasons of prudery, not, in the case
of *Touch*, because the poems are "anatomically correct." It's more in the spirit of Edith
Hamilton's translation of an early Homeric hymn on the rites of Eleusis: "'mysteries
which no one may utter, for deep awe checks the tongue'" (53).

The Poem Revisited

I've merely mentioned the mythological dimension of *Touch To My Tongue*. This (the
story of Demeter and Kore/Persephone) is braided with some of the other strands: as
a seasonal myth it decorates the narrative (a progress through the seasons which is
unobtrusively observed in several poems); in its feminist re-vision (Adrienne Rich's
term) it's a major component of the marginalizing or diminishing of the male.

Marlatt remakes the myth, not forgetting but tokenizing its male figures/principles. Her story is not, then, about the abduction of Persephone by Hades and Zeus's compromise by which she ends up spending a third of the year underground. Hades is dismissed ("only the latest technician") from the poem called "prairie" which imagines Persephone caught in dangerous currents in the Red Deer River, rather than stolen by the lord of the underworld. The underworld, or *an* underworld, is reconfigured spatially and temporally, as both the long season of distance between the lovers and a place of "sudden descent into the dark" (31) caused by sickness. If Hades is identified in the original myth as the instrument of division (of winter from summer, mother from daughter, underworld from upper world), then his place is perhaps supplied in *Touch to My Tongue* by the "mother of giving turned terrible mother, blood-sipper, sorrow Durga" (20). The self-containment of the female world of the poem involves, not a whitewash of what it means to be a woman (no banishment of the dark side), but a confidence in the sufficiency of female mythology to supply from within its own economy the antagonist, the principle of separation, of chaos.

Marlatt chooses as the kernel of the myth the mother-daughter relationship emphasized by Nor Hall, in *The Moon and the Virgin,* from whom Marlatt quotes in her "notes":

> the story of Persephone's abduction by Hades and her subsequent reunion with Demeter is uniquely the story of the relationship between daughter (kore, maiden) and mother (De- meter, earth mother). It forms the heart of the rituals celebrated at Eleusis. "It was her own daughter who was buried under earth, and yet the core of *herself* died with her and came back to life only when Persephone - flower sprout, grain sprout - rose again from the earth" (35-36).

The underworld of *Touch to My Tongue* is a place of separation, not loss, sweetened by memories and anticipation of desire fulfilled: "and earth? i have seen her open up to let love in, let loose a flood, and fold again, so that even my fingers could not find their way through all that bush, all that common day rolling unbroken" (26). This is not "the king of the multitudinous dead," rising up "through a chasm in the earth" (Hamilton 50), but rather Demeter, "amorous Demeter, you with the fire in your hand (23), as she appears in the poem called "kore." It makes no sense to try fixing one of the lovers as Kore and the other as Demeter, because the roles either reverse or are played by both women at once. There's no point in taking too literally the incestuousness of the erotic in the mother-daughter connection, either. "lost daughter, other mother and lover" is a triple configuration, capable simultaneously (as in the act of love) of being "amative and nurturing," of "sucking and suckling" (23). At such mo ments identity, both personal and archetypal, is fluid. In fact Marlatt's syntax can quietly blend and blur, or double—as if obeying a principle of fluidity in definition—the identities of these lovers. In "astonished your hand covers mine walking lowtide strands of Colaba," there is no syntactical indication of which of the two is astonished;

so they both are. And are they literally both walking the lowtide strands, or are they figuratively together as Marlatt recounts her Indian experience? No way to know (no *need* to know) from the text; once again there is that satisfying increment of possibility.

Kore and Demeter are one in the lover, "amorous Demeter" whose skin (Kore as maiden/sprout) is "smooth as fruit" (23). The same woman is at once "excessive and radiant storehouse of sun" (displacing the god of light in the original story) and earth. And "kore" is a poem which shows the climax of lovemaking as the bursting of a seed (Kore/Demeter's) from underground: "spurt/spirit opening in the dark of earth, *yu!* cry jubilant excess, your fruiting body bloom we issue into the light of, sweet, successive flesh ..." (23). Movement into the light is also the theme of the second last poem, "coming up from underground," where the light is lunar rather than solar, as are the lovers, "lunar and pulled beyond reason," "the blaze of light we are, spiralling" (31). They fold into themselves the identity of Artemis/Diana, the huntress-moon, who is introduced in "houseless," ("your body, its radiant bow-woman arched over me ..." 20). Both of these poems enact in little, but differently, what the poem as a whole is doing with the rhythm of descent and rise, apartness and togetherness.

∾

Lorraine Weir throws out the observation that "the pattern of Marlatt's work is that of an epic journey through the underworld ..." (60); that is as true of individual (long) poems as it is of the work as a whole, those spirals around and down again, and up. Very often Marlatt (the character/narrator) is the adventurer, assuming the role traditionally held for the male—facing the minotaur in *How Hug A Stone*, for example, stalking the monster in *Ana Historic*—and thus belatedly if anxiously realizing childhood fantasies that crossed the patriarchal grain:

> tomboy, her mother said. tom, the male of the species plus boy. double masculine, as if girl were completely erased. a girl, especially a young girl, who behaves like a spirited boy—as if only boys could be spirited. who read Robin Hood, wore scarlet, identified with Lancelot and the boy who wanted to join the knights of St. John (all trespassers, law-breakers in the guise of saviours ...) (*Ana Historic* 13).

For Marlatt it has been a long way down, or back ("going forward may be the same as going backwards," says Gertrude Stein in the epigraph to "In the Month of Hungry Ghosts") to a time before history opened up its swallowing plot. Even now, being human, she is not home free. *Touch to My Tongue* "says" that the ground has shifted, still keeps shifting, under Marlatt's feet, but also that a strand of her identity rests, rooted, in another woman, in a sufficiency called Woman.

Works Cited

Barrie, J.M. *Peter Pan and Wendy*. London: Hodder and Stoughton, 1911.

Bowering, George. "Given This Body: Interview with Daphne Marlatt." *Open Letter* Fourth Series, 3 (Spring 1979), 32-88.

Cooley, Dennis. "Recursions Excursions and Incursions: Daphne Marlatt Wrestles With the Angel Language." *Line* 13 (Spring 1989), 66-79.

Cotnoir, Louise. "S'écrire avec, dans et contre le langage." *Room of One's Own* 8, 4 (January 1984), 47-49. Trans. Barbara Godard, "Writing Ourselves With, In and Against Language," 50-52.

—. "Territoires Critiques." *Contemporary Verse 2* 11, 2 & 3 (Spring/Summer 1988), 106-110. Trans. Erika Grundmann, "Critical Territories," 111-115.

Davey, Frank. "Words and Stones in *How Hug a Stone*." *Line* 13 (Spring 1989), 40-46.

Hamilton, Edith. *Mythology*. New York: New American Library, 1940.

Kroetsch, Robert. "My Book is Bigger Than Yours." *The Lovely Treachery of Words*. Toronto: Oxford, 1989.

Marlatt, Daphne. *Zocalo*. Toronto: Coach House Press, 1977.

—. "In the Month of Hungry Ghosts." *The Capilano Review* 16/17 (1979), 45-95.

—. *What Matters: Writing 1968-70*. Toronto: Coach House, 1980.

—. *How Hug a Stone*. Winnipeg: Turnstone, 1983.

—. *Touch to My Tongue*. Edmonton: Longspoon, 1984.

—. *Ana Historic*. Toronto: Coach House, 1988.

—. "Correspondances: Selected Letters." *Line* 13 (1989), 5-30.

Warland, Betsy. *open is broken*. Edmonton: Longspoon, 1984.

Weir, Lorraine. "Daphne Marlatt's 'Ecology of Language.'" *Line* 13 (Spring 1989), 58-63.

OUT OF THE BLANK: *ANA HISTORIC*

The ideal template is held up in front of every person observed in daily transactions. This means that variance, when perceived, is viewed as monstrous, to be safe is to be identified with the ideal type, of which a separate form exists for all ages, social groupings and classes. This template is an extension of symbolic logic acting in areas which are not properly its domain. In human beings variation is the norm. This variation is viewed as monstrous or entropic by the viewers who implicitly subscribe to the alibi of serial ideal templates.

> Christopher Dewdney, *The Immaculate Perception*

Gothic

To begin, two circles. The first appears in one of the passages of patriarchal discourse that provide the documentary background against which the lives of Daphne Marlatt's women are lived in *Ana Historic*. The second is William Patrick Day's tracing of the trajectory of the Gothic fantasy:

> 'Women in their course of action describe a smaller circle than men, but the perfection of a circle consists not in its dimensions, but in its correctness, says the logical Hannah More' (72).

> *

> The Gothic world, like a black hole in space, allows no energy to escape, but traps it in a closed system. Action can never be progressive, only circular; whatever the protagonist tries to do, his action must result in his own disintegration. The more energetic his motion the sooner this will occur. Gothic fantasies portray actions that move from point *a* back to point *a*, except that in this movement, the identity of the actor erodes. The Gothic protagonist achieves only the illusion of meaningful action, for every movement is in fact the same movement, a downward spiral to destruction (44).

Nowadays Hannah More (1745-1833, author of *Strictures on the Modern System of Female Education* and other books) might be seen as kin to the sort of colonial Negro King who sells his own people into slavery in exchange for personal power or authority, granted by whites. *Ana Historic* dramatises the lives of three women history has invited to dream within Hanna More's "perfect" sphere, but who wake up instead

172

in the gothic trap. These women are anything but serene about occupying this small circle, anything but happy with a correctness defined for, not by, them. Hannah More's circle, in fact, tightens around one vital life and chokes it to death. This is what happens to Ina, the mother of the principal narrator Annie. The strand of the novel that tells Ina's story is gothic. Strip away all the extravagant exotic paraphernalia of the gothic novel, that is, and you might be left with a story like hers.

This is a quicksand story, a nightmare story, with no rescue and no awakening. It is the more horrifying to observe, to watch the powerless Annie retrospectively recounting, *because Ana Historic* is not fantasy; its depiction of a routine that is domestic and banal is realism. What is this closed, constricting circle in the novel? It's the interior of Ina's house ("long hours of the mind alone in its trap turning the wheel" 26), the confining limits of social convention. Also it's a line of narrative, the script of marriage with a subordinate role already written down for women, or of history which erases these female lives of servitude: "history is the historic voice (voice-over), elegiac, epithetic. a diminishing glance as the lid is closed firmly and finally shut. That was her. summed up. Ana historic" (48). History: Ina's coffin: a "hope" chest. And there are other interlinked images of gothic confinement: impasse, frame, blank, silence. But *Ana Historic* is the act of an escape artist.

Frankenstein

Ina's story is gothic, but *Ana Historic* is not a gothic novel. Rather, it's a feminist teasing or deconstruction of the gothic genre represented by Mary Shelley's no-outlet tale, *Frankenstein*. In *Ana Historic*, Shelley's monster serves as a vane for the anxiety and fear that afflicts the lives of the women characters. He enters the novel in its opening scene, as the present-day Annie awakes in anxiety and remembers the routine of checking for the monster in the family wardrobes on the nights of her girlhood when she was left alone to babysit her two sisters. Later he merges with the men her mother warns her about, maybe lurking in the woods behind the house where she always loved to play. And he is the one she hysterically seeks to throw herself at one night during her adolescence in the era when her mother is, perhaps, crazy and the family in danger of being poisoned. But the older Annie, the narrator, knows better: "it was night - it was moonlight and briars, it was the fascination of desire for what lay out of bounds. Not Frankenstein, but the touch of the terrible ... " (77).

Not Frankenstein

Out of bounds is outside the woman's small circle, the prison which Ina in her paranoia for her daughters represents to them as a charmed circle of obedience. Stay inside it—as good girl and then good wife—and the monster won't get you. Out of bounds is into "undefined territory" (81), which exercises a powerful, frightening attraction for Annie. She senses the flaw in her mother's small-circle version of life long before she finds herself closed inside it. She causes her character, Mrs. Richards, to throw the *Frankenstein* parallel into doubt quite early in the novel. "[T]his was not

Europe," Mrs. Richards feels, "and Mary Shelley's monster would never speak his loneliness here" (16). The adult Annie, figuratively looking over Mrs. Richards' shoulder as she (Mrs. Richards) writes, understands: "it isn't Frankenstein you're looking for but some elusive sense of who you might be: she, unspoken and real in the world, running ahead to embrace it. She is writing her desire to be, in the present tense, retrieved from silence" (46). The "you" here is Annie; the "she" is primarily (more on Marlatt's pronouns later) Mrs. Richards, functioning as Annie's probe for identity, as her surrogate adventurer in a gothic patriarchal world so familiar that its circumference is difficult to locate.

Masks of the Monster

Not Frankenstein. The image of the monster is introduced and then allowed to metamorphose, is explored and eventually set aside as inapplicable to a woman's experience, for all that the creator of Victor Frankenstein, creator of the monster, was a woman. The monster, in a passage I'll return to later, turns into "a man's name for man's fear of the wild, the uncontrolled" (142), for the out of bounds. But before that understanding is reached, all the women in the novel try on the identity of monster. Mrs. Richards, addressing her English father, her personal representative of authority, has a backsliding moment when her desire for independence outside the circle allowed her sex falters: "Perhaps I am the monster you feared I would become—Is it that I want what womanhood must content itself without? (72)." An unnatural creature (a monster): a woman who wants to live "a man's life."

"I suppose you see me as the monster hidden at the heart of [the story]", Ina says (dead but, like Mrs. Richards' father, internalized and fiercely disputing with her daughter still), and her daughter replies no, "there *is* a monster, there is something monstrous here, but it's not you" (24).

On one level Annie's writing is her search for the monster's identity. She is tempted with the role of monster in her turn, when Zoe, her friend and reader, nudges her into imagining a lesbian relationship between two of her characters, Mrs. Richards and Birdie Stewart. Lesbian in 1873? That much freedom? "but this is a monstrous leap of the imagination," Annie protests, immediately wondering whose voice has spoken (it's her mother, speaking from inside her).

so be monstrous then, [Zoe] says.

but the monster is always someone / something else. the real monster is fear, or the monster is what i always feared as real: the violence behind the kiss, the brutal hand beneath the surgical glove, the one who punishes you for seeing (through) him (135).

One of the reasons *Ana Historic* works so well as fiction, despite its component of overt feminist essay, is that Annie, narrator and principal character, *is* a character, one whose perspective on herself and her life is limited, if growing. She herself is learning and changing until the last page of the novel. She finds out how to analyse the gothic circle of patriarchy (replacing her mother's pain of obliviousness with her own pain of consciousness) long before she discovers she has a choice: in or out. Before she finds her lesbian identity. The last deflection of the monster she presents is on the last (numbered) page of her story, when she removes her fictional mask (Mrs. Richards) and cleaves to Zoe. She is now stepping out of bounds, into the undefined, into the space where fear and desire are one: "it isn't even Frankenstein but a nameless part i know. terror has to do with the trembling that takes you out of yourself" (142). This is what, without knowing it, she has been looking for through(out) her story: a passionate letting go, uninhibited expression of desire for/with another person, in complete safety. Why the terror, then?

The gothic circle has defined Annie's life into middle age; it has been her reality, a reality in which she was conditioned to be passive. Nobody just steps from one reality into another without suffering trauma, but, Annie (like many women), acting on what she finally sees to be true for herself, even obvious, braves a terrible feeling of transgression. Emotionally, declaring complete independence is like suffering a second fall. "i am trying very hard to speak, to tell it" (49), she says. One of the reasons *Ana Historic* doesn't (can't) settle into a single, stable narrative technique is the intense difficulty its narrators experience in constituting an unfragmented subject/narrator to act in the verb of the narrative.

Bluebeard

Mary Shelley's novel would be merely one of the more important minor motifs in the novel if not for the way the spirit of the gothic genre fits Ina's story, if it weren't for the power of the gothic story/trap to attract women into it. "Bluebeard," that folktale distillation of the gothic, is mentioned only once in *Ana Historic* (80), but even once is sobering: each of the wives hanging in the locked room of Bluebeard's castle represents one cycle of a story so plausibly horrible that it won't rub off, even after its monstrous "author" is eliminated.

Not Bluebeard

When Annie drops her fiction of Mrs. Richards and calls out to Zoe, she escapes the gothic spiral she is in, the dissolution-in-progress of her identity ("falling apart. we are, i am. we have fallen apart. the parts don't fit. not well. never whole. never did./ / Zoe!" 150). But not before she has tasted it, not before she has come to read the riddle of the circle: a thicket of thorns grown around her imperceptibly. Like her mother, she got married, had children, slid into middle-age with no sense of accomplishment, certainly not for her work as research assistant on her husband's "Big Book" (79) on Vancouver history. One generation later, then, history once again is repeating itself in a patriarchal arrangement for which no one in particular is at fault. The men in the novel (Ina's husband Harald, Annie's husband Richard) are no Bluebeards but decent

Stan Dragland

people—*Ana Historic* is anti-patriarchy, not anti-male—themselves uncritical, because unconscious, of the patriarchal script. They don't experience "the small space a life gets boxed into" (59), so they can't understand what torments their wives.

Binaries

If one could imagine *Ana Historic* having been written and published in the fifties or early sixties, one could also imagine its reception by reviewers then: "Some powerful writing, but the research shows; the raw materials have not been integrated into the narrative." In Annie's imagined version of Richard's reaction to her bricolage, we have much the same response. Nowadays we're used to reading mixed-genre fictions in exploded form. It's no criticism to say of *Ana Historic* that it carries unmasked ideological content. The novel's thought obviously dovetails with that of feminist theorists of the male gaze, deconstructors of the feminine as lack and so on. The novel *is* a theoretical text, includable in but not quite covered by Linda Hutcheon's classifiction, "'historiographic metafiction'—fiction that is intensely, self-reflexively art, but is also grounded in historical, social and political realities" (13). *Ana Historic* is nearer fiction/theory in Nicole Brossard's sense, but Marlatt herself has recently coined the term "fictionalysis" to describe the particular hybrid of fiction and autobiography in *Ana Historic*: "a self-analysis that plays fictively with the primary images of one's life, a fiction that uncovers analytically that territory where fact and fiction coincide" (15). To some readers, Marlatt's discourse appears not only explicit but simplistic, based in a binarism that splits the sexes and what they represent too neatly in two. Whatever one thinks of the split—Frank Davey objects to it in *How Hug a Stone* and Lola Lemire Tostevin has reservations about it in *Ana Historic*—there's no denying its presence in both texts. In the novel, male energy keeps that gothic circle turning; female energy shatters it.

"While lesbian-maternal texts are crucial in exploring the unrepresented, the unthought," Lemire Tostevin says,

> it is important they not be prescriptive in their attempt to describe women's writing and lives. ... Now that the leap of the imagination has been made, it seems more vital than ever that the mutual containment of binaries that has traditionally defined our society be deciphered and unraveled so that the female subject writing herself on to "the blank" page of history conceive herself not only as *the* difference, but as a multiplicity of differences that cut across sexuality, gender, form, class, race. It would seem more vital than ever that in our newly created spaces we discover not only the multiple differences that exist between men and women, between women and women, but perhaps more importantly, within each woman (39).

But might not this bothersome binarism have some important function in *Ana Historic*? Robert Kroetsch says, in *Labyrinths of Voice* that two good readers wanted

The Bees of the Invisible

What the Crow Said elaborated out of its skeletal patterning, but that he knew from what they told him about it that they got the story. Why finish it for them (11)? Perhaps one reason why I find the polarization of binaries, the ideological "incompleteness" of *Ana Historic*, appealing is that I feel competent to fill in the greys myself. I understand what Frank Davey says in *Reading Canadian Reading*, that "each text, through the language structures by which it constitutes itself, serves some ideology" (47)—though the word "serves" collapses a possible gamut of relationships between ideology and text—and I admire his reading vigilance, but I don't believe that the function of criticism is to correct a text's ideology. I expect the text to be a thread of what James Reaney, speaking of national identity, calls "a web of adjusting visions" (7). Criticism is a web of adjusting visions too. I read Marlatt's binarism as an armature of rhetoric about which play the eloquent multiples of language, characterization, narrative technique and structure. I read that aspect of the novel the way I read romance and satire, two genres (working incognito in *Ana Historic*) which intentionally polarize and oversimplify experience by way of clarifying it.

I read *Ana Historic* as an historical novel not only about Mrs. Richards of Gastown, but about Annie, who was a teenager in those technicolor dark ages, the 1950's. This is a novel that presents and explores personal experience of a sexism enlightened people naturally like to feel they're beyond. I am writing this on the day of the annual Take Back the Night March (dedicated this year to the women massacred at the École Polytechnique in Montreal), which is a sad reminder that Bluebeard lives, that women often have no choice but to divide the world's human population into Them and Us. Not only on this continent. Travelling by train with Betsy Warland in the Australian desert, Daphne Marlatt finds herself (her selves) still within the gothic cul de sac:

> she wants to migrate she wants to mutate she wants to have no natural predators be nothing looking at nothing thrive in her own absence be out of focus out of range of The Gaze hide out from The Law under assumed names but there's no way out ... (*Double Negative* 51).

"wants to have no natural predators": a heartbreakingly simple desire.

Marlatt has always been searching for the grounding in herself of "a common condition," sensing "a narrative that wasn't only mine, though i participated in its telling & was thereby told" (*What Matters* 7,8). *Ana Historic* tells a very common story indeed, a story so grim that even if we *were* now beyond this tale of male power and violence on the one hand, women's fear and frustration and growing resistance on the other, the *experience* of feeling it's "them" versus "us," would it ever be obsolete? "But The Somme, the Somme:" says Colleen Thibaudeau of the World War I battle so disastrous for Canadian soldiers, "could we ever live days enough / to give it enough holding?" ("Letter Six" 99). No, the indignity of being born and treated like nothing, like a blank, has to be lived through again and again, has to be told over and over. No one powerful text, no *A Room of One's Own*, can s/lay the ogre by itself.

Multiple: Character

In fact only one pole of the male-female binary is stable in *Ana Historic*. The novel itself answers Tostevin's call for female multiplicity. None of the female characters is unitary; Annie certainly isn't, often to her pain. She is her (patriarchal) mother and she is the instinctually enlightened Mrs. Richards. For much of the novel she is rended in mind and body, yearningly aware that no adult compensation has arrived for the oneness she felt before puberty. It's because she can't bear to see Ana boxed into the limited career of a wife that she resists and finally refuses to write her marriage to Ben Springer:

> what if that life should close in on her like the lid of a hope chest? if she should shrivel and die inside, constricted by the narrow range of what was acceptable for Mrs. Springer? if all the other selves she might be were erased—secret diarist, pioneer pianist, travelling companion to Birdie Stewart—unvalidated, unacceptable, in short. because they weren't the right words. try artist, try explorer—prefaced always by lady, no, it wasn't a choice anyone sane would make (146).

Perhaps the best evidence of this multiplicity in characterization is the first name Annie gives to the woman she has discovered in the Vancouver archives bearing only her husband's name. Mrs. Richards, quietly on page 39, in a slightly estranging combination of Annie and Ina, becomes Ana. On one of the novel's six divider pages, someone (Ina? Richard? a skeptical reader?) objects to this invention and someone else (Annie? Marlatt?) responds with definitions:

you misspelled her name

Ana

that's her name:
    back, backward, reversed
    again, anew (43).

In *Webster's Third New International Dictionary*, the definitions of ana (prefix) are 1: up: upward, 2: back: backward, 3: again: anew. A fourth definition is inapplicable. "Up" is dropped out, to emphasize the "horizontal" return, renewal, that Annie makes through Ana. The addition of "reversed" calls attention to the palindrome (works both ways) in the name, less a proper name than a combiner or "intensifier" (Urday 26). Or a proper name that functions more like a pronoun, a shifter, than a noun. What frustrates the spelling police expresses out-of-rangeness, possibility. So when we read "that was her. summed up. Ana historic" (48), we have to look again. This is not "a-historic," not a blank. The lid may be closed on the box, but Ana isn't in it.

Multiples: Plot, Point of View

The narrative multiplies too. The story of Mrs. Richards is foregrounded, because we see it in the process of being made (the story of Annie and her mother "just happens" to unfold in the background); we watch Annie struggling with it, trying different stratagems (first person journal, in which Mrs. Richards, like Annie, struggles to word her experience; second person address; or third person limited omniscience); we see her extending the story through her own editorial/narratorial comment on it, through discussions about it with Zoe, and through suffering the imagined hostile criticisms of her mother and her historian husband Richard.

But it doesn't do to think of the three stories as separate. Each of them infiltrates the other, as each is highlighted in various ways by the documentary voices woven through the novel; each story is an exploration for a different generation of the power of that gothic narrative. In life or fiction, can it be escaped? To pay attention to the telling of each story is to see that the total narrative technique, always metafictionally self-conscious, is extremely fluid. There is not only no single or stable technique for telling any of the woven strands of the narrative, but a definitive beginning of each of them is difficult to fix, and the beginnings are scarcely begun when the endings begin. In fact beginnings of one sort or another (*of* a story, *in* a story) are brushing against endings from the second page, when Annie's story begins with Ina's death. The technique is metafictional, metalinguistic, multiply multiple.

Annie/Marlatt

Of all the real life characters whose lives flowed into *Ana Historic*—"fictionalysis" is *roman à clef* with a mission—the most fascinating is Daphne Marlatt, because she is the maker of the fictional characters (who are not merely plucked out of life and tucked intact into the fiction). One has a pleasant, only mildly vertiginous feeling, imagining Marlatt writing Annie writing Ana writing... More importantly, *Ana Historic* dramatises the painful eking out of a feminist ideology and aesthetic, and much of what Annie discovers about language and writing has its parallels elsewhere in Marlatt's work, some of it written in her pre-feminist phase. Lorraine Weir calls Marlatt's "feminist ecological poetics" "part of a consistent pattern of critique and resistance reaching its logical outcome" (63n) in the revolutionary *Touch to My Tongue* and *Ana Historic*. At the core of that pattern is Marlatt's engagement with writing. What Annie says and does, then, mirrors what Marlatt does, and vice versa, though the reflection is inexact.

So Annie's writing is illuminated by something Marlatt says in the preface to *What Matters*, a much earlier text. I'm thinking not only of the echo in her identification of the problem of writing ("an effort to fight off the closed terms of our culture") of the closure of a gothic life, but also of her constant employment of writing as a kind of close reading, as the only way she can truly find things out: "Making sense became the work," she says of the urgency of her aesthetic, "generated by the fear that if i could not make sense of what was happening, then my life was indeed senseless and immaterial" (8).

Stan Dragland

Writing

Annie's writing has one sort of origin in the research for her husband's book. In fact it begins, hesitantly, as an answer to that book, to Richard's linear method, to the virtual absence of women from his sources; it begins as a reaction against history in which women are a-historic. But the main impetus is visceral; it's desperation, the need to find a way out of the closed system she inherited from her mother:

> She was knocking on paper, not wood, tapping like someone blind along the wall of her solitude … ./ / but there was the page, her tapping there, looking for a way out of the blank that faced her—blankety-blank—and not that tug either, the elliptical tug of memory which erased this other. she was looking for the company of another who was also reading—out through the words, through the wall that separated her, an arm, a hand—(45)

Knocking, tapping, tapping, looking, looking … reading: these are metonyms for writing. "Also reading" is a compact way of describing the way Daphne Marlatt's writing functions for her, as a reading of the world where she meets it in the body of language, where she meets others also reading.

Reading

In the novel, writing and reading are identical acts, a novelty a reader registers with pleasure, without prompting. Why it happens, though, what the shift is undoing, is explained by Marlatt in a meditation on writing and reading called "Writing Our Way Through the Labyrinth":

> writing goes back to a Germanic word, *wrītan*, meaning to tear, scratch, cut, incise. it is the act of the phallic singular, making its mark on things (stone, wood, sand, paper). leaving its track. "I was here," the original one in the world. reading goes back to Indo-European *ar-*, to fit together, appears in Old English as *rǣdan*, to advise, explain, read. advise and care for seem to be enduring aspects of its meaning and still survive in the word rede, counsel or advice given, a decision taken by one or more persons; or, to govern, take care of, save, take counsel together. always there is this relating to others (47-48).

Writing as reading is intended to detach the process of making with words from the Freudian "phallic signifier, its claim to singularity, the mark of the capital I (was here)." In a passage echoed in *Ana Historic*, one that I'll return to, Marlatt goes on to say, "language is no 'tool' for [women], no extension of ourselves, but something we are 'lost' inside of" (49). "writing my way through" (46) is what Marlatt has always been doing, though not always as a declared feminist.

In *Ana Historic* this writing/reading is a reaching, to go back to the "knocking on paper" passage—reaching to or for whom? Mrs. Richards? She is perhaps the one erased, all but erased, in the historical record. For Zoe? Zoe has not been introduced into the novel when Annie begins tapping, which means only that there is yet no name, no person, to make incarnate a need Annie can already feel. Annie may even be reaching out to the reader. But it's actually more than a person she's tapping for. Beyond the arm, the hand (beyond the dash) waits the whole body, erotically charged, of an other. When Annie arrives at this body, in Zoe, reading and writing are eroticized. The last line of the last, unpaginated, entry in the novel is an echo of its opening—that anxious awakening in the dark—but now "it isn't dark but the luxury of being has woken you, the reach of your desire, reading us into the page ahead." "hot skin writing skin"—there has occurred a melting of difference not only between writing and reading but also lovemaking, between the physical body and the body of language, on the move.

The Drift

Lola Lemire Tostevin says of the "powerful ending of the novel," which she also calls "its climax," that it is "unexpectedly conventional in its utopian vision" (38). She is referring to the scene, entitled "Not a Bad End," in which Mrs. Richards admits that she desires Birdie Stewart. But that scene lasts only a page and a half, and there's a problem with declaring it *the* ending (in fact there is a different version of the scene at the end of section five), there being almost as many endings as beginnings in *Ana Historic*, and since the last line pushes ahead, into the page ahead, which is (or is it?) blank. Skin contains the body: the body ends where it meets the air. But it certainly gets around.

Insofar as it makes sense to speak of the closing pages of *Ana Historic* as ending (the feeling is of arrival and re-beginning), it's true that the ending is happy. "Utopian" didn't always have the connotation of idealist evasion it has picked up in some contemporary literary theories, though. The Greek origin of the word fits *Ana Historic* best: nowhere. That's where the novel arrives, at a space, a nothing, a by-now-plenitudinous blank. By the end, as in Marlatt's other books, there has been a gain in clarity for the writer/character, but, as is also usual, there has been much resistance to the straight-line approach to discovery. "the plot-line is the drift," Marlatt says in *What Matters*, "which circles back on itself while still moving towards some recognition—this rather than a plotted crescendo of conflict & resolution" (71). This is circle as verb. This circling is of Marlatt's choice. In *Ana Historic*, technique contributes much of the buildup of centrifugal energy that shatters the gothic circle.

Ina's departure for boarding school as a "child with serious eyes and a delicate mouth" (89), is a beginning that appears in the middle of the novel; her death, her ending, is announced at the beginning of the novel, and then the circumstances of her decline to it are filled in in such a way that she dies, as it were, before our eyes. Annie's story begins (in 1950) where Mrs. Richards' does (in 1873), with arrival in Vancouver. Annie's discovery of the slight information about Mrs. Richards in the Vancouver archives is another sort of beginning—of the novel within the novel—but this one, like the writing Mrs. Richards does within it, is marked by "false" starts, crossed out words or parenthesized alternatives, and other signs of work in progress. There is the feeling that the novel is being made while we watch—a little reminiscent of James Reaney's drama in that respect, with its elimination of the line between stage and backstage. We're not simply watching the novel of Mrs. Richards unfold before our eyes; we're also being teased with alternative choices of narrative path and point of view. Choices are *not* made between these, of course (as they would be by a writer who wished to produce a transparent text), so we're left with a sense of narrative and subject in process, with a telling that is kept very loose (in the sense of flexible), very mobile. All three riming stories are dispersed between so many narrative stances that they get told, especially those of Ina and Annie, without seeming to, while the foreground is occupied by concern with the process (the problems) of writing Ana's story. Annie's difficulties with beginning and ending, leading to the crisis of her dropping Mrs. Richards' story entirely, are signs that she has not succeeded in getting herself together—"i don't even want to 'pull yourself together,' as Richard urges (myself? yourself? theirself?)" (17). But Annie's failure, if failure it is, is Marlatt's success. "Getting it together," stringing it out in a line, imposing author-ity on the text—this is the way of telling that she associates with patriarchy, history, "relentless progress towards some end" (81); this is the way that has come to be associated with the exclusion of women. Marlatt lets the story lie there, apparently in pieces, "circling around the same idea" (81), the sum of Annie's indecisions and indirections. Which is not to say that Marlatt hasn't shaped her material. *Ana Historic* is intricately structured; it just isn't locked up.

The Blank

After she drops her story of Mrs. Richards and calls out to Zoe ("which is not the end. the story is 'only a story' insofar as it ends./ / in life we go on" 150), we are still in a fiction, one layer nearer the skin of the onion. Then, without forgetting the use of the term in shock therapy (see p. 144), Annie's ending/beginning with Zoe is glissando, a slide, into "the page ahead." It doesn't come down any *where*. That Annie is happy in the last pages means that something has happened to the gothic blank, which appears in the novel as obstruction, impasse, wall, emptiness, silence.

One effect of the many spaces appearing in the text is to render the reading somewhat spasmodic, a physical punctuation of the thematic search among words and within a voice so deeply inscribed with male experience that the feminine skids right off it. The sense of displacement, of inauthenticity in occupying these words ("what if our heads are full of other people's words? nothing *without* quotation marks" 81), that makes Annie's writing such a struggle, is one of the commonplace urgencies of feminism. It's also uncannily like that expressed by Dennis Lee in "Cadence, Country, Silence: Writing in Colonial Space." In fact an essay by W.D. Ashcroft, which quotes Lee's essay, helps me to see *Ana Historic* as metaphor for an intersection of oppositional elements in feminist and post-colonial discourse. "[F]or both feminism and postcolonialism," Ashcroft writes, "the 'authentic' language is one whose authenticity itself is constructed in the process of constructing the feminine and post-colonial subject" (27). But first, for both, there's the burden of imperialism. "[I]f we live in space which is radically in question for us," Lee says,

> that makes the barest speaking a problem to itself. For voice does issue in part from civic space. And alienation in that space will enter and undercut our writing, make it recoil upon itself, become a problem to itself (502).

There is in fact a version of this particular problem, the large linguistic problem in little, in *Ana Historic*. Annie is growing up Canadian in an English household. She has "two languages. two allegiances" (23). One of these is the past and must be erased if she is to fit into the new Canadian context that her mother finds inferior: "my difference i was trying to erase. my English shoes and woolly vests. my very words./ / impasse: 'my very words' were yours" (23). To the normal generational conflict is added this hassle over lifestyle and words.

But, more significantly, Marlatt's equivalent of Lee's imperialism—withering the roots of the very language he occupies—is history. Part of her disillusionment has been to discover that the language of history, which carries the past into the present, the language she was brought up in, is a foreign tongue to her as a woman. At least she can't find herself in it.

> but i don't want history's voice [Annie says]. i want … something is wanting in me. and it all goes blank on a word. want. what does it mean, to be lacking? empty. wanton, vanish, vacant, vacuum, evacuate. all these empty words except for wanton (lacking discipline, lewd). a word for the wild. for the gap i keep coming to (48-49).

The wild, according to Hannah More and her ilk, is outside a woman's proper sphere, that invisible circumference Annie's mother did her utmost to accept, and to make her daughter accept, the limit that Annie raged against as adolescent and young woman, and still somehow ended up bounded by.

Marriage is the proper ending for the story of single maidenhood to those who hold that heterosexual relationships are the correct sort. But "what do you do when the true you feel inside sounds different from the standard" (18)? Annie's inability to locate herself in history, in her "own" language, has been a sadly common enough experience for women. But something else about Annie's identity is buried so deeply (there being virtually no public image to call it out): the true of her sexuality. That such a fundamental aspect of her identity could be so hidden from her is a measure of the power of the heterosexual script that was written for her. She is a middle aged woman before she finds out how to read the repressed inklings of lesbianism she experienced as a young woman. This she does by writing out the story of Mrs. Richards, writing

Ana as a woman also struggling to account for herself, also looking for words that are her own. Writing to her father of her life in the new world, Ana breaks off in frustration, unable to convey anything "of these sawdust byways" (83). "her real story," Annie says of Ana, "begins where nothing is conveyed. where she cannot explain, describe—" (83) and Annie, too, breaks off. The identity of these two women is established in the structure long before Zoe spells it out.

She

"A book of interruptions" (37), a book of blanks. Beyond the limit is the blank, the gap, the silence, the wild—all negatives? The novel pivots a reader into revaluing the experience they name. In it, one gradually realizes, nothing is *conveyed.* This nothing, zero, o, opposite to Hannah More's circle, is limitless, and, to overstate the matter, it's under the protection of a goddess. Let's return to Annie's assessment of *Frankenstein* preceding her release of the wildness in herself. We're now in a position to comment on the context: "—actually Frankenstein was the man who created him. did you ever read the book? and now we call the monster by his name. a man's name for man's fear of the wild, the uncontrolled. that's where *she* lives" (142).

Who is *"she?"* The italics confer importance on the pronoun, but the immediate context identifies no referent. A detour will bring us back to *her,* the long way round.

Daphne Marlatt's personal pronouns always need watching, never more so than in *Ana Historic.* Her sliding use of pronouns is in fact an index of the relational way her work makes meaning. Often the charge you feel a certain word or phrase emitting is not a property of the word or phrase in itself, but the halo of associations it has gathered, the aura of possibilities generated by the whole (finite but unlimited) verbal field. Meaning in her work doesn't seem quite so up for grabs as it does in a formulation of Charles Bernstein's, but Bernstein is helpful, especially as he makes personal pronouns the principal sign of the provisionality of meaning he endorses in poetics (and what he says about that subject transfers well, or should, to other sorts of imaginative writing, including criticism):

> Strictly speaking, it's absurd to be for or against subjectivity; yet the subject may be an area of poetic contest that forces philosophically odd, but poetically comprehensible, polarizations. Key categories like these, or ones such as form, process, tradition, communication, subject matter, abstraction, representation, concreteness, plainness, voice, meaning, clarity, difficulty, content, history, elegance, beauty, craft, simplicity, complexity, prosody, theme, sincerity, objectification, style, imagination, language and realism have no unitary or definitive sense within poetics; they are, like the personal pronouns, *shifters,* dependent for their meaning on the particular context in which they are used (68).

Pronouns are very active in *Ana Historic,* often arranged for maximum shift ("a-historic / she who is you / or me / 'i' / address this to" 129), and the context for a pronoun, like the "*she*" in the passage about *Frankenstein*, is sometimes the whole novel. For this particular pronoun, in fact, I think the most important context is *How Hug a Stone*, with its core of feminine mystery, The Great Mother, discovered in the quest for Marlatt's own mother, Edrys, who "is" Ina in *Ana Historic*.

> although there are stories about her, versions of history that are versions of her, & though she comes in many guises she is not a person, she is what we come through to & what we come out of, ground & source. the space after the colon, the pause (between the words) of all possible relation (73).

The Goddess is everywhere in the spaces, between the lines of *Ana Historic*. Bride (with the e pronounced)—the principal name she goes by in *How Hug a Stone*—makes a brief appearance in *Ana Historic*, as "Bridie or Birdie with the wandering 'r'" (108). There need be no stampede to the conclusion that Birdie Stewart (reminiscent of Lulu Sweet—"White as the moon, who was she?—the madam who gave her name to Lulu Island in Marlatt's *Steveston* 21) *is* The Goddess. History is male myth in *Ana Historic*; myth as archetypal story is not much in evidence, though if one *were* picking up what there is in that line, then plain-speaking, self-assured Birdie Stewart, secure in her female lineage, makes a wonderful counterbalance to the Eve through whom women were cursed to shame and passivity in the Christian tributary to patriarchy. Annie has to prise this tradition out of her mother. It's hidden in the answer to questions like why must women wear hats to church? The other overt hint that the Goddess might be presiding over the narrative is the "rite, an ancient place [Ana] had been admitted to, this crossing over into life" (123) during Jeannie Alexander's accouchement. And I sense her presence in Ana's autoerotic fantasy of joining two women in a warm forest pool: "They beckoned to her. Rain fell warm around them, the brown water pulled at her skirts—it hadn't mattered, clothes fell away—she was about to change into something magical and sure ... (86).

You tiptoe up to The Name and then withdraw, moving outward from The Goddess who is nowhere, back to Bride, to "*she*" in the passage we began with. Thence to other "shes" and "hers" in the novel whose identity is not exhausted by the possible referents nearby. They lift and shift as you watch, and many seem tinged with an unspecifiable largeness. Some hand or shadow moving through the words. Some readers may wish to slide back into the heart or the mind, the forearms or the womb—wherever *she* is felt—back, beyond gender, to Marlatt feeling her way with words about a nameless "ground" in a 1974 letter to Warren Tallman:

> But what are these *formless* messages, these 'vibrations' we keep getting thru the grid of our own knowledge, & contain ones standing in the desert like crazy signposts gesturing: *all* meaning, every silhouette, every shadow (Don Juan), every contour of the landscape-language all previously established (brain) cir-

cuits make of everything OUT there shadowless & absolute, as if, we begin to see, thru the shadows our own forms cast, that there is some *other* ground these forms we take to be landmarks (ours) barely signify (anything) in.

I suppose that the only peculiarly American gift will be learning to be lost—unmapt country, over & over ("Correspondances" 13).

Then over to George Bowering, writing to Dennis Lee about the "nerve" of the man who, in "Polyphony: Enacting a Meditation," tries "to speak those things that are unnameable but experientially there. Experientially? Pah. I mean there. There" (*Tasks* 196). "It" is approached again and again by the writers whose work is addressed in this book. The meaning shifters, sometimes under the sign of the trickster, are wording their way towards (within) Presence.

Writing

The writing, in *Ana Historic,* is formulating a poetics of cooperation with the nameless real, with "the thick being [Ana] could feel between things" (41). In the twentieth century Annie, this becomes also a poetics of opposition to a way of writing (reading) aligned with the axe, the saw, with technology. "our writing, which we also live inside of," she says, "is different from men's, and not a tool, not a 'pure instrument for getting a grip on the world.' 'it contains menaces,' traps, pitfalls … " (133). A poetics which seeks to revalue what has been marked as lacking. In the passage just quoted Annie is working with the words (those in quotation marks) of Simone de Beauvoir, a "woman of your generation … Ina" (133), to sharpen the focus of the usual postmodernist critique of humanism, Charles Olson's for example, so that the particularly male component of it stands free. Here is de Beauvoir on the female body, a (one might say) gothic view that Annie inherited from her mother:

'(Her body) is a burden: worn away in service to the species, bleeding each month, proliferating passively, it is not for her a pure instrument for getting a grip on the world but an opaque physical presence; it is no certain source of pleasure and it creates lacerating pains; it contains menaces: woman feels endangered by her "insides"' (Marlatt 133; de Beauvoir 619).

Annie knows what de Beauvoir means; she lost her sense of unitary self when she entered womanhood (without much help from Ina, with no nurturing ritual to mark the rite of passage, beyond being furtively handed a box of sanitary pads). No wonder she is nostalgic for "that child, one with her body. not yet riven, not split into two—the self and the body that betrays the self. bleeding, leaking, growing lumps, getting pregnant, having abortions and miscarriage (89).

So Annie's Penelopean "untelling," "trying to get back the child who went too far, got lost in the woods, walked into the arms of Frankenstein" (141), her reaching back into the "magic circle" (148) of once-intact family is motivated by no nostalgic expectation of return. Rather, she wants to counter the dominant view of it all as a fall, as the (gothic) inheritance of a curse. The main shift that Marlatt/Annie makes, recontextualizing de Beauvoir's words, is the substitution of "writing" for "body," in answer to a need she calls, writing of Ana's writing, "the unspoken urge of a body insisting itself in the words" (46). Each of the narrative beginnings these two women make is an assertion of identity, a physical articulation, a bodily speaking or writing that carries much more than "menace." With them, *Ana Historic* is annotating an assertion of H.D. that is one of the epigraphs to Marlatt's *Touch to My Tongue*: "The brain and the womb are both centres of consciousness, equally important."

The Body

In this positive, celebratory view, menstruation—notwithstanding all the mental and physical difficulty associated with it (see Sarah Murphy's "Putting the Great Mother together again, or how the cunt lost its tongue" in *A Mazing Space*)—is writing, "a secret pleasure," the source of

a childish astonishment, *i made that!* the mark of myself, my inscription in blood. i'm here. scribbling again.

writing the period that arrives at no full stop. not the hand manipulating the pen. not the language of definition, of epoch and document, language explaining and justifying, but the words that flow out from within, running too quick to catch sometimes, at other times just an agonizingly slow trickle. the words of an interior history doesn't include ...

that erupts like a spring, like a wellspring of being, well being inside ... (90).

Why all those beginnings in *Ana Historic*, then, all that resistance to endings? The book is a female body. The menstrual period is periodic; it describes a monthly circle. Begin, Begin again. It's the rhythm of a woman's body—in orgasm and in labour as well. That is clear in Annie's comments, unpunctuated for maximum flow, on Jeannie Alexander's labour. Her references to competition detach the female birthing scene from a race between two boats, the Pearl and the Annie Fraser, referred to in the documentary passages that are threaded through this section:

woman a rhythm in touch with her body its tides coming in not first nor last nor lost she circles back on herself repeats her breathing out and in two heartbeats here not winning or losing labouring into the manifest (125).

It's appropriate that Mrs. Richards witnesses this birthing scene, and narrates part of it, with Annie shadowing her closely (as earlier Annie watches at Mrs. Richards' shoulder while she writes), because this natural instinctive process of great power is

Stan Dragland

analogous to her own struggle with writing. An ancient metaphor—literary creation as child-bearing—is given explicit physicality:

> Ana caught a glimpse of dark almost purple flesh and stood up, shocked. How dark it looked, an angry powerful o, stretched, stretched, hair springing black above. This was Jeannie, this was something else not Jeannie, not anyone, this was a mouth working its own inarticulate urge, opening deep—(125).

And the mouth speaks: "a massive syllable of slippery flesh" (126), a baby, astonishing Mrs. Richards and filling her with wonder. "This secret place between our legs we keep so hidden—is yet so, what? What words are there? If *it* could speak!—as indeed it did: it spoke the babe, and then the afterbirth, a bleeding mass of meat" (126). Metaphor this may be, but it's also literal physical birth, a bloody marvel female flesh accomplishes. Not wishing to confine the feminine to women, one would not wish to dismiss those *idea* births that men have been so fond of—Dylan Thomas, for example, labouring to bring forth the poem—but they look bloodless compared to this. And in the absence of female writing on the subject, men are vulnerable to the charge of usurpation.

O

When Annie arrives at the body of Zoe, of the eroticized writing, their love feels to me as if it takes place under the aegis of The Goddess, who is retrospectively revealed to have been between the lines, in the spaces of this novel, from the beginning. Of course sometimes an attribute of her appears *in* the words. That's her o that Ana sees giving birth (a zero, vagina, become speaking mouth). In *How Hug a Stone* it, *she*, appears as "a hollow space or place, enclosing object, round object, a lump, mound in the surrounding sea of grass. *Ku-* , *Kunte*, to, wave-breaking womb: Bride ... " (72) who, "*winged* from *buried*" (75), attends a seasonal and psychological birth/rebirth.

A man is writing this, fascinated by *Ana Historic*, this body, this "traffic of the mind around a gaping hole" (123), the cunt. Feeling sometimes like an interloper, but coming to understand some matters in the way that Marlatt wants to understand all things: for herself, "not as knowledge but as experience, that is where the writing [reading] starts" (*What Matters* 25). Experiencing in *Ana Historic* (as in "Rings," Marlatt's poem of the birth of her son, *How Hug a Stone* and *Touch to my Tongue*) a hypersexual corroboration of my own fascination with the cunt. The marvel, for me, reading Luce Irigaray's *This Sex Which Is Not One* was not so much in how deftly the notion of penis envy is made to look ridiculous; the marvel was that I hadn't found the notion ridiculous when I first heard of it. Those who are called envious have incentive to original thinking on the subject, of course; males are even more subject to blindness than women who accepted so much of what they were told about themselves (*Ana Historic* is founded on this fact) though their very experience denied it.

The Stoned Horse in Ed Dorn's *Slinger* shakes his head at the narrow view of grasses taken by American suburbanites: "Out of all that great tribe they planted lawn grass" (Book III)! I shake my head too, wondering at that magnificent organ reduced to a hole to shove a prick into. The men who see it that way are the ones who seized the night. Freud, with his idea that there's nothing between a woman's legs, is somewhere behind them. Women have been finding the words to take back the night from Freud; men need to be doing this too, rooting their words in an instinctive granting of physical complementarity to the sexual organs of both sexes. There needs to be a felt basis for renovating patriarchal language and thought—by no means an easy task: "secretly looking [vagina] up in French [Annie] was astonished to discover it was masculine. le vagin. there must be some mistake, i thought, not knowing its history, a word for sheath, the cover of a sword, it wasn't a sword that i was promised" (163).

Ina

The healthy Ina, most "herself," "the mother who'd laughed at 'Hokey-Pokey,' loved Abbott and Costello, read 'The King asked the Queen and the Queen asked the Dairy-Maid' in funny voices" (144) is juxtaposed towards the end of *Ana Historic* with the Ina whose repression, depression, whose hysteria has fetched her up in a lull of unmotherhood caused by the shock treatment which destroys her personality. (In the Gothic, Day says, "The identity of the actor erodes.")

The ending of Ina's story is intolerable; therefore it's a beginning. What she became, so will she always be to her daughter (a complex knot of the creative and the repressive, the rigid and the perceptive), but she bequeaths to Annie a blank of understanding that Annie must write her way into: however could her mother have ended that way, causing so much searing of her family in the process? Who is responsible? The answer lies in the quotations that Annie sprinkles ("improperly," she imagines Richard saying about her technique) throughout her text, in the male histories that smugly ignore women; in the "how-to-heal / how-to-fix yourself books" (35) in which women try, within the circle described by Hannah More, to make a virtue of being a slightly less static part of a man's background than, say, his house; in the psychiatric diagnoses of hysteria made by men who fail to trace this vicious circle back to its social origins, leaping instead at a tangent to women's bodies, to a shocking fantasy of absence: no penis. *Ana Historic* raises to consciousness this sort of gothic circle. Against (around?) the background of the humanist/patriarchal line of thought, Marlatt weaves case studies, her own counter diagnoses, and a celebratory view of woman—mind and body—that is a new beginning.

Works Cited

Ashcroft, W.D. "Intersecting Marginalities: Postcolonialism and Feminism." *Kunapipi* XI, 2 (1989), 23-35.

Bennett, Donna, Russell Brown and Karen Mulhallen, eds. *Tasks of Passion: Dennis Lee at Mid-Career.* Toronto: Descant, 1982.

Stan Dragland

Bernstein, Charles. "Optimism and Critical Excess (Process)." *Writing* 23/24 (Fall/ Winter 1989), 62-88.

Davey, Frank. *Reading Canadian Reading.* Winnipeg: Turnstone, 1988.

——. "Words and Stones in *How Hug a Stone.*" *Line* 13 (Spring 1989), 40-46.

Day, William Patrick. *In the Circles of Fear and Desire.* Chicago and London: University of Chicago Press, 1985.

de Beauvoir, Simone. *The Second Sex.* Trans. and ed. H.M. Parshley. New York: Knopf, 1957.

Dewdney, Christopher. *The Immaculate Perception.* Toronto: Anansi, 1986.

Dorn, Edward. *Slinger.* Berkeley: Wingbow, 1973.

Hutcheon, Linda. *The Canadian Postmodern.* Toronto: Oxford, 1988.

Irigaray, Luce. *This Sex Which Is Not One.* Trans. Catherine Porter with Carolyn Burke. Ithaca, N.Y.: Cornell University Press, 1985.

Kamboureli, Smaro and Shirley Neuman. *A Mazing Space.* Edmonton: Longspoon/ NeWest, 1986.

Lee, Dennis. "Cadence, Country, Silence: Writing in Colonial Space." *Open Letter* Second Series, 6 (Fall 1973), 34-53.

Marlatt, Daphne. *What Matters: Writing 1968-70.* Toronto: Coach House, 1980.

——. *How Hug a Stone.* Winnipeg: Turnstone, 1983.

——. *Touch to My Tongue.* Edmonton: Longspoon, 1984.

——. *Ana Historic.* Toronto: Coach House, 1988.

——. and Betsy Warland. *Double Negative.* Charlottetown: Gynergy, 1988.

——. "Correspondances: Selected Letters." *Line* 13 (Spring 1989), 5-30.

——. "Self-Representation and Fictionalysis." *Tessera* 8 (Spring 1990), 13-17.

Murphy, Sarah. "Putting the Great Mother together again, or how the cunt lost its tongue." Shirley Neuman and Smaro Kamboureli, eds. *A Mazing Space.* Edmonton: Longspoon/NeWest, 1986.

Neuman, Shirley and Robert Wilson. *Labyrinths of Voice: Conversations with Robert Kroetsch.* Edmonton: NeWest, 1982.

Reaney, James. "A Letter From James Reaney." *Black Moss* Series 2, 1 (Spring 1976), 2-10.

Thibaudeau, Colleen. *My granddaughters are combing out their long hair.* Toronto: Coach House, 1977.

Tostevin, Lola Lemire. "Daphne Marlatt: Writing in the Space That Is Her Mother's Face." *Line* 13 (Spring 1989), 32-39.

Urday, Lawrence and Alexander Humez, eds. *Prefixes and Other Word-Initial Elements of English.* Detroit: Gale Research, 1984.

Weir, Lorraine. "Daphne Marlatt's 'Ecology of Language.'" *Line* 13 (Spring 1989), 58-63.

Other books by Stan Dragland published by Coach House Press:
Wilson MacDonald's Western Tour, 1923-4 (1977)
Peckertracks (1978)
Journeys Through Bookland (1984)

Also available in this series:

Fear of the Open Heart
Constance Rooke

A collection of lucid, passionate essays about contemporary Canadian writing that celebrate the intimate relationship of the reader and writer. Includes essays on P.K. Page, Margaret Laurence, John Metcalfe, Mavis Gallant, Michael Ondaatje, Alice Munro, Sheila Watson and Margaret Atwood. The extraordinary title essay develops a theory of intimacy in relation to Gallant, Munro and Laurence.

Editor for the Press: Michael Ondaatje
Cover design: Gordon Robertson
Cover painting: James Reaney

COACH HOUSE PRESS
401 (rear) Huron Street
Toronto, Canada M5S 2G5